What's Wrong with Terrorism?

For Brian Barry

What's Wrong with Terrorism?

Robert E. Goodin

polity

First published in 2006 by Polity Press

Polity Press
65 Bridge Street
Cambridge CB2 1UR, UK

Polity Press
350 Main Street
Malden, MA 02148, USA

ISBN: 0-7456-3497-4
ISBN: 0-7456-3498-2 (pb)

A catalogue record for this book is available from the British Library.

Typeset in 10.5 on 12 pt Berling
by SNP Best-set Typesetter Ltd, Hong Kong
Printed and bound in Great Britain by MPG Books Ltd, Bodmin, Cornwall.

The publisher has used its best endeavours to ensure that the URLs for external websites referred to in this book are correct and active at the time of going to press. However, the publisher has no responsibility for the websites and can make no guarantee that a site will remain live or that the content is or will remain appropriate.

Every effort has been made to trace all copyright holders, but if any have been inadvertently overlooked the publisher will be pleased to include any necessary credits in any subsequent reprint or edition.

For further information on Polity, visit our website: www.polity.co.uk

Contents

Preface

I wish, twice over, that I did not have any need to acknowledge the contribution of the first-order political actors whose activities occasioned this book: first and most obviously, those who think that death and destruction is a fitting means to political goals; but second and as sincerely, those 'democratic' politicians who deliberately frighten people further for their own narrowly partisan purposes.

September 11, 2001, found me visiting Britain, where I had lived for the decade marking the height of IRA bombing campaigns. Of course there was shock and horror at the pictures from New York and Washington; of course there was concern for friends and family living there; and there was of course the sympathy of common humanity for all those caught up in the horrors of that day. But having learned to live with medium-grade terror over dozens of years of IRA violence (and the high-grade terror of the Blitz, a generation before), Londoners also seemed to be taking a much more balanced and realistic attitude to the real magnitude of the new threat. The attitude seemed to be, 'Okay, steer clear of the pillar boxes and don't go near Canary Wharf for a while': but otherwise, it was business as usual.

When I returned home to Australia, and still more when I visited Washington a few months later, it was all very different. Ordinarily sensible people were clearly scared witless (literally, in my view). People whom I know to have taken a fair few reasonable risks in their lives were suddenly stockpiling duct tape to seal their windows against gas attacks. Every public office, even the most innocuous, was barricaded behind razor wire and concrete crash barriers. The 'government of the people' had become a 'gated community'. So too had all the great public monuments to liberty along the Mall, that great avenue of the Republic. Draconian new police powers had been voted into law by congressmen who, by their own confession, had not even paused to read the legislation.

Clearly, people were spooked. And they were all the more spooked by the precautions that were supposedly protecting them. It is hard even for a jaundiced observer, stuck in a long queue waiting to have his bags inspected before entering the Library of Congress, not to succumb to the thought that 'There must be a real, substantial threat, for them to go to all this trouble.' One then pinches oneself, of course, if one is sufficiently jaundiced, and reminds oneself that 'it's all just campaign advertising, at public expense (twice over)'.

But how many people are sufficiently jaundiced? Plenty, in Britain: or so the opinion polls and election returns from there seem to suggest. Not nearly as many in the US, judging from the opinion polls and election returns there. In Australia, on the verge of a federal election as the Twin Towers fell, the panic lasted long enough to re-elect the government after a shamelessly xenophobic campaign, subsequently confirmed to have been based literally on a lie. The War on Terror, or anyway the war on Iraq so disingenuously linked to it, might have cost Tony Blair his job had there been a more credible Opposition or a braver leader-in-waiting within his own party. Other members of the 'Coalition of the Willing' are less willing than they once were, and many are slipping away quietly or otherwise. But the US remains hegemonic, and the neuroses whipped up there in response to the threats of terrorism, real and imagined, cannot help shaping the world that all the rest of us have to share with it.

I have few illusions about the power of a book by an academic (even if it is deliberately less 'academic' in its style than my other academic books) to change any of that. Not directly or immediately, anyway. But over the long haul, with enough of us chipping away at that crazy consensus, the general tide of opinion might eventually begin to turn. Terrorism might come to be reduced to its rightful place as a cruel nuisance to be marginalized as best we can, but unworthy as a major preoccupation of a great people. Politicians attempting to fix our focus on it for their narrowly partisan purposes ought be seen as subverting democracy, just as surely as the bombers themselves.

Weetangera, 1 July 2005

* * * * * *

Final manuscript for this book was delivered to the publishers shortly before the London transport bombings of July 2005, and I have been unable to take any account of those events and reactions to them. From what I am able to tell from half a world away, however, is seems that Londoners' reactions to those attacks are radically different from Americans' to those of 11 September 2001, in the ways that my text anticipated – and of which I wholly approve.[1]

Weetangera, 2 August 2005

Acknowledgements

Naturally, all of us have talked with a great many people over the past months and years about terrorism, how to understand it and what to do about it. When one's academic project abuts issues dominating public discourse in this way, it is hard to disentangle all the many contributions others have made to one's thinking on the subject.

I know that not all influences were academic. I vividly recall the scepticism of a taxi driver, clearly a denizen of darkest Washington SE, who pointed and said, 'That be the State Department; you can tell by the black clouds hovering above it.' We had a good discussion, but I'm afraid I didn't catch his name.

Those who I know influenced my thinking, through conversations or correspondence, include Brian Barry, Chuck Beitz, Geoff Brennan, Jerry Cohen, Angelo Corlett, Raymond Das, Lina Eriksson, Amitai Etzioni, Richard Falk, Andreas Føllesdal, Bruno Frey, Christel Fricke, Diane Gibson, Al Hájek, Renée Hájek, Jennifer Hochschild, Julian Le Grand, Catherine Lu, Larry May, Gill McAndrew, Jeff McMahan, Helen Nissenbaum, Bhikhu Parekh, Carole Pateman, Thomas Pogge, Martin Rein, Chris Reus-Smit, James Rice, David Rodin, Sam Scheffler, Jeremy Waldron, Adrian Walsh, Burleigh Wilkins and Andrew Williams. I am grateful more generally to various conference and seminar audiences in Armidale, Canberra, Oslo and Pasadena, and to my publishers' anonymous referees, as well as to Naomi Sussmann and her University of Haifa students who trialled it in the classroom. Finally, I am grateful to my publishers, especially Louise Knight and Ellen McKinlay, for their continuing faith in this venture.

This book is dedicated to Brian Barry. As mentor and friend, he taught me well – not only how to chew, but also when to swallow and when to spit.

1

Introduction

Let me be clear from the outset: the title of this book is anything but rhetorical. There are a great *many* things wrong with terrorism.[1]

Indeed, it is my thesis in this book that there are even *more* things wrong with it than commonly appreciated. The further, under-appreciated wrongs of terrorism I shall be concentrating upon in this book are of a predominantly *political* character.

The fundamental thought lying behind my argument is just this. Of course terrorists do *all sorts* of terrible things. They kill people. They destroy buildings and aeroplanes not belonging to them. They kidnap people and chop off their ears. All that is true, and it is morally enormously important. But pause to consider: what is the *distinctive* wrong of terrorism? The offence of 'killing people' is already on the moral statute books. So too are those of 'kidnapping', 'maiming' and 'destroying property not belonging to you'. What makes terrorists different from, and morally *even worse* than, ordinary murderers, kidnappers and so on? What is the moral disvalue of 'terrorism', over and above the moral disvalue of the particular acts (of murder, kidnapping, and so on) through which it is carried out?

I take it that any sensible definition of 'terrorism' simply must include, as a central feature, the fact that it involves the strategic use of terror. That is to say, terrorism is fundamentally strategic, and it is fundamentally aimed at instilling terror.

Terrorism as I shall be depicting it is first and foremost a *political* tactic: frightening people for political advantage. That is its core element. No doubt there are many other elements, of various familiar sorts, that it would also be necessary to add for a complete characterization of 'terrorism'. And no doubt there are a lot of other political tactics that involve frightening people for political advantage that do not constitute 'terrorism'.[2] Nonetheless, looking at terrorism as a subset of that larger class of more familiar political manoeuvres usefully brings to the fore the distinctively political wrong that is involved in terrorism.

Note well, however: if 'frightening people for their advantage' constitutes the analytic core of 'terrorism', then that is something that can be done by Western political leaders as part and parcel of their War on Terrorism as surely as it can be done by extremists in the course of their War of Terror. To what extent Western political leaders are actually guilty of doing that depends crucially upon their intentions. I do not pretend to have any privileged access to those; maybe we never really will know for sure. At least for now, I must therefore content myself with making a more philosophical point in a more hypothetical fashion.

Still, the point in this suitably hypothetical form remains. *If* (or *insofar as*) Western political leaders are intending to frighten people for their own political advantage, *then* (to *that extent*) they are committing the same core wrong that is distinctively associated with terrorism. Such, anyway, will be the argument of this book.

'Can that possibly be right?', one naturally asks oneself. 'Surely those who fly aeroplanes into buildings, killing thousands of people and destroying property, are guilty of *additional* moral crimes – and far *worse* moral crimes – than politicians who do nothing more than "frightening people for political advantage".'[3]

Certainly they are. My point is merely that those are *other* offences. What makes the terrorist pilots' behaviour not merely (*sic*) 'murder' and 'vandalism', but also 'terrorism', is that they act with the intention of instilling fear in people for their own political purposes. *That* is the distinctive feature that makes 'terrorist murderers' not merely 'murderers' but also 'terrorists'. And *that* is a feature that the behaviour of murderous terrorist pilots shares with the behaviour of politicians who commit no further moral offences (beyond merely frightening people for political advantage).

Very much the worst thing about mass-murdering terrorists is that they are mass murderers, not that they are terrorists. My account of 'terrorism' is a deflationary one: it is not as bad as we think, focusing just on the distinctively 'terrorist' element of a terrorist's act. But my account is also an expansionary one: there are more terrorists around than we might ordinarily imagine (Western political leaders mounting wars against terrorism being potentially among them).

More will be said over the course of this book to try to make those propositions convincing. But be warned that that is where the argument is heading.

* * * * * * * *

Be warned, too, about the nature of this book. It is largely an exercise in political philosophy, in the hard-nosed analytic mode.

I draw on facts as appropriate – probably more heavily than most of my peers in academic philosophy. Facts matter in any attempt at applying philosophical precepts to the real world. They are not the only things that matter, and not all of them matter equally. But certainly we should do our best to get the relevant facts wherever we can, to tailor our philosophizing to the actual world to which it is meant to apply.

Academic philosophers typically attempt to finesse the facts through toy examples. They abuse that procedure badly when they ask us to imagine some utterly fanciful scenario. 'What would we say in *that* case?', they enquire; but if the scenario is too outlandish, too far from the circumstances of ordinary life around which our intuitions have been shaped and to which they are adapted, it simply does not matter what we would say (and indeed, we may not even have anything much to say). 'Crazy cases' count for naught in attempting to apply moral philosophy to the real political world.[4]

In its proper place, however, that procedure can be absolutely invaluable. There are certain things we just do not (now) know that we would need to know to judge real-world actors. To help us see exactly what we would need to know – on what facts our judgements would actually turn – it can be enormously helpful to think our way through philosophical-style hypotheticals. 'We do not know exactly how the world actually is, but suppose it were this way: would the person be guilty of terrorism in that sort of case?' By then varying the scenarios ever so slightly and repeating the question, we can discover where exactly the cutting point comes, for us, between a terrorist and a non-terrorist. Thus, while I draw on facts where possible and appropriate, I also (in chapter 5 especially) employ philosophical-style hypotheticals to determine what facts might actually matter.

Although this is a philosopher's attempt to come to grips with the phenomenon of terrorism, it is designed to be generally accessible to all interested readers. Scholarly apparatus is kept to a minimum. Notes are used sparingly, and placed unobtrusively at the back of the book. Fine-grained philosophical analyses are eschewed in favour of a more 'big picture' approach. I hope (and fear) it is still evidently the work of a professional philosopher. But I hope it is also one that anyone interested in the topic can read with both profit and perhaps even pleasure.

* * * * * * * *

In this book, I shall be making much of 'definitions'. That is not merely the preoccupation of a philosophical fusspot. Definitions carry political consequences.

There is a lot of loose talk about 'terrorism'. Public officials are wont to describe just about anyone making political trouble for them, these days, as a terrorist.[5] Here are a couple of the more egregious examples I have come across:

- In announcing increased penalties for anyone convicted of illegal logging in eastern Philippine provinces prone to flooding as a result of deforestation, President Gloria Arroyo said, 'We are determined to make those responsible for death and destruction pay the price for their misdeeds, and we shall prosecute them' as 'terrorists'.[6]

- US Education Secretary Rod Paige, meeting with state governors at the White House in February 2004, 'said the National Education Association, one of the nation's largest unions, was like "a terrorist organization" because of the way it was resisting many provisions of a school improvement law pushed through Congress by President Bush.' His subsequent apology was singularly unapologetic: more in elaboration than retraction, Paige said, 'It was an inappropriate choice of words to describe the obstructionist scare tactics that the NEA's Washington lobbyists have employed against No Child Left Behind's historic education reforms.'[7]

But this misuse of the label 'terrorist' to tar any political opponent is not just the product of overstatement on the part of zealous junior officials. This sort of inflated definition is sometimes found at the highest levels, and sometimes even works its way into legislation.

Consider, for example, India's Prevention of Terrorism Act, 2002. There, a 'terrorist act' is defined as any act done 'with intent to threaten the unity, integrity, security or sovereignty of India' (followed by the more standard formulation 'or to strike terror in the people or any section of the people').[8] But note well: the former clause could well deem any opposition parties, however loyal, 'terrorist organizations'. After all, it is the job of the opposition to oppose, thereby engendering 'disunity and dissensus'.

Well, words mean whatever we say they mean, in an observation that Lewis Carroll attributes to Humpty Dumpty. And the law is whatever lawmakers say it is. But big words such as 'terrorist' carry mighty consequences, and we ought be correspondingly careful how we use them. Fussing over definitions in such circumstances is anything but pure pedantry. Figuring out what exactly terrorism is and what exactly makes it so wrong is crucial to framing an appropriate response to that evil.

2

Terrorism as Unjust War: Killing Innocent Civilians

Nowadays terrorism is typically defined as involving most fundamentally 'violence against' (and in the limiting case 'the killing of') 'innocent civilians'. The wrongness of terrorism then follows almost automatically from the simple analytic fact that it is wrong, by definition, to harm (especially kill) 'the innocent'.[1]

That is very much the orthodox way of approaching such problems. Theories of 'just war' handed down to us from medieval Church fathers have been assimilated into international law, culminating in the Geneva Conventions.[2] Because that is our received way of moralizing about the use of force, it is also the most natural way for us to begin to think about the use of force by terrorists, be they foreign or domestic.

Among academics, Michael Walzer, whose *Just and Unjust Wars* constitutes the leading exposition of just-war theory for our time, did much to champion that characterization of terrorism as well.[3] As he summarizes that position,

> Terrorism is the deliberate killing of innocent people, at random, in order to spread fear through a whole population and force the hand of its political leaders.

Elaborating, he writes,

> The victims of a terrorist attack are third parties, innocent bystanders; there is no special reason for attacking them; anyone else within

a large class of (unrelated) people would do as well. The attack is
directed indiscriminately against the entire class.[4]

A plethora of academic commentators follow Walzer's lead
in defining terrorism as essentially involving violence against
innocent civilians.[5]

It is not just academics who think this way, however. This
view of 'terrorism' as violence against innocent civilians is
enshrined in US law. Title 22, section 2656f(d) of the *US Code*
defines terrorism as:

> pre-meditated politically motivated violence perpetrated against
> non-combatants, targeted by sub-national groups or clandestine
> agents, usually intended to influence an audience.

This is the definition on which both the US State Department
and the CIA rely in their official pronouncements on terrorism,
and it is presumably this definition that guides their efforts
against it as well.[6] The same is true of the US Army. Its *Field
Manual* on the subject instructs soldiers that:

> In contrast [to terrorism], war is subject to international law. Ter-
> rorists recognize no rules. No person, place or object of value is
> immune from terrorist attack. There are no innocents.[7]

This is also the dominant mode of public discourse about
terrorism. 'Terrorism as an attack on innocent civilians' was
the central, recurring motif in discussions of the attacks of
September 11. Just reflect on these examples:

- In his address to the US Congress shortly after those
  attacks, President George W. Bush pointedly remarked,
  'The terrorists' directive commands them to kill Christians
  and Jews, to kill all Americans, and make no distinction
  among military and civilians, including women and
  children.'[8]
- The Preface to the official *9/11 Commission Report* identifies a 'new enemy', terrorism, the defining feature of which

is that 'it makes no distinction between military and civilian targets. Collateral damage is not in its lexicon.'[9]

- It comes as no surprise that theologically oriented commentators such as Jean Bethke Elshtain talk of terrorism in those terms: 'Surely there can be little doubt in anyone's mind that the attacks of September 11 constituted an act of aggression aimed specifically at killing civilians. . . . If we cannot distinguish the killing of combatants from the intended targeting of peaceable civilians . . . we live in a world of moral nihilism. In such a world, everything reduces to the same shade of grey and we cannot make distinctions that help us take our political and moral bearings. The victims of September 11 deserve more from us.'[10]

- More surprisingly, perhaps, is the way in which even radical commentators see the significance, and peculiar wrong, of those attacks similarly: 'There is no doubt', Noam Chomsky for example writes, 'that the 9-11 atrocities were an event of historic importance, not – regrettably – because of their scale, but because of the choice of innocent victims. . . . The sharp break in the traditional pattern surely qualifies 9-11 as a historic event, and the repercussions are sure to be significant.'[11]

All seem agreed: the chief sin of the September 11 attackers was one of fighting dirty, 'killing innocent civilians' in contravention of established norms of civilized conduct, codified in the international law of war.

Note, finally, that this just-war approach to terrorism also pervades international thinking on these matters. A UN resolution on 'Human Rights and Terrorism', for example, begins by

> *Profoundly deploring* the increasing number of innocent persons, including women, children and the elderly, killed, massacred and maimed by terrorists in indiscriminate and random acts of violence and terror, which cannot be justified under any circumstances.[12]

And the UN's 1999 International Convention for the Suppression of the Financing of Terrorism defines terrorism as:

> Any . . . act intended to cause death or serious bodily injury to a civilian, or to any other person not taking an active part in the hostilities in a situation of armed conflict, when the purpose of such an act, by its nature or context, is to intimidate a population, or to compel a government or an international organization to do or to abstain from doing any act.[13]

Perhaps the most telling evidence of the extent to which the just-war model pervades international-organizational thinking about terrorism is found, however, in the 'short legal definition of terrorism' commended by the UN Office on Drugs and Crime:

> Act of Terrorism = Peacetime Equivalent of War Crime.[14]

Three problems with the just-war analysis of terrorism

For my own part, I doubt that this 'just-war' fixation on the 'killing of innocent civilians' is the best way to analyse what terrorism is and what is (especially) wrong with it. My doubts are rooted in several thoughts. Those thoughts point in several different directions. But they all, I think, pull us away from any easy 'just-war' assimilation of the wrongness of terrorism to off-the-shelf analyses of the wrongness of 'killing innocent civilians'.

In setting out these problems with the just-war style analysis of terrorism, I ought acknowledge at the outset the intricate casuistry that characterizes just-war theory. Just-war theorists will always be able, with enough twisting and turning, to wiggle out of any tight spots they find themselves in. Whether the casuistry is credible, whether the escape attempts ultimately succeed, are matters that I will not discuss here: this is not intended principally as a book about just-war theory, and getting sucked into its endless twists and turns would take us much too far from this book's intended focus.

The fact that so much twisting and turning would be required to rescue the just-war analysis of terrorism is in itself something of a bad sign. But let us leave whether it can eventually succeed as an open question. Suffice it to say that the problems to which I point constitute, at the very least, a 'case to answer' for the just-war analysis of terrorism.

* * * * * * * *

First, how exactly does the 'killing innocents' formulation distinguish terrorism from simple murder? Murder victims are innocent, too. (Or, if not 'innocent' in some absolute, theological sense, certainly they have done nothing that suffices to justify the fate inflicted on them.)[15] If the wrongness of terrorism is exhausted by the wrongness of 'killing those who are innocent', then terrorists have done nothing morally worse than ordinary murder. Were that true, it would powerfully deflate what we ordinarily regard as the wrongness of terrorism.

(Of course, I want to deflate it too – just not *that* completely. Much the worst thing the terrorist murderers do is to commit murder. But doing so for terrorist purposes is an added wrong on my analysis, in a way it seems not to be on the just-war analysis.)[16]

Of course terrorists who kill many people at once are not 'simple' murderers but are, instead, 'mass' murderers. Morally, of course it is worse to commit multiple murders than a single murder; and it may also be worse, morally, to commit 'mass murder' than merely 'multiple murders'. Then terrorists engaged in mass murder would be deserving of those heightened degrees of moral censure. Still, what on this analysis they would be deserving is censure for (mass) murder: nothing less, but also nothing more.

The moral wrongness of terrorism would, on this analysis, be put on a par with that of a common or garden lunatic gone on a (highly successful) killing spree. Again, that simply does not seem right. Terrorism seems worse than that, somehow.

* * * * * * * * * *

A second worry, one that often arises within discussion of 'just war' itself, is that there are gradations of complicity and inno- cence. Given those gradations, there may not be all that many people who are completely innocent. Thus, in just-war connec- tions, we can question whether workers in munition factories, although undeniably 'civilians', are truly 'innocent' of complic- ity in the war in a way that ought render them immune from deliberate targeting. And, in a broader sense, we might even question whether perhaps all Germans who were eligible to vote in the 1933 elections were not to some extent complicit in bringing Hitler to power.

In assessing the attacks of September 11, we might ask similar questions. In the Lords debate, Paddy Ashdown, an ex- SAS officer and former leader of the Liberal Democrats, described the events of that day as 'an attack . . . on the centres of global power and the heart of global capitalism'.[17]

For Lord Ashdown that was a source of particular horror. But had the attackers been sensitive to just-war concerns, that same fact might well have been a point of honour. The attack- ers or their apologists could point with just-war pride to the fact that the attacks were carefully targeted. They were aimed precisely at the command centres of the US military-industrial complex: the Pentagon and the self-styled 'World Trade Center'.[18]

True, not everyone in those buildings was actually directly complicit in all the acts of the US military-industrial complex as a whole (if such a thing exists at all). But the same is true of any well-focused attack on legitimate targets in a just war of a more ordinary sort. Even in the General Headquarters in some genuine military campaign, there are always some people sweeping floors or making tea; there are always some civilians on site; and so on.

The basic just-war point is that, insofar as GHQ is indeed the command centre of the military campaign, it and the commanders operating there constitute a legitimate target. Assuming all the other conditions of a just war are met, opposing forces are morally permitted intentionally to target it for destruction. They are morally permitted to do so, even in the knowledge that some innocents may (or maybe even will, with certainty) be harmed in the process, as long as that collateral damage to innocents is an unintended (albeit foreseeable) by-product. Hence, on standard just-war theory, if the Pentagon and World Trade Center really were command centres of a military-industrial complex that just-war standards allowed opposing forces to target, and all other conditions of a just war were met, then even the (foreseeable but unintended) deaths of children in the creche would have been morally permissible.

The children in the creche were pretty undeniably 'innocent', by any sensible standards. But we might well query just how innocent many of the others were. True, the janitors at the Pentagon were not making any command decisions; they might even have been civilians cleaning the building under contract. The GHQ during a conventional military campaign might similarly bring in local ladies to clean or cook, as well. Still, just-war theorists might go on to say that nobody working in GHQ, or the Pentagon either, could credibly claim not to know what the core business of that enterprise was. And, although the case is a little less clear, perhaps something similar might be said of people walking past the sign styling their workplace 'the World Trade Center' every day on their way to work.

In such situations, claims to 'innocence' in any naive sense would be unsustainable. Such people knew, or could and should reasonably have known, what was going on there. They may not have played a very important part in those operations. But just-war theory makes no distinctions on that score: the lowest signals corpsman is as legitimate a target as the highest general.

Either way, the same basic conclusion follows on just-war logic. *If* there is such a thing as a US military-industrial complex, and *if* it is guilty of moral atrocities, and *if* various other conditions of a 'just war' are met, then its command centres would under just-war theory be legitimate targets. Not all those working in those command centres are necessarily directly complicit in the wrongs in view, but none can complain if they are caught in the legitimate targeting of those buildings, any more than can a contract janitor in GHQ during a military battle. Let me be clear on two points, here. The first is that I do not believe that this sort of argument actually justifies the attacks of September 11. There are simply too many unsustainable 'ifs' in the above chain of argument: '*if* there is such a thing as the US military-industrial complex'; '*if* all the conditions of a just war against it were met'; and so on. And even if all those 'ifs' were sustained, a just-war theorist would still pause at the manner in which the attacks were carried out. A just-war theorist might complain, for example, that they were 'sneak attacks' without any formal warning or any declaration of war;[19] or a just-war theorist might complain over the lack of a 'just cause for going to war', saying those attacks were 'unprovoked' by anything that the US had done.[20]

My point is just this: I think it is a morally damning fact about 'just-war' theory and its peculiar analysis of the wrongness of 'killing innocents' that it *could* have accepted those attacks and the resulting devastation as morally legitimate, if the facts had lined up differently. Of course facts matter. And of course war is a dirty business that is better for its being governed by some standards than by none at all. The standards of just-war theory might, for all I know, be the best ones available (or even conceivable) for governing military engagements of conventional and perhaps even many non-conventional sorts. But trying to shoehorn the analysis of what is morally wrong with terrorism into that theory seems to me a step too far.

* * * * * * * * * * *

There is a third and yet more powerful reason, I think, to resist conflating the wrong of terrorism with 'killing innocent civilians'. That locution suggests something that I think we ought not readily concede – certainly not anyway in each and every case of terrorism, as we would be doing if defining the generic wrongness of terrorism in those terms.

The implication of charging terrorists with the just-war crime of 'killing innocent civilians' suggests – implicitly, but nonetheless powerfully – that, while these particular targets were 'innocent civilians', there were others who would have been legitimate targets of similar attacks. The category of 'civilian' makes sense only as a contrast case to 'combatant'. Were *everyone* a civilian, there would be no particular point in describing anyone in particular in that way.

The standard application of just-war theory is to military campaigns, of course. There, complaints about 'killing innocent civilians' make sense, precisely because there are indeed combatants who ought to have been targeted instead. But except where terrorism is being conducted as part of a literal war – which is true in only a tiny subset of all cases of terrorism – there are no combatants who ought have been targeted instead.

Just-war theory is essentially a framework for governing state-on-state violence. In trying to shoehorn terrorism into that framework, we are implicitly agreeing to treat terrorist groups 'as if' they were states and 'as if' they were waging war. Sometimes that model works tolerably well. It does, for example, when terrorism is part of a guerilla war, or a revolutionary struggle, or a struggle for national liberation. There, the terrorist group constitutes in effect a 'government-in-waiting'; and there, the terrorists' complaint is indeed with the existing state, its officials and its soldiers. In other cases, however, the terrorist group is not a quasi-state and its complaint is not principally with the existing state, its officers or soldiers: at most, terrorists want to bring pressure to bear (whether on innocent civilians or duly authorized agents of the state) in order to make some *other* people do something differently. Shoehorning that different sort of terrorism into a quasi-state model, and trying to make just-war theory fit, is inevitably going to work less well.

Just-war talk of 'innocent civilians' implicitly contrasts them with 'non-innocent non-civilians'. In any community there are

always some 'non-civilians' – armed people in uniform, be they
in the army or the police. But depending on the particulars of
the terrorists' complaint, those non-civilians might be wholly
innocent of what they are complaining about and wholly powerless to do anything to alter it.

Just-war theory, in the context of literal wars, renders all
soldiers 'non-innocent' and legitimate targets for attack.[21] In
analysing terrorism in those terms, we would be implicitly
extending that proposition much more broadly.[22] Any group
with a complaint legitimated by *jus ad bellum* standards and
pursued in *jus in bello* ways would be permitted to attack any
officers of the state (police or soldiers) that they liked.

Even accepting that those conditions of just war will rarely
be met, are we really all that comfortable with that implication? Potentially legitimating indiscriminate cop-killing seems
to be one further implication of the just-war analysis of terrorism that ought give us pause.[23]

* * * * * * * * * * * *

Besides, how much comfort, exactly, can we take from the
thought that the full conditions of a just war will rarely be met
in the case of terrorist campaigns?

Less than we might initially suppose, I think.[24] Here is why.
In ordinary just-war thinking, *jus in bello* (just conduct in the
course of a war) is treated as a wholly separate issue from *jus
ad bellum* (the justice of going to war). The two issues are
traditionally taken to be 'logically independent', in the words
of the pre-eminent scholar of just war in the present
generation.[25]

Of course, all parties to a war ordinarily claim (however
disingenuously) that they had justice on their side in going to
war; so, from the point of view of the participants themselves,
jus ad bellum conditions always seem to be met. But even if
they were not, we would not want to exempt combatants from
the constraints of *jus in bello*. Suppose midway into a war I
learn (indeed, suppose my leader announces) that our grounds
for going to war were wrong: in error, or even unjust. Surely

that does not exempt me as a soldier from conducting myself in the course of that war according to just-war *jus in bello* standards. If anything, I would then have a reason to be more scrupulous, not less, in my adherence to *jus in bello* standards, lest I aggravate the moral crime involved in our initiating an unjust war in the first place.

That disconnection between *jus in bello* and *jus ad bellum* seems right, civilized, as regards the standard application of just-war doctrine to ordinary wars and ordinary combatants. But transposing just-war thinking along those lines to the case of terrorism seems to lead to less comforting conclusions. In particular, it seems to provide even more of a licence for cop-killing than the argument sketched previously. It says to the would-be terrorist: 'Bracket the issue of the justice of your cause; just make sure you kill only combatants (police etc.).'[26]

Note one further disquieting feature of the disconnection between *jus ad bellum* and *jus in bello* that is traditional in just-war thinking. Ordinary foot-soldiers are prosecuted as war criminals only for violations of *jus in bello*, for things such as killing innocent civilians in the course of the war. Ordinary foot-soldiers are not prosecuted as war criminals responsible for violating *jus ad bellum* by initiating an unjust war; they are held responsible only for violations of *jus in bello* when fighting a war unjustly.[27] It is only their leaders, who took them to war, who are liable to prosecution as war criminals on grounds of violation of the standards of *jus ad bellum*.

Again, that seems reasonable and proper in the standard cases to which just-war thinking is traditionally applied, to cases of state-on-state violence. But it has worrying implications, once again, when we transpose it to the case of terrorism. This aspect of just-war theory would have the effect of exempting terrorist foot-soldiers from worrying about the justice of their cause. *Jus ad bellum* is a problem only for their leaders; ordinary foot-soldiers only need concern themselves with *jus in bello*. So as long as the terrorist foot-soldier intentionally targets only combatants (police, army, etc.), he is on morally safe ground, or anyway ought be immune from prosecution if we are thinking about terrorism along just-war lines.

But that conclusion seems highly problematic. And, worse still, none of the obvious ways of evading that conclusion seem particularly promising. True, terrorist foot-soldiers are volunteers: but so too are the foot-soldiers in a great many armies of the world. True, the terrorist groups' leaders are typically unelected and indeed often literally self-appointed: but, again, that is true of lots of leaders of sovereign states. True, terrorist groups typically do not 'declare war' but, rather, strike randomly and in unexpected ways: but, again, some states have done the same.

With states and state officials that are sub-optimal in all those respects, we nonetheless want to apply just-war doctrine to them in all the ordinary ways. They should go to war only on *jus ad bellum* conditions; they should fight wars only on *jus in bello* terms; ordinary foot-soldiers should be liable only for their own violations of the latter, while it is leaders who should be liable for the former (and systematic violations of the latter). If that is the right thing to say about states even of those sub-optimal sorts, why is it not the right thing to say about terrorist groups displaying the same features?

One reason (discussed further in chapter 4 below) might be that just-war doctrine, by definition, applies only to 'war' and that 'war' is something that, by definition, states alone can engage in. Of course, groups aspiring to form new states, through revolutionary action or wars of national liberation, would resist that claim. (We might even want to adjust the definitions above so that 'wars' can be engaged in by either 'states' or 'proto-states', thus counting among the latter any group that aspires to statehood.)[28]

This may well be the most promising way around the predicaments I have been describing.[29] But note well how it avoids those predicaments: by denying that terrorists can conduct wars, strictly speaking. And the implication of that would be that terrorism, and what is morally wrong with it, cannot properly be analysed in just-war terms. If terrorist groups are not the sorts of entities that can logically conduct what are properly called 'wars', then they cannot do so 'justly' or otherwise. It is simply a 'category mistake' to apply the term to their conduct.

This conclusion may or may not be right.[30] But in any case, it is stronger than I strictly need for the argument I am here making. Whether or not just-war doctrine is analytically inapplicable to the behaviour of terrorists, purely as a matter of definition and logic, I want to argue that just-war doctrine does not provide the best way to analyse what is most fundamentally and distinctively wrong with terrorism, morally.

A different sense of 'innocence'

So far I have been speaking of 'innocence' in a fairly colloquial, non-technical way. But in some versions of just-war theory it takes on a very particular meaning. When talking of 'innocence' or 'guilt' ('complicity in wrong-doing', etc.), we are ordinarily talking about 'moral innocence': people have done something wrong, for which they are to blame. But just-war theorists sometimes try to disassociate themselves from that simple notion of 'moral innocence', redefining 'innocence' in a way that better tracks whom they think ought be legitimate military targets in a just war.

Here are a couple of examples of the sorts of embarrassment that arise for them from the ordinary notion of moral innocence. Imagine a conscript soldier, who is personally opposed to the war he is being forced to fight, who even voted against the government waging the war and evades orders whenever he possibly can. He is morally innocent – he is fighting under duress.[31] But if forced he will obey orders to attack. Insofar as that is true, he poses a threat to those whom he would attack; and just-war theory had better deem him a legitimate target for attack by soldiers on the other side.

Or, for a second awkward case, imagine a civilian who is not in any sense engaged in war work but who is a fervent supporter of the regime and its war effort. She makes speeches, buys war bonds, does all manner of things to lend 'aid and comfort' to the perpetrators of the war. She is in some sense 'morally guilty', even if her aid and comfort are in no way essential or even remotely helpful to the war effort. Still, just-war theorists feel they should insist that, as a civilian non-combatant, she is not a legitimate target for attack by opposing armies.[32]

To accommodate counter-examples such as these, just-war theorists tend to redefine 'innocence' broadly in terms of 'self-defence'. This redefinition works in either, and usually both, of two ways. Sometimes it is said that the 'innocent' are those who are 'defenceless'; other times it is said that the 'innocent' are those who pose no threat to opposing soldiers. Civilians, by definition, are unarmed; and captured or incapacitated soldiers are disarmed. The fact that they can neither defend themselves nor harm others explains why on just-war precepts none of them ought be harmed.[33]

This analysis is sometimes carried across to just-war style analyses of the wrong of terrorism. What is wrong with taking innocents captive, for example, in order to bargain for the release of jailed members of some terrorist gang? Well, on this account, it is precisely the fact that there is nothing that those innocent hostages can themselves do to comply with the terrorists' demands. Terrorists are guilty of the Kantian offence of 'using people as means', rather than respecting them as 'ends' in their own right.

* * * * * * * *

I have my doubts about defining 'innocents,' for just-war purposes, as those who are unthreatening and defenceless. I do not think that tracks our intuitions about who ought be immune from attack in today's sort of military combat. Neither do I think that that tracks our intuitions about who ought be immune from attack by terrorists.

In the military case, consider high-level aerial bombardment of emplacements that lack anti-aircraft weapons capable of reaching the aeroplanes attacking them. Then the ground troops pose no threat to the bombardiers, and they are defence-less against them. If 'innocence' is defined purely in those terms, and purely on a dyadic basis (a soldier on the ground *vis-à-vis* a bombardier in the plane), then the ground troops do indeed qualify as 'innocent' and hence they should be immune from attack on just-war principles interpreted in that way. But that seems absurd. Aerial bombardment may often be morally suspect, but surely not on *those* grounds.

Perhaps the absurdity arises from seeing the situation in too narrowly dyadic a perspective. Perhaps instead of looking at it as a matter of the ground forces' threats to and defences against particular bombardiers, we ought be looking at it in a more systemic perspective. The ground troops are part of an armed force that is posing a threat to elements of the armed forces of which the bombardiers are a part.

But press the 'systemic' point and you begin to see an unravelling of the banker's daughter's immunity to being taken hostage by terrorists seeking finance for their activities. She is herself 'innocent' in the sense of posing no threat to, and having no defence against, her captors. But she is part of a system – a kinship network, in her case – that does have the capacity to meet her captors' demands, and in that way defend her against their threats to kill her.

The argument here in view suggests that there ought be immunity against terrorist threats for (and only for) people who are 'innocent' in the sense of posing no threat to and having no defence against the terrorists. But does that mean that there should be no immunity against terrorist threats for people who *do* pose a threat to the terrorists (police chiefs, judges)? Or for people who are *not* defenceless, in the sense that there is something they could do to meet the terrorists' demands (millionaires, heads of state)?

Again, that seems absurd. The absurdity in both cases rests, I submit, with the definition of 'innocence' in terms of self-defence – posing no threat and having no defence.

* * * * * * * *

My aim in entering all these objections to the just-war model of terrorism as 'killing innocent civilians' is not to offer excuses for terrorists. My objection to that way of analysing terrorism is precisely that it allows them too much room for excuses, and for excuses that (in my view) operate at the wrong places to boot.

War crime, ordinary crime or a special offence?

One of the virtues of applying just-war principles to terrorism is, perhaps, that that takes seriously a self-conception that terrorists often harbour. They see themselves as engaged in a war: a holy war against infidels, or axes of evil; a war of national liberation against unjust occupiers; a revolutionary war against a domestic tyrant or an oppressive socio-politico-economic system. 'In Northern Ireland, members of the IRA starved themselves to death to press their demands that they be treated as prisoners of "war" rather than as ordinary criminals.'[34]

Spokespersons for the state apparatus under attack in this way have often insisted on calling campaigns against those terrorists 'police actions'. They insistently reserve for states alone the prerogative to wage wars (justly or otherwise). Declaring a 'war on terrorism' at least pays the terrorist groups the respect of being taken seriously in the terms in which they wish to be regarded, and being recognized as the sort of entity that *can* enter into a war.[35]

Of course, if they are waging a war, then terrorist groups ought morally be bound by the standard canons commonly recognized at international law as to what constitutes a *just* war. Among other things, that means not deliberately targeting innocent civilians. Under just-war canons, non-combatants may be harmed in the course of a just war only as the unintended (albeit perhaps foreseeable) effect of an attack on some other legitimate target. (That, as noted before, has the morally worrying consequence that even the deaths of the children in the Twin Tower creche might – given a long string of 'ifs' – have been a morally permissible by-product of a just war.)

* * * * * * * * *

International lawyers have a reason of their own for wanting to conflate the crime of terrorism with ordinary war crimes. The reason is simple: we already have a rich set of international legal instruments (the Geneva Conventions, etc.) governing war crimes.[36] If we could simply apply those to terrorism, we would not have to negotiate any new treaties to cope with that phenomenon. So the suggestion is this:

> [Ra]ther than trying to negotiate new treaties on terrorism that are not likely to be ratified or enforced, nations should apply the laws of war, to which almost all have agreed. Terrorists . . . should be dealt with as soldiers who commit atrocities. Nearly all countries have agreed to try to extradite soldiers who commit atrocities in international armed conflicts. Why should persons not explicitly granted soldiers' status be given greater leeway to commit violence? Under the laws-of-war approach, terrorism would comprise all acts committed in peacetime that, if committed during war, would constitute war crimes.[37]

The pragmatics of that approach are beyond criticism. It is better that bad behaviour be subject to some law than no law; and if the 'law of war' is the only law that realistically could ever be brought to bear on terrorists, then let that law apply. For legal purposes, let us treat terrorism 'as if' it were a war crime.

We may well be forced to think of terrorism that way in international law. But that does not mean that we should necessarily think of it that way outside those narrowly international-legal contexts. As we well know, the law is full of fictions that are absolutely essential for its effective functioning. Still, just because the law is forced, for its narrow purposes, to treat corporations 'as if' they were persons, that is no reason for us to do so outside those narrow contexts. (So, for example, those of us opposed to capital punishment for flesh-and-blood people need not extend that opposition, on the grounds 'corporations are persons', to 'corporate capital punishment': winding up corporations that have egregiously violated company law, for example.)

The exigencies of law, international as well as domestic, force us to pretend that all sorts of things are 'just so' when we know well that they are not. Here is another example from the realm of the international law of terrorism. Article 11 of the International Convention for the Suppression of Terrorist Bombing stipulates that

> none of the offences [covered by the Convention] ... shall be regarded, for the purposes of extradition ... as a political offence or ... as an offence inspired by political motives. Accordingly, a request for extradition ... based on such an offence may not be refused on the sole ground that it concerns a political offence.[38]

Now, of course it is absurd to suppose that the terrorist offences covered by that convention are never 'inspired by political motives' (almost invariably they are). But that is a necessary fiction within international law, because extradition treaties typically exempt people accused of political crimes from extradition. If terrorists are to be extraditable under this Convention at all, it has to pretend that their crimes are not political, when clearly they are.[39]

In like manner, it might be convenient for the reasons given earlier to treat terrorism 'as if' it were a war crime, at international law. That may be the best, perhaps the only, way in which international law can be brought to bear on terrorists. But just because international law has to think of terrorism that way does not mean that that is the best way for us to think about the phenomenon, morally or politically, outside those narrowly international-law contexts.

* * * * * * * *

Some commentators try to fudge the question of the distinctiveness of terrorist offences in another direction. They say that, when terrorists kill innocent civilians, it makes no difference whether we regard the terrorists as being engaged in a war or a crime.

The RAND Corporation launched a pioneering analysis, and ongoing chronology, of terrorism in 1972. Early on, the team leader reports, they 'concluded that an act of terrorism was first of all a crime in the classic sense such as murder or kidnapping, albeit for political motives.' So the question naturally arose, 'Should [we] . . . deal with terrorism as crime or as a mode of warfare?'[40]

Maybe it makes no difference. 'All terrorist acts are crimes', the RAND thinking goes, 'many of which would also be war crimes or "grave breaches" of the rules of war if we accepted the terrorists' assertion that they are waging war.'[41] If the terrorists are engaged in a war, then deliberately killing innocent civilians is a war crime. If they are not engaged in a war, then deliberately killing innocent civilians is just plain murder. Either way, it is clearly wrong. For determining that bottom-line moral judgement, there is no need for us to decide precisely which sort of wrong it is: war crime, or ordinary crime.

This fudging of the issue – treating terrorism sometimes as a violation of the ordinary criminal code, sometimes as a violation of the international law of war – pervades the US response to the events of September 11. As David Luban observes,

> In the immediate aftermath of September 11, President Bush stated that the perpetrators of the deed would be brought to justice. Soon afterwards, the President announced that the United States would engage in a war on terrorism. The first of these statements adopts the familiar language of criminal law and criminal justice. It treats the September 11 attacks as horrific crimes – mass murders – and the government's mission as apprehending and punishing the surviving planners and conspirators for their roles in the crimes. The War on Terrorism is a different proposition, however, and a different model of governmental action – not law but war.[42]

Throughout the ongoing campaigns against the terrorist threat, the US government has continued to vacillate, treating terrorism as lying 'in a twilight zone somewhere between criminal law and the law of war'.[43]

* * * * * * *

I can appreciate the appeal of fudging the issue in that way. But I also see dangers in it, ones that are far more serious than any difficulties that the fudge allows us to evade.

The cost of this fudge comes in deciding what it is permissible for us to do in response to the terrorists' wrong or threatened wrong. In deciding that, it turns out to be pretty important *which* sort of wrong the terrorists' wrong is (or would be).[44]

According to the conventions that define the rule of just wars, it is permissible to kill enemy troops simply because they are enemy troops, regardless of what they happen to be doing at the moment. It is permissible to kill enemy troops on grounds of the threat that they might pose, sometime in the future, rather than (necessarily) on grounds of what they have done in the past or are doing at present. It is permissible to exercise potentially lethal force against enemy troops on grounds of their intentions, even if those have not yet issued in action. Under the rules of just war, no particularly high standard of proof is required – merely 'plausible intelligence'[45] – before firing on someone as an enemy soldier. Under the rules of just war, it is permissible to inflict unintended (albeit foreseeable) harm on innocent civilians in pursuit of legitimate military objectives.[46]

None of that is permissible under the conventions that define the rule of law, in the domestic non-war context. Officers of the state may (after due process of law) detain and imprison people for what they have done. But people can be justly detained and imprisoned, under the rule of law, only for what they have done – not merely for what they might do or even intend to do in the future. Under the ordinary rule of law, police officers can exercise lethal force only against those who are actively threatening them or others. Under the ordinary rule of law, people may justly be detained and imprisoned (much less shot) only upon the basis of much stronger evidence than just war requires.[47] And under the ordinary rule of law, it is not permissible for police (in a way it would be, under the rule of just war, for soldiers) to blow up a building harbouring criminals who are firing on them, if they know that a number of other innocent people in the building would also die in the blast.

There are also important differences between what one can appropriately do to people detained and imprisoned under the rules of just war and those detained and imprisoned under the rule of law. Under the rules of just war, embodied in the Geneva Conventions, enemy soldiers may be held captive but not punished; and once the war is over, they must be released and repatriated.[48] Under the ordinary rule of law, convicted criminals may properly be punished (so long as it is not in ways that are 'cruel and unusual'); and they have no claim to be released until their just sentence has been served.[49]

* * * * * * *

Of course, in 'emergency' situations the rule of law can be and often has been suspended.[50] The US Constitution allows the right of habeas corpus to be suspended, and prisoners to be held without formal charges, 'when in cases of rebellion or invasion the public safety may require it'.[51] The Roman Constitution made much more elaborate provisions. In both those cases, though, the emergency suspension of the ordinary rule of law was strictly time-limited: for a specific period of time, in the Roman case; or for the duration of the emergency, in the US case.[52]

The striking thing, frequently commented upon, about the 'emergency' defined by the War on Terror is that it is an emergency without end. That is said to be one of 'the principal differences between the current war against terrorism and more conventional wars: . . . this war may never end.'[53] The president has in effect 'been ceded the power to define the beginning, duration and end of our current state of "war". This power has allowed the Executive to place our nation in a perpetual state of crisis'; and 'in war the laws are silent' ('*inter arma silent leges*', as the Latin maxim puts it).[54]

That is not merely the judgement of some excitable civil libertarians. President Bush admits as much. He said at one point, of the War on Terrorism: 'I don't think you can win it.'[55] The president prefers nowadays to put it less bluntly: 'We went to war because we were attacked, and we are at war today because there are still people out there who want to harm our country and hurt our citizens.'[56] But when has that not been true, of someone somewhere in the world? 'Terrorism is not a threat that is temporary', quite simply because we 'cannot count on ending a phenomenon that can be brought about by any small group in a world of seven billion people.'[57]

The official US *9/11 Commission Report* agrees:

> We do not believe it is possible to defeat all terrorist attacks against Americans, every time and everywhere. A president should tell the American people, 'No president can promise that a catastrophic attack like that of 9/11 will not happen again. History has shown that even the most vigilant and expert agencies cannot always prevent determined, suicidal attackers from reaching a target. But the American people are entitled to expect their government to do its very best.'[58]

'Doing its best' refers, of course, to the 'emergency measures' that will, on the Commission's own analysis, therefore be required to remain in force indefinitely, perhaps in perpetuity.

The US military concurred when setting about constructing at Guantánamo Bay permanent jails 'modeled on US medium-security civilian prisons and made of steel and concrete in place of the welded shipping containers used as cells' at present for the terrorist suspects being held there indefinitely without trial. 'Since global war on terror is a long-term effort, it makes sense for us to be looking at solutions for long-term problems', a Pentagon spokesperson explained.[59]

The Director-General of the Security Service in Britain agrees, writing in the preface to the Home Office's discussion paper on *Counter-Terrorism Powers*, 'I see no prospect of a significant reduction in the threat posed to the UK and its interests from international terrorism over the next five years, and I fear for a considerable number of years thereafter.' On that basis, the Home Secretary argues for continuation of emergency anti-terrorism powers beyond the date they were initially due to lapse.[60]

It is not just that Bush and Blunkett, like President Nixon before them, have a seemingly never-ending list of 'enemies' to be pursued seriatim. More importantly, killing terrorists *creates* terrorists. As in any blood feud, so too in the war on terror: measures and counter-measures form a never-ending cycle, with each side regarding the other's last step as compelling grounds for its own next step.[61]

Furthermore, the problem with waging war on non-state groups without any settled internal structure of authority is that there is no one with authority to negotiate the termination of hostilities. (Traditional just-war prohibits killing the head of the opposing state or its ambassadors precisely in order to avoid that awkwardness.)

In short, terrorists will always be with us. Any given individual might be killed or might surrender. Any given group might be broken up, if never quite vanquished. But there is no one empowered to surrender on behalf of 'terrorists' *tout court*.[62] The only way for the War on Terror to come to an end is (in the old Vietnam era slogan) for its prosecutors to 'declare victory and go home'. And, for reasons discussed in chapter 7 below, there does not seem to be any immediate prospect of that happening.

And the upshot of that, in turn, is that 'the "emergency" steps that we take today to combat terrorism – the "temporary" compromises we strike with our liberties – are likely to become part of the permanent fabric of our legal and political culture. Sunset provisions written into laws restricting our freedoms will be less effective in the context of terrorism than in other contexts, because the sun will never set on terrorism and the fear it provokes.'[63]

* * * * * *

It does therefore make a big difference – both to those deemed 'terrorists' and to the civic quality of the society fighting them – whether we regard the struggle against terrorism as a War on Terror (subject to the rules of just war) or as an ordinary police action (subject to the rule of law). Each puts a distinctive set of powers in the hands of public officials; each also brings with it a distinctive set of constraints on how government may legitimately pursue the struggle.

Neither set of rules seems to be being applied systematically in the War on Terror, however. In both the US and UK, the rules being invented to govern the War on Terror are a code of 'permanent emergency rule', in which the constraints of the ordinary rule of law are suspended indefinitely (possibly in perpetuity) but the constraints involved in the rules of just war are ignored as well. Suspected terrorists have been detained indefinitely without trial; and even when those practices were declared to be illegal (in contravention of the European Convention on Human Rights and the US Constitution)[64] similar practices persisted (house arrest in place of jail; delaying tactics in place of refusal even to arraign suspects). The CIA has, contrary to international law, flown captives to countries where they could be interrogated using torture.[65] In this hybrid, neither the rules of just war nor the rule of law are respected. Governments, evoking a notion of 'permanent emergency', proceed unconstrained by either code.[66]

For those who cherish the notion of limited government, this is a sorry state of affairs indeed. That state of affairs is all the sorrier for its being, at least potentially, a state without end.

* * * * * * * *

This, I submit, is a second sort of havoc wreaked by invoking the notion of just war in relation to the response to terrorism. It licenses the invocation of the different set of rules with respect to the nation's enemies; and, through notions of 'emergency', it invites suspension of the ordinary rule of law as well. The upshot is a lawless state, immune to either the constraints of the rule of law or the rules of just war.

The problem, here once again, lies in thinking of the response to terrorism in just-war terms at all.

3

Terrorism as a Political Tactic: Intending to Instil Fear

Terrorism often involves 'killing innocent civilians', or anyway lots of people who in no sense 'deserve to die'. That is a very bad thing; that is most definitely one of the largest wrongs of terrorism. But analysing the wrongness of terrorism fundamentally in terms of that wrong mistakes what is uniquely, peculiarly wrong about terrorism; for the wrong of killing innocent people is not unique to terrorism. Furthermore, trying to understand and react to terrorism as if it were purely a matter of 'killing innocent civilians', as if an unjust war, leads us into the many morally uncomfortable lacunae exposed in the previous chapter.

Let us now step back from the fixation on 'killing innocent civilians', and the just-war model that that involves, to see if some other ways of looking at the phenomenon might not afford us a better perspective on what terrorism is really all about and what its truly distinctive (albeit morally lesser) wrong might amount to.

To foreshadow: I am going to be arguing here that terrorism is best understood not as a psychopathology or as an ideology but, rather, as a distinctive political tactic the essence of which lies in its attempt to frighten people for political advantage. I thus propose to put 'terror' – or anyway the attempt to terrorize – back at the heart of our analysis of 'terrorism': what is morally distinctive about it and what is morally wrong with it.

What sort of 'ism' is terrorism?

Sometimes terrorism is treated as an ideology (like 'anarchism' or 'communism'), sometimes as a psychopathology (like 'sadism'). There is some warrant in the theory and practice of terrorism for both descriptions. But neither, in the end, proves terribly enlightening.

* * * * * *

Here are some of the sorts of things people tend to say when suggesting that terrorism is basically a psychopathology:

- In the post-9/11 words of the British opposition spokesperson for foreign affairs, there is something 'invariably distorted and perverted in the psychopathic terrorist mind'.[1]
- In the words of political theorist Benjamin Barber, a terrorist's actions 'are predominantly the consequence of pathology and yield neither to rational analysis nor understanding. Divested of any moral principle, [the terrorist] has no moral sense, no moral controls, and is therefore capable of committing any crime, like a killing machine, without shame or remorse.'[2]
- In the words of Benjamin Netanyahu, one-time Israeli prime minister, terrorism involves a 'disposition toward unbridled violence' and the 'shedding of all moral inhibition'. The terrorist is 'a new breed of man which takes humanity back to prehistoric times, to the times when morality was not yet born. Divested of any moral principle, he has no moral sense, no moral controls, and is therefore capable of committing any crime, like a killing machine, without shame or remorse.'[3]
- In the words of a US Army *Field Manual*, 'Terrorists do not even consider that they may be wrong and that others' views may have some merit. Terrorists tend to project their own antisocial motivations onto others, creating a polarized "we versus they" outlook. They attribute only evil motives

to anyone outside their own group. This enables the terrorists to dehumanize their victims and removes any sense of ambiguity from their minds.'[4]

In terms of psychopathology, certainly it is true that terrorists characteristically – perhaps even 'necessarily', in order to practise their craft effectively in the modern world – display a callous disregard for the lives and well-being of innocent people who are randomly brutalized by their actions. Terrorists pick their victims largely indiscriminately, and they intentionally subject them to terrible and terrifying fates.

Furthermore, that is an intrinsic rather than incidental feature of adopting a policy of terrorism in the modern world. 'Old-school terrorism was direct; it intended to produce a political effect through the injury or death of the victim.' And in that world, it was possible for terrorists, like just-warriors, to practise their trade discriminately. 'In late nineteenth-century Russia, radicals planning the assassination of tsar Alexander II aborted several planned attacks because they risked harming innocent people', for example. But that changed with the rise of the bureaucratic state:

> Modern governments have a continuity that older, personalistic governments did not. Terrorists found that the death of a single individual, even a monarch, did not necessarily produce the policy changes they sought. Terrorists reacted by turning to an indirect method of attack. By the early twentieth century, terrorists began to attack people previously considered innocents [and immune from old-school terrorist attack] to generate political pressure.[5]

Nowadays no one who intentionally adopts a policy of terrorism can realistically hope to avoid imposing indiscriminate suffering on many who do not deserve it.

Those who wish to assimilate terrorism to a psychopathology, such as 'sadism', point to those plain facts, thinking that they suffice to establish their case. But do they? Among terrorists, certainly there are many psychopaths. They may even predominate. But all the talk of what is 'necessarily so', in the previous paragraph, ought cause us to hesitate rather than rush to the judgement that terrorism is a psychopathology and nothing more.

'Necessity', remember, can sometimes serve to excuse, maybe even to justify.[6] 'Necessity' ties together means and ends into a single inseparable package. In such a package, morally worthy ends can sometimes justify morally disreputable means (just as, by the same token, morally disreputable means can sometimes discredit morally worthy ends).

The fact that random innocents will suffer might be accepted as an unfortunate 'necessity' by perfectly rational and perfectly moral agents, on the basis of careful balancing of all the relevant moral considerations in play. Road traffic engineers do so all the time, in deciding that straightening a mildly dangerous stretch of road at vast expense but modest savings of life would just not be worth the cost. Acceptance of such unfortunate necessities does not necessarily reflect psychopathological indifference to, much less welcoming of, the suffering of others (not *necessarily*: however common that attitude might or might not actually be among terrorists). It would be wrong – dangerously imprudent, as well as morally short-sighted – to dismiss all acceptance of the suffering of innocents as being inevitably the unreasoning product of psychopathological impulses alone. That inference would be just as wrong when it is applied to terrorists as when it is applied to road traffic engineers.

Thus, it is wrong to think of terrorist acts as being necessarily ones of 'mindless violence'. More typically, terrorists act in pursuit of objectives; and someone who is 'mindlessly violent' would typically be 'more of a liability than an asset' in pursuit of those objectives.[7]

* * * * * *

If terrorism is not well characterized as a psychopathology, like sadism, might it be better characterized as an ideology, like anarchism?

Terrorism is indeed animated by a 'philosophy', of sorts. So it seemed, anyway, to Johannes Most, who entitled his late nineteenth-century anarchist tract *The Philosophy of the Bomb*. But, as ideologies go, that particular philosophy is singularly devoid of any ideals, any ultimate ends, any vision of a better world. The central propositions of that 'philosophy of the bomb' are of a more pragmatic sort:

1 outrageous violence will seize the public imagination;
2 its audience can thus be awakened to political issues;
3 violence is inherently empowering, and a cleansing force;
4 systematic violence can threaten the state and impel it into delegitimizing reactions;
5 violence can destabilize the social order and threaten social breakdown (the 'spiral of terror' and counterterror);
6 ultimately the people will reject the government and turn to the 'terrorists'.[8]

Far from offering the sort of utopian vision we characteristically associate with ideologies, this 'philosophy' of terrorism offers instead little more than a how-to manual for displacing existing governments. It is a technique – 'propaganda of the deed', in a famous phrase adopted by the anarchist movement as it turned to terrorism.[9] The content of the message is left open to be filled in by those whose deeds they are.

What terrorists want

What do terrorists want?

Different things in different cases, obviously. Some are pursuing nationalist ends, campaigning for self-determination: of Algerians, in the case of the FLN; of Basques, in the case of ETA; of Israelites, in the case of the Stern Gang; of Palestinians, in the case of Al Aqsa Martyrs Brigades; of Irish in the remaining six provinces, in the case of the Real IRA; of Tamils, in the case of the Tamil Tigers. Other terrorists are pursuing revolutionary ends of a more socio-economic sort, as in the case of the German Rote Armee Fraktion or the Italian Brigate Rosse. Still others are pursuing nihilistic ends of a more purely anarchist sort.

* * * * * * *

What terrorists have in common is not what they want but, rather, how they proceed. Terrorism is first and foremost a *tactic*, adopted for *socio-political ends*.[10]

It is the defining feature of terrorists that they intentionally adopt the 'production of generalized terror' as a proximate end. Furthermore, they do that as a means to some larger socio-political purpose (more of which below). Terror as a proximate end, serving as a means to some larger socio-political purpose, is what Waldron calls the 'complex structure of the intentionality of terrorist action'.[11] That structure is common across terrorist groups quite generally. It is also common across a wide range of definitions of 'terrorism', both official and academic, both political and legal.

Note the recurring emphasis on terrorism as a *tactic*, and one deployed for *political* purposes, in the following characterizations:

- The US 9/11 Commission puts it plainly: 'Terrorism is a tactic used by individuals and organizations to kill and destroy.'[12]
- The 1796 *Dictionnaire de l'Académie Française* defines 'terrorism' as 'the systematic use of terror or unpredictable violence against governments, publics or individuals to attain political objectives'.[13] Modern dictionaries echo that original formulation, equating 'terrorism' with 'intimidation' (*Webster's*) or 'the employment of methods of intimidation' (*Oxford English Dictionary*), and a 'terrorist' with 'any one who attempts to further his views by a system of coercive intimidation' (*OED*).
- The official US definition, relied upon by the US State Department and CIA, defines 'terrorism' as 'pre-meditated, politically motivated violence perpetrated against non-combatants, targeted by sub-national groups or clandestine agents, usually intended to influence an audience'.[14]
- The US FBI defines it as 'unlawful use of force and violence against persons or property to intimidate or coerce a gov-

ernment, the civilian population, or any segment thereof, in furtherance of political or social objectives'.[15]

- The UN defines terrorism as 'criminal acts intended or calculated to provoke a state of terror in the general public . . . for political purposes'.[16] Elsewhere it adds that 'the purpose of such an act, by its nature or context, is to intimidate a population, or to compel a government or an international organization to do or to abstain from doing any act.'[17]

- The US Army *Field Manual* tells us that 'The essence of terrorism is the intent to induce fear in someone other than its victims to make a government or other audience change its political behavior.'[18]

- The RAND Corporation definition itemizes a cluster of characteristics associated with terrorism which ends: 'And finally – the hallmark of terrorism – the acts are intended to produce psychological effects beyond the immediate physical damage.'[19]

- Academic commentators offer a plethora of definitions. The most succinct defines 'terrorism' as consisting in 'committing acts intended to instill public fear, against more-or-less randomly chosen victims who themselves are powerless to meet their attackers' demands'.[20]

Obviously, emphases vary. But what is common across all these definitions is that terrorism is a tactic of coercive intimidation, for socio-political ends. (International-legal definitions that explicitly deny that terrorist acts are committed for political ends do so for purely pragmatic reasons concerned with extradition, as already discussed in chapter 2.)

* * * * * * * * * *

Note that I define 'terrorism' in terms of the *intention* to produce fear for socio-political purposes.

Of course, it is perfectly possible for terrorist acts to misfire or even backfire and 'give rise, not to the spread of fear and demoralization, but to defiance and a strengthening of resolve'.[21]

Terrorist acts do not cease to be terrorist acts simply because they misfire or backfire in that way, failing to produce the fear that was intended. 'Any act may fail to have its intended consequence.'[22] 'Terrorism', strictly speaking, must therefore be defined in terms of 'acting with the intention of instilling fear'. (That is a cumbersome phrase, and I shall ordinarily refer to it in more abbreviated fashion in what follows; but that ought always be seen as shorthand reference back to this fuller and more precise formulation.)

Suppose a terrorist shoots a missile at a plane full of people, intending to kill an important public official on board and frighten the rest of the country into granting the terrorist's political demands. There are several ways in which the terrorist's intended act of terrorism might fail: the missile might miss the plane; the government official might not be on board; or the downing of the plane might not produce the public fear envisaged. In the first case, the terrorist would be guilty, not of an 'act of terrorism' perhaps, but rather of 'attempted terrorism'. In the latter two cases, however, the terrorist would undoubtedly be guilty of an 'act of terrorism'. Shooting down a plane full of people with the intention of instilling fear for a political purpose *is* an act of terrorism, whether or not the terrorist's missile hit the wrong target and whether or not it succeeded in producing the further effects intended (fear; the granting of the terrorist's demands).

There is another way in which intentions and actual effects might come apart, in ways that suggest that terrorism should be defined in terms of intentions rather than actual effects. Something that you do might actually frighten others, and it might do so in ways that rebound to your own political advantage; but it might do so without your in the least intending to frighten them. (Maybe it was not even possible to foresee that they would be frightened.) Were 'terrorism' to be defined in terms of having the effect rather than the intention of instilling fear for political advantage, then unintentionally and unforeseeably frightening people in that way would count as terrorism, when it clearly ought not.

There are, to be sure, costs to defining people as 'terrorists' or 'attempted terrorists' purely by reference to their intentions rather than their accomplishments. Imagine a would-be terrorist, Bozo the Crown. Bozo's intentions are genuinely terroristic: his aim is to frighten people into crowning him king. But Bozo is a hopeless terrorist. His antics evoke laughter, not fear. No one takes his antics remotely seriously. There is simply no realistic prospect that anyone will ever be frightened by anything he does. Still, his clear intention was to frighten people for political advantage, and that marks him as a 'terrorist' on my definition.

In one sense, that simply does not seem right: but in another sense, it seems absolutely right. Consider another sad case, that of the hapless shoe-bomber, Richard Reid.[23] He was lots more dangerous than Bozo, no doubt: if he had ever managed to ignite his shoe bomb, a planeload of people would have been killed. Still, it was such a hare-brained attempt that one cannot help but feel a little sorry for him, rather as one would Bozo.

The point remains: terrorists can be sad cases, and nonetheless remain terrorists. However sad they suppose Richard Reid's case to be, no one can doubt that he was caught in the act of committing a terrorist offence. And that would have remained true even if there had been absolutely no prospect of his plan's ever working (had the explosive packed into his sneaker not been ignitable by the heat of a mere match or cigarette lighter, for example). Ditto, I think, Bozo. His antics should surely count as acts of attempted terrorism, because that was what he was intending. And they should count as such, even if there was no realistic prospect of his attempted terrorism ever terrorizing anyone. Intentions, not accomplishments, are indeed what ought count in defining terrorism.

* * * * * * * * * *

Terrorists typically adopt 'the production of generalized terror' as a proximate end towards some larger socio-political end. Just occasionally, the proximate end might be the ultimate end as well. No doubt we can imagine – perhaps we can even find – people who intentionally terrorize others, purely for the sake of terrorizing them and with no further end in view. We might well be tempted to say that anyone who intentionally terrror-izes others is, *ipso facto*, a 'terrorist'.

Those, however, are distinctly non-standard sorts of cases. Certainly street gangs delight in terrorizing the neighbourhood. Like gangs of roving bandits, however, they usually do so at least partly with other ends in view: generically, 'exacting tribute', sometimes in the form of 'booty', sometimes in the form of sheer 'respect'.[24]

And certainly, among the terrorist groups we are here dis-cussing, there are socio-political ends in view. They may be vague and imprecise. They may involve little more than 'smash-ing the existing system' in hopes that something better might follow. Vague and imprecise as such ends may be, they are nonetheless clearly socio-political in character.

Usually terrorists intentionally produce generalized terror as a means to some other end, and that further purpose usually takes a socio-political form: 'Brits out'; 'exposing the true char-acter of an oppressive regime'; and so on.

* * * * * * * * *

'Socio-political' here needs to be understood expansively, if it is to capture the broad range of ultimate ends animating ter-rorists across diverse times and places. And even then, it might miss out certain cases of purely nihilist terrorism.

Historically, the classic cases of nihilist terrorism cluster towards the end of the nineteenth century. Here is the sort of passage from Bakunin that leads history to remember him as an advocate of wholesale, aimless destruction:

> Revolution requires extensive and widespread destruction, a fecund and renovating destruction, since in this way and only this way are new worlds born.[25]

But even the Nihilists destroyed for a purpose, and a recogniz-ably political one at that. Their aim was to create the 'new worlds' to which Bakunin refers, and which he actually sketched in some detail elsewhere in his writings.[26] 'On reading the declarations of the condemned [nihilist terrorists] of that period', Camus remarks,

> we see that all, without exception, entrusted themselves, in defiance of their judges, to the justice of other men who were not yet born.... The terrorists undoubtedly want first of all to destroy – to make absolutism totter under the shock of exploding bombs. But by their death ... they aim at recreating a community founded on love and justice, and thus to resume a mission which the Church has betrayed.[27]

It is often said nowadays (as it has often been said in previous eras) that there is a 'new terrorism' abroad in the world. Today's terrorists undoubtedly pursue rather different strategies towards different specific ends than did their predecessors. But what exactly is there, in this 'new terrorism', to suggest that it is a different 'type' of action altogether? It cannot simply be, for example, that the 'new terrorism' is 'new' insofar as it attaches to 'identity politics'.[28] How other than as a manifestation of 'identity politics' are we to characterize terrorism that has long been associated with nationalist campaigns for self-determination?

RAND analysts suppose that we might increasingly face a form of 'post-modern terrorism', which 'is divorced from any coherent political agenda, motivated instead by transcendental or nihilist objectives, or simply rage at the failure of some societies and the success of others.' That latter phrase is not just an echo of the simple-minded post-9/11 discussions of 'why do they hate us?' The RAND analysis actually predated that, and is rooted in more careful case studies of the ethnography of terrorism in various places around the world. Here are some of the sorts of examples the RAND writers had in mind:

> The horrific violence in Algeria springs from a political crisis, but is increasingly divorced from any coherent political explanation. What began as a struggle between the military government and extremists bent on the establishment of an Islamic state has dete-

riorated into a shadowy war of all against all, in which personal and clan vendettas, factional struggles, and criminal infighting probably account for much of the 'terrorist' violence. Despite the government's claims to have contained the terrorism, the country hovers on the verge of anarchy. The most clearly discernible impetus behind the violence is the profound alienation – rage is perhaps the more accurate term – of younger Algerians with no economic or social prospects. Terrorism in Algeria is a striking case of a phenomenon also seen elsewhere. Arguably, Rwanda, Haiti and Somalia provide other examples where political crises have given way to terrorist behavior and popular rage, often divorced from any clear political agenda.[29]

In Habermas's view, 'the global terror that culminated in the September 11 attack bears the anarchistic traits of an impotent revolt directed against an enemy that cannot be defeated in any pragmatic sense. . . . Global terrorism is extreme . . . in its lack of realistic goals.'[30] Still, to say that the goals are not 'realistic' is not to say that the acts are not goal-directed. And, remember, 'destroying something that is bad', even if you have no clear idea what will follow it, is a perfectly pragmatic ambition.

It is also sometimes suggested that terrorism practised by religious fundamentalists is of a different character, in taking as its ultimate aim some transcendental goal rather than a socio-political one. RAND analysts, for example, say that

> The rise of religious terrorist movements over the past two decades is significant in [that] . . . it represents a significant shift away from the measured political agendas associated with ideological and national liberation groups active in the 1960s and 1970s, . . . as a result of its transcendental or 'total' character.[31]

There has, on this analysis, been 'a change in the quality of terrorist violence, as ideologies based on religion have replaced political ideologies and specific national goals' of a more political character.[32]

No doubt there are occasional cases like that. Among contemporary examples, the standard ones offered are 'fringe

cults . . . like the Aum Shinrikyo' that are said to 'rest on millenarian visions that cannot conceivably be realized by any
human agency.'[33] Insofar as acting on those millenarian impulses
involves instilling terror in people – and doing that intentionally (rather than as the unintended by-product of some other
imperative, such as salvation, purification or pleasing the deity)
– perhaps we might still be tempted to call these cases of 'terrorism', albeit perhaps in some attenuated sense.

But note that even Aum is more political than it might first
appear. It is para-political in its structure. 'Its leaders had
official-sounding titles of Minister of Education, Minister of
Health and Human Services, and so on . . . [The Aum leader]
Asahara may also have created a miniature government to
prepare his seizure of power in Japan.'[34] Furthermore, even its
millenarian aspect has its political side: 'Aum's idea on Armageddon is in line with an eschatological view that we are now living
through the last remnants of the period of *mappo* where the
forces of evil will destroy themselves through war that only the
blessed few (those who achieve enlightenment through Aum)
will survive.' Translated into realpolitik terms: Aum's faithful
will be the only voters left in town, come Armageddon.[35] Seen
in this light, even seemingly other-worldly groups such as Aum
are not without a definitely socio-political side to them.

The same is true of earlier examples of 'holy terrorist' groups
such as the Thugs. For them, 'the primary audience is the
deity . . . They intend their victims to experience terror and to
express it visibly for the pleasure of Kali, the Hindu goddess
of terror and destruction. . . . Having no cause they wanted
others to appreciate, they did things that seem incongruous
with our conception of how . . . terrorists should behave.' Still,
as Rapoport goes on to observe, 'virtually all activity was
hemmed in by self-imposed restraints' which 'the Thugs seem
to believe are of divine origin' but 'in each of which we can
trace a shrewd *practical* purpose'. Finally, the 'list of persons
immune from attack' under those rules 'suggests, perhaps, that
the cult may once have had a political purpose', even if the
Thugs had long since ceased to seek the publicity we would
expect of a political movement.[36]

* * * * * *

Finally, and perhaps most tellingly, note well that the most famous recent instance of religious fundamentalist terrorism – the September 11 attacks on the US – was explicitly political in its aims. Osama bin Laden's announced aims were of a highly socio-political sort: the removal of infidel troops from the holy lands of Saudi Arabia, and so on.[37] The terms of his 1996 Declaration of War on the Americans occupying the Land of the Two Holy Places 'directly related to US foreign policy (it included a historical account of US policy since Franklin D. Roosevelt's time as well as detailing the corruption and un-Islamic policies of the Saudi state).'[38]

The US Army *Field Manual* is surely right in regarding that as the more typical case. It begins by acknowledging the diversity of possible terrorist motivations. 'Terrorism may be motivated by political, religious or ideological objectives', it observes. It goes on to add, however, that 'in a sense, terrorist goals are always political, as extremists driven by religious or ideological beliefs usually seek political power to compel society to conform to their views.'[39]

Townshend observes that, 'For all their messianic semitones, Hezbollah and Amal are very real political forces engaged in an earthly power struggle, as indeed is Hamas in Palestine.'[40] Remember, as Habermas reminds us, that 'some of those drawn into the "holy war" had been secular nationalists only a few years before', suggesting that 'today's Islamic fundamentalism is also a cover for political motifs.'[41] Recall, for example, that the reason Rabin's assassin was so upset might have been millenarian, connected with the Oslo accords' and the threat he perceived them as posing to the continued existence of Israel, and hence to the building of the third Temple where Muslim shrines now stand; but the act was, nonetheless, the assassination of a head of state carried out in response to an act that he had performed in that official capacity.[42]

Note also that, even when the religiously inspired act is of a more purely transcendental form, the aim is rarely *purely* of that form. Executing the *fatwah* against Salman Rushdie might be seen by some as the performance of a transcendental duty; but it will hardly escape their notice that it would also serve the purpose of setting an example for other would-be blasphemers against Allah. Similarly, the assassin of Theo Van Gogh did not stop at punishing Van Gogh for his blasphemous film *Submission*. He also left a five-page letter addressed to Ayaan Hirsi Ali, the Somali-Dutch MP who had collaborated with Van Gogh in that film. And it was left in a highly public place (affixed by dagger to the corpse in the street) to ensure maximum publicity for its message to anyone who might be tempted to follow their blasphemous leads.[43]

Fear is the key

It would be etymologically odd (to say the least) for the analysis of 'terrorism' to lose track of its root, and fail to analyse 'terrorism' first and foremost in terms of 'terror'. As one philosopher puts it, 'we will look pretty silly if we do not mention terror in our account of terrorism.'[44] Yet that is precisely what the just-war analysis of 'terrorism' as 'killing innocent civilians' has somehow managed to do.

In so doing, it is untrue not only to the etymology of the term. It is untrue also to the purposes of the terrorist groups themselves. Terrorists (the vast majority of them, anyway)[45] kill innocent civilians not as an end in itself, but rather as a means towards some further purposes. Their ultimate purposes are as varied as terrorist groups themselves, but the proximate aim by virtue of which they earn the designation 'terrorists' is the production of terror among the target population from which their victims are randomly drawn.[46]

* * * * * * * * *

Just look back at some of the most standard definitions of 'terrorism', lexicographical as well as political, to confirm that 'terror' – the intention of instilling fear in the target population – does indeed constitute the core:

- Elaborating on its primary definition of 'terrorism' as 'the employment of methods of intimidation', the *Oxford English Dictionary* goes on to describe that terrorism is 'a policy intended to strike with terror those against whom it is adopted'.
- Historically, the first use of the term 'terror' in a political context occurred in France where, recall, the Académie Française defined it in the 1796 supplement to its *Dictionnaire* as 'the systematic use of terror or unpredictable violence against governments, politics or individuals to attain political objectives'.[47]
- The first international convention on terrorism, drafted under the auspices of the League of Nations in 1937 (but which never went into force), defined terrorism as 'all criminal acts directed against a State and intended or calculated to create a state of terror in the minds of particular persons or a group of persons or the general public'.[48]
- Under the UK Prevention of Terrorism Act 1974, '"terrorism" means the use of violence for political ends, and includes any use of violence for the purpose of putting the public or any section of the public in fear.'[49]
- The RAND Corporation's definition of 'terrorism', recall, ends the long cluster of characteristics associated with terrorism quoted earlier by saying, 'And finally – the hallmark of terrorism – the acts are intended to produce psychological effects beyond the immediate physical damage.'[50]

And again, several scholarly analyses follow in those footsteps, emphasizing that terrorism amounts to violence intended to instil fear.[51] The intention of producing a psychological effect – fear, terror – is absolutely central to the act of terrorism.

* * * * * * * * *

The recurring mantra that terrorism paradigmatically involves 'killing or threatening to kill innocent civilians', while misleading in the many ways I have already discussed, actually fits well with this terror-based analysis of the true nature of terrorism and what is really wrong with it.

Let us begin by noting this peculiarity: terrorism is not merely a matter of 'killing innocent civilians'. If pressed, most people would doubtless agree that the term should also extend to people who in similar circumstances and with similar intentions destroyed buildings (anyway, non-military buildings) that they knew to be uninhabited at the time of the attack.[52] The 1997 UN Convention for the Suppression of Terrorist Bombing, for example, also covers 'extensive destruction of . . . a place, facility or system, where such destruction is likely to result in major economic loss'.[53]

But property damage is very much a lesser theme, compared to 'killing innocent civilians', in most discussions of terrorism. Indeed, in many international agreements property damage goes unmentioned altogether (as in the International Convention for the Suppression of the Financing of Terrorism) or is included only 'if the act created a collective danger for persons' (as in the European Convention on the Suppression of Terrorism).[54] In 1973 the UN convened an ultimately inconclusive Ad Hoc Committee on Terrorism, where the US proposed a terrorist be defined as 'any person who unlawfully kills, causes serious bodily harm or kidnaps another person'; the US draft convention did 'not include crimes against property' and indeed 'few nations suggested . . . that crimes against property be covered'.[55]

So, to the peculiarity: why this fixation on sudden death in the standard discussions of terrorism? Well, one reason is that crimes against persons are morally worse than mere crimes against property: murder is worse than simple theft or vandalism. But another reason is that sudden, random death is so much more *frightening* than loss of property, however valuable or cherished. And the really distinctive feature of terrorism is its instilling a general sense of terror across the relevant population.

On this point the 1997 UN General Assembly Resolution on Human Rights and Terrorism is particularly perspicacious. In its preamble we are reminded that 'the most essential and basic human right is the right to life' and that 'terrorism creates an environment that destroys the right of people to live in freedom from fear.'

Similarly, in its 1994 Resolution on Measures to Eliminate International Terrorism, the General Assembly declared:

> Criminal acts intended or calculated to provoke a state of terror in the general public, a group of persons or particular persons for political purposes are in any circumstance unjustifiable, whatever the considerations of a political, philosophical, ideological, racial, ethnic, religious or any other nature that may be invoked to justify them.

Let us pause to unpack that a little. 'Criminal acts' by definition are always 'unjustifiable', legally at least (i.e., within the body of law that renders the acts criminal in the first place). Legally, 'criminal acts' may sometimes be 'excused' (if, for example, committed under duress or in unavoidable error). But at law criminal acts can never be literally 'justified'.

The point of the UN General Assembly's referring specifically to 'criminal acts intended or calculated to provoke a state of terror . . . for political purposes' is not, I submit, to identify a particular subset of criminal acts which are unjustifiable. (That is true of all criminal acts.) The point of referring to that *subset* of criminal acts is, I submit, to point to the particular aspects of certain criminal acts that make those constitute acts of 'terrorism' (the subject of the Resolution in question). The defining feature of terrorism, for the UN General Assembly, is thus that it is 'intended or calculated to provoke a state of terror' in some target group, *'for political purposes'*.

Summing up

The business of this chapter has been to put the notion of 'terror' – acting with the intention of instilling fear – back at the centre of our understanding of what 'terrorism' involves. Terrorism often involves the intentional killing of innocent civilians, as the just-war analysis of it points out; and that is of course very wrong. But that wrong is not unique to terrorism: that is a wrong that terrorism shares with ordinary murder. And, as I have shown in the previous chapter, thinking of terrorism in just-war terms morally misleads us in many important ways.

The suggestion of this chapter has been that we think of terrorism, instead, as fundamentally a political tactic, involving the deliberate frightening of people for political advantage. That is not the worst wrong that terrorists commit. But it is the *distinctive* wrong that terrorists commit, making them terrorists and not mere murderers.

In this judgement I am joined by none other than Michael Walzer, whose writings on just war were so influential on that way of analysing terrorism. But here is what Walzer has to say on the subject, at the very beginning of his own major paper on the topic, 'Terrorism: A Critique of Excuses':

> This, then, is the peculiar evil of terrorism – not only the killing of innocent people but also the intrusion of fear into everyday life, the violation of private purposes, the insecurity of public spaces, the endless coerciveness of precaution.[56]

Walzer makes nothing more of this key observation in his own subsequent discussion, which is couched very much in just-war terms of the sort that have been discussed and dismissed in chapter 2. I shall be making much more of his passing insight, however, in subsequent chapters of this book.

4

States Can Be Terrorists, Too

Is it impossible for state officials to qualify as 'terrorists'? Does being an authorized agent of a state conceptually immunize one against charges of terrorism?

Asked straight out, such questions seem almost purely rhetorical. 'Surely not' is obviously the right response. But insinuations to that effect are rife in the post-9/11 world.[1] National leaders speak in offended tones of 'war' having been declared on the 'civilized world' by agents who lack legitimate standing to do so.[2] The insinuation is that states alone can go to war (and even then only on certain 'just-war' terms, if it is to be a legitimate war), whereas non-state actors cannot legitimately go to war on any terms.[3]

On the line of analysis implicit in such rhetoric, 'terrorism' is not so much 'unjust war' (or 'acts committed in peacetime that would have been war crimes if committed in wartime'), per the analysis discussed and dismissed in chapter 2. Instead, on this line of analysis, 'terrorism' is 'war conducted by agents not entitled to go to war'.[4]

On this analysis, violent acts by non-state actors would always count as 'terrorism' (provided perhaps they meet a few other conditions: that they are for 'political ends', for example). Violent acts by state actors, on the other hand, would never count as 'terrorism' on this analysis – for state actors are always, by definition, the sorts of agents 'entitled to go to war'. Whether or not they are just in going to war on any given occasion, or just in their conduct of the war, depends on certain further just-war conditions being met. But they are always the sorts of actors entitled to go to war. Statehood in and of itself suffices for that.

This analysis is, as I say, typically only implicit in the post-9/11 rhetoric. Much that is said in those connections would be in logical tension with that analysis, if it ever were made sufficiently explicit for such logical worries to come to the surface.[5] Leaving the analysis implicit, such worries never arise. Still, this is a sufficiently pervasive gestalt in post-9/11 thinking on terrorism that it is worth putting it in the spotlight, and addressing it at some length.

To foreshadow: our initial impulse to regard the questions with which this chapter opens as rhetorical will turn out to be well founded. *Of course* the state can engage in terrorism, both against its own people and against other states; states have done just that with depressing frequency over the years. The *Dictionnaire* of the Académie Française said as much, in the original 1796 introduction of the term 'terrorism' into the political lexicon:

> Terrorism has been used by political organizations with both rightist and leftist objectives, by nationalistic and ethnic groups, by revolutionaries and by the armies and secret police of governments themselves.[6]

Of course. Still, ours is a world of rhetorical politics in which too much already proceeds by nods and winks, general impressions and lines left unspoken. In such circumstances, it is worth belabouring the point rather than just leaving it at a simple, 'Of course'.

* * * * * * * * *

The *raison d'être* for the state, for Locke as surely as Hobbes, is to secure social order. A state that systematically undermines social order by practising terrorism, against its own people or others, is not doing what states are supposed to do. It is not a good state; such a state may not even be a legitimate state. Maybe states systematically practising terrorism against their own people and others thereby sacrifice any claim to the loyalty of their own citizens and the forbearance of others.

Still, bad states remain states regardless. Were it the case that states ceased to be states at all when practising terrorism, then that would make it analytically true that states could never practise terrorism: they then could not practise terrorism without ceasing to be a state; they then could not remain a state without abstaining from terrorism.

But that is simply not how statehood works, any more than it is how personhood works. States that do things they are not supposed to do do not cease to be states, any more than people who do things that they are not supposed to do cease to be people. They are bad states, or bad people. But they are nonetheless states, nonetheless people.

* * * * * * * *

Terrorism is typically characterized as a 'weapon of the weak'.[7] The strong complain that those deploying that tactic seek to achieve through fear what they cannot accomplish 'legitimately' (through persuasion or the just application of force). That, no doubt, is one reason why terrorism is often associated with non-state actors.[8]

But, remember, states too can be weak as well as strong. 'Weapons of the weak' are not the province of non-state actors alone. Weak states, or vying warlords in failed states aspiring to the status of quasi-states, often attempt to achieve by terror what they cannot achieve otherwise.[9]

In the converse case, it can also often prove true that the stronger the state the stronger the temptation to rule through a regime of terror. That was Aristotle's assessment of rule by tyrants of antiquity and Montesquieu's of despotic governments such as the Ottoman empire.[10] Judging from the experience of totalitarian regimes of the twentieth century, ranging from the Soviet Gulags to the Argentinian *desaparecidos* (more of which below), it remains true to our own day. Thus there is no reason to think that terrorism can be practised only by non-state actors.

Remember too (again, more of which below) that some of the clearest cases of 'terrorism' – understood as the intentional adoption of the 'production of generalized terror' as a proxi-mate end, serving as a means to some larger socio-political purpose – came through deliberate state action in World War II. The terror bombings by the Nazis of London and by the Allies of Tokyo and Dresden were designed to instil generalized terror in the home populations of their opponents, and thus to help achieve their political ends in the war. That the actual effects often turned out to be the opposite of those intended does nothing to change the terrorist intentions, or hence the terrorist nature of the acts.

So states, and their duly authorized officials, can be terrorists, too – both *vis-à-vis* their own populations and *vis-à-vis* others. We must not let the persuasive definitions promulgated by state actors (the US Department of State and suchlike) cloud that obvious fact. That, in brief, is the argument that this chapter will be pursuing at length.

The definitional ploy

On the definitions of 'terrorism' promulgated by certain states, officers of the state would be definitionally immune from counting as 'terrorists', no matter what they did. Recall the definition written into the *US Code*, upon which the US State Department and CIA rely. 'Terrorism', according to that defini-tion, is:

> pre-meditated politically motivated violence perpetrated against non-combatants, targeted by sub-national groups or clandestine agents, usually intended to influence an audience.[11]

When previously examining this definition, we focused on other aspects of it: the emphasis on 'non-combatants' (in chapter 2) and on terrorism as a tactic for political ends (in chapter 3). For present purposes, let us shift our focus to the clause restricting terrorism to 'sub-national groups or clandes-tine agents'.

The upshot of that clause is to exclude states and their authorized agents from the category of actors who could conceivably count as terrorists. They might do everything else that constitutes the defining acts of terrorism under this definition: they might perpetrate 'pre-meditated politically motivated violence . . . against non-combatants', and their intention may be 'to influence an audience'. But insofar as they do not qualify under the intervening clause – they are not 'sub-national groups or clandestine agents' who are doing the targeting – their acts do not qualify as ones of terrorism.

This is obviously a terribly convenient definition, from the CIA and State Department's point of view. Under it, virtually no matter what they do, those agencies of the state can never be committing terrorist acts. They can provide all the support they want, either openly or clandestinely, to insurgent groups who practise systematic terrorism against their countryfolk in their attempt to overthrow their government. But the State Department or CIA would not be committing terrorism themselves, nor (unless the insurgents can be seen as 'clandestine agents' of those agencies) can the State Department or CIA even be said to be complicit in the terrorism of others. Convenient: very convenient.

* * * * * * * * * *

Here is a parallel, from earlier times. Under customary international law, now codified in international treaties, it has always been definitionally impossible for people who are acting on the authority of a state to commit an act that strictly speaking counts as one of 'piracy'.

'Piracy', at international law, consists in 'any illegal acts of violence, detention or any act of depredation, committed for *private ends* by the crew or passengers of a *private* ship or a *private* aircraft'.[12] As if that were not clear enough, the American Law Institute Reporter summarizing the implications for *The Foreign Relations Law of the United States* goes on to emphasize, 'Wrongful acts by government ships are not included in the definition of piracy.'[13]

People acting on the authority of a state can commit many wrongs that are strictly analogous to those committed by pirates. But they cannot commit the particular wrong of 'piracy', which by that international-law definition is doing those things 'privately' (rather than on authority of some state). Sir Francis Drake may have behaved much as Blackbeard. But Drake acted on commission from the queen of England, and that made all the difference.

The *US Code*'s definition of 'terrorism' would have us think of it in the same way: states and their official agents can commit many wrongs strictly analogous to those committed by terrorists, perhaps; but they cannot commit the particular wrong peculiar to 'terrorism', which is (as with 'piracy') doing those things 'privately' rather than on the authority of some state.

* * * * * *

It is not just state officials who strive to write themselves exemptions from charges of terrorism. Academic commentators often accede in that practice.[14] Charles Townshend bemoans that fact. 'State terrorism', he complains,

> occupies only 12 of the 768 pages in the *Encyclopedia of World Terrorism* (1997), and five of those are about 'state-sponsored terrorism', a rather different phenomenon. (But at least this section is there; in many books on terrorism it is not.)[15]

There certainly are academic writers – distinguished ones – who strongly share Townshend's view that 'it is important to grasp how far state terror has dwarfed the puny efforts of rebels in the 20th century.' Among the most distinguished is Michael Walzer, whose early work on *Just and Unjust Wars* pointedly emphasized that 'the systematic terrorizing of whole populations is a strategy of both conventional and guerilla war and of established governments as well as radical movements.'[16]

Still, the definitional ploy – precluding the possibility of 'state terrorism' purely by definition – is one that is common enough, both politically and academically, to merit sustained consideration and critique.

* * * * * * * *

What should we make of that definitional manoeuvre that would, at one fell swoop, exempt any and all state officials from charges of terrorism? One is initially inclined to respond pretty dismissively.

Of course, words mean whatever we say they mean. We can always stipulate that that is what we mean by 'terrorism'. Politicians have a clear interest in such a stipulation. International conventions organized by politicians naturally tend to reflect those preferences and predilections.

There is something morally suspicious, however, about people making laws that apply to everyone except themselves.[17] The sheer fact that politicians have entered into a mutual-protection pact not to prosecute one another as 'terrorists' cannot change any logical or deontological facts of the matter. If what they do is otherwise indistinguishable from what is done by non-state actors that we would deem to be terroristic, then the acts of the state officials doing the same thing would be morally equally wrong for just the same reasons. If that wrong is not technically termed 'terrorism', under conventions that politicians succeed in establishing as international law, that fact is simply of no *moral* consequence.

* * * * * * *

That is a tempting response. But before we climb onto that moral high horse, we ought also weigh two further facts that might be offered in mitigation.

One is that the definition of terrorism of which the CIA and State Department are so fond is not universally endorsed, even within the US government, much less by other governments. The FBI, for example, operates according to another definition of terrorism which contains no such clause explicitly exempting state officials. The definition written into British legislation also contains no such explicit exemption.

We ought not allow ourselves to become too impressed with this fact, however. What the CIA/State Department definition does explicitly, other official definitions often do implicitly. The FBI definition, for example, identifies 'terrorism' as:

> the unlawful use of force and violence agains persons or property to intimidate or coerce a government, the civilian population, or any segment thereof, in furtherance of political or social objectives.[18]

The reference to 'unlawful' there serves to guarantee that, however much their acts might otherwise resemble those of *bona fide* terrorists, officers of the state in the lawful exercise of their official duties cannot by definition commit terrorism.[19] There are similar let-out clauses in British legislation defining terrorism.[20] So perhaps we should not be too reassured on that first score: the CIA/State Department definition is just making explicit the exemption for state officials that all the other official definitions prefer to leave implicit.

* * * * * * * * *

The second fact, which is somewhat more reassuring, is that, while officers of the state may be exempt from being charged with 'terrorism', that exemption comes at the cost of their being liable in *other* ways for their actions.

In the piracy case, for example, the American Law Institute Reporter is at pains to emphasize that state agents are not immune from blame for the pirate-like wrongs that they do, just because they cannot qualify as 'pirates'. Instead, those are wrongs that 'are addressed by general principles of international law governing state responsibility for violations of international obligations'.[21]

Something similar is found in the International Convention for the Suppression of Terrorist Bombing. As its preamble notes, 'the activities of military forces of states are governed by rules of international law outside the framework of this Convention.' For that reason, Article 19 (2) explicitly exempts armed forces from the provisions of that Convention, in the following terms:

> The activities of armed forces during an armed conflict, as those terms are understood under international humanitarian law, which are governed by that law, are not governed by this Convention, and the activities undertaken by military forces of a State in the exercise of their official duties, inasmuch as they are governed by other rules of international law, are not governed by this Convention.

But, as the preamble is at pains to emphasize, 'the exclusion of certain actions from the coverage of this Convention does not condone or make lawful otherwise unlawful acts, or preclude prosecution under other laws.'[22]

Here again, officers of the state (here, soldiers) are exempt from prosecution (here, for terrorism). But they are exempt from prosecution under that heading, precisely on the grounds that they are liable to prosecution under other headings (for war crimes).[23]

How reassuring that thought ought be turns on how serious the alternative liability would actually be: whether officers of the state can reasonably expect sanctions commensurable to those that non-state agents could expect to receive for similar terrorist offences. Sometimes, presumably, they can. Not all war criminals are caught and prosecuted, any more than all terrorists are; but when they are, the punishments meted out by War Crimes Tribunals (or, in some places, courts martial) are of broadly the same magnitude that terrorists guilty of similar offences outside the military might expect.

In other cases and other ways, however, the alternative liability visited upon officers of the state seems substantially less likely and less severe than that visited upon non-official terrorists performing analogous actions. Anti-terrorist laws often make it an offence merely to be a 'member' of a proscribed organization, for example; but no soldier would be prosecuted merely for being a member of a company of soldiers that conducted an illegal massacre during a period he was himself on leave or in hospital. There also seems to be more scope for officers of the state to claim 'honest error' than non-official terrorists, who are typically treated as bearing more strict liability for the consequences of their actions.

In part officers of the state get preferential treatment in those ways because there is some legitimate purpose which their organization could be serving, and there are some acts similar to those for which they are being prosecuted which they could legitimately have performed. In contrast, terrorist organizations are sometimes said to serve no legitimate purpose. People never have any excuse for belonging to them; and there is no situation for which they could have 'honestly mistaken' their present one in which it would have been legitimate for them to perform the act for which they are being prosecuted. If that is true, then perhaps that much differential treatment might indeed be permissible. (Whether it is true is something that might of course be queried in countries with a history of terrorism at their foundation: by the Sons of Liberty in the US, Etzel in Israel, the ANC in South Africa.)

* * * * * * * *

Of course, in practice how good the 'alternative liability' argument is depends on the reliability of the institutions charged with imposing it.

Where officers of the state are notionally liable but effectively immune, because of the inability or unwillingness of the institutions to act, then the 'alternative liability' is a chimera. Consider the example of the AAA death squads in Argentina. They were absorbed into the official state apparatus after the 1976 military takeover, making them notionally subject to courts martial in consequence. But there was no realistic prospect of that.[24]

One form of 'alternative accountability' that is sometimes evoked to excuse elected officials from criminal prosecution for their conduct in office is 'democratic accountability'. Elected officials are not accountable in courts of law (at least for their conduct in office), because they are accountable in the court of public opinion instead.

In general, that judicial reticence is doubtless a good political practice. It ensures the effective functioning of government that would otherwise be subject to constant harassment through court challenges. But when it comes to grave offences against humanity such as war crimes, it seems less plausible to say that the international community should desist from prosecuting state officials for war crimes merely because those officials have been duly elected and re-elected by their own people. Neither, I submit, should we say that in cases of terrorism, whether practised against their own citizens or against others.

As a contingent fact, democratically elected state officials may well engage in less state terrorism than non-democratic ones. And as a purely practical matter, the best way to deal with democratically elected state terrorists on any given occasion may well be to wait for the next election, in hopes they will be turned out of office. But in general, the fact that the state terrorists have been democratically elected and re-elected – with their terroristic practices being known at the time of election – ought not bolster but, instead, undermine our confidence in that 'alternative mechanism of accountability' actually holding them to account for their terrorism.

States terrorizing other states

From time to time, agents of one state commit acts that would be construed as 'terrorist' ones, even on the strictest definitions written into international law.[25]

Hijacking an aeroplane, for example, clearly counts as a terrorist act, and is condemned as such by international conventions. That is something that many terrorist groups attempt to do from time to time. But it is also something that states do from time to time. For example:

On August 10, 1973, Israeli jets intercepted a Middle East Airlines jetliner outside of Beirut, Lebanon, and forced the plane to land in a military airfield in Israel. The purpose of the diversion was to capture four leaders of the Palestinian Liberation Organization and to hold a show trial in Israel. The leaders were not on board the aircraft, and after a few hours of inspection and questioning Israel permitted the airliner to resume its flight. The incident provoked widespread protests in the international community, culminating in a UN Security Council Resolution condemning Israel by a vote of 15–0.[26]

Or, again, kidnapping for political purposes is a clear case of terrorism, and is condemned by international conventions as such. But terrorist groups are not the only ones who do that. So too do states, from time to time. For example,

On August 9, 1973, Kim Dae Jung, the leader of the opposition to South Korean President Park Chung Hee, was abducted from a hotel in Tokyo . . . [T]here is evidence to suggest that it was the work of the South Korean CIA. Mr. Kim was released . . . in Seoul five days later . . . only after the Japanese Government reacted vehemently to the infringement of its sovereignty.[27]

Or, again, politically motivated murder counts as terrorism when done by non-state actors. But that too is sometimes done by agents of the state. For example,

Six foreigners, including two Israeli agents, [were] charged in the murder of a Moroccan waiter slain on July 21, 1973, in Lillehammer, Norway. The Moroccan . . . was mistakenly thought to be a member of a Palestinian guerilla organization. The incident assumed international proportions when the two Israeli agents were discovered hiding in the home of an Israeli Embassy security officer. On Aug. 14, 1973, the Norwegian Government expelled the Israeli security officer.[28]

Or, for another example, consider the Rainbow Warrior affair, in which agents of the French secret services sank a Greenpeace boat moored in Auckland harbour to prevent it from sailing into France's nuclear testing zone in an attempt to stop the testing, killing a photographer on board.[29]

All those are precisely the sorts of acts that, if committed by non-state groups for political purposes, would qualify as prime exemplars of terrorism. Unless agents of the state are definitionally precluded from ever counting as terrorists – which I have just argued they should not be – the same sorts of acts performed by agents of the state should also count as terrorism. And insofar as those agents of the state were acting on the authority of their state, as clearly they were in all these cases, their acts should surely count as terrorism conducted by and on behalf of the state itself.

* * * * * * * * *

Precisely because the acts just described are so obviously analogous to acts called 'terrorist' when committed by non-state actors, they constitute perhaps the clearest evidence that states can commit terrorism, too. The more classic cases of states terrorizing the citizens of other states, however, come in the course of war.

Terrorizing civilian populations has long been part of warfare. The ancient and medieval practice of 'sacking of captured cities', for example, 'was plainly intended to intimidate the inhabitants of other fortified posts (whether combatant or noncombatant).'[30] But the practice of state-on-state terrorism was perfected in connection with modern 'total war'. The 'razed earth' tactics of Napoleon or Sherman might claim to have aims that are at least partly military, being designed at least in part to prevent enemy soldiers from 'living off the land'. But no such military excuses can be found for some of the most classic cases of one state terrorizing citizens of another by aerial bombardment.

An early instance was the bombing of Guernica in the course of the Spanish Civil War.

> [O]n April 26, 1937 ... the Condor Legion of the German Luft-waffe, in support of Franco's war against the Spanish Republic,

bombed the Basque capital, Guernica, on a market day, killing 1654 people out of a population of 7000.[31]

Clearly, this was a case of targeting civilians, for political rather than military purposes.[32]

During World War II 'virtually every aspect of human production became a legitimate target.'[33] The fire-bombing of Dresden and Tokyo by Allied forces was terrorism pure and simple.[34] The targets were of no direct military value. The aim was to demoralize enemy non-combatants, 'to kill civilians in such large numbers that their government is forced to surrender'.[35] So too, arguably, was the dropping of the atomic bomb on Hiroshima and Nagasaki – which the Chairman of the combined British/American Joint Chiefs of Staff and Chief of Staff to the US President insisted at the time 'was of no material assistance in our war against Japan'.[36]

Clearly, the populace of those cities had no direct control over the wartime decisions of their political masters; there was nothing they could do to comply with the demands of those initiating the attacks against them. At most, they might have been quasi-military targets only insofar as their morale made any material difference to the enemy's war effort. Still, the case seems pretty clearly one of terrorism: frightening one group of people, in order to produce some change in the political actions of some others.

* * * * * * *

Of course, war by its nature is a terrifying business. Those engaged in war often intentionally make it even more terrifying than strictly necessary, as a deliberate strategy for winning the war. And what is 'winning the war', except a political objective? So, on the face of it, if we define 'terrorism' as I have done as 'acting with the intention of instilling fear for socio-political objectives', it looks as if all warfare (and not just extreme cases such as fire-bombing civilians in Dresden) is going to count as 'terrorism'.[37]

There are two possible responses to that sort of objection. One response is the pacifist response: to agree that all war really is terrorism, and should be morally condemned on the same grounds as we condemn terrorism by non-state actors.[38]

That is not to say that there are no moral distinctions to be made among all the acts that pacifists morally condemn. Even those who think that war is always morally evil can agree that some wars are more evil than others: a war that kills millions is surely worse than one that kills only hundreds, even from the point of view of a pacifist who thinks that both wars are morally wrong. Pacifists can surely agree that war is less evil (although still beyond the threshold of moral unacceptability) if it is constrained by rules like those written into the Geneva Conventions. And pacifists may well go on to agree 'terrorism' was less evil (although still morally unacceptable) when it was practised only against political leaders rather than the population at large.[39] But, to the pacifist's way of thinking, it is perfectly right that both war and terrorism should be morally condemned, in just the same way and for just the same reason.

The second broad line of response would be to try to find some way of distinguishing 'terroristic' forms of war from other forms of war. The standard way is, of course, to do so according to 'just-war' standards: where *jus in bello* standards are being respected, acts of war are not terroristic; where those standards are not being respected (as, for example, when civilians are intentionally targeted), those acts of war are terroristic. Standard though it may be, however, this just-war way of defining terrorism faces all the problems I have pointed to in chapter 2.

Here is another way of making that distinction between terroristic and non-terroristic acts of war. It does so in terms of my definition in chapter 3 of 'terrorism' as 'acting with the intention of instilling fear for *socio-political* advantage'. Certainly, we may agree, some terrifying things are done, with the intention of frightening people, in the course of war. British infantry charges were traditionally led by massed bagpipes, emitting frightening squeals designed to disconcert the enemy.

But the advantage in view there is *military* – at least in the first instance. Ultimately, of course, military victories will lead to political ones, culminating in the surrender of one's opponents. But the direct intended consequence of frightening armed opponents in the course of a military campaign is to win the battles. Instilling fear in one's opponents in order to gain some battlefield advantage is to pursue a military objective, not a political one.[40] Hence that should not count as 'terrorism', on the definition here offered.

States can, however, sometimes engage in genuinely terroristic behaviour in the course of war. They do so, insofar as they aim to instil terror for genuinely political advantages. That is what they do when they engage in frightening activities with the direct intention of 'breaking the will', not just of soldiers on the other side, but of the other country as a whole. That was the aim of fire-bombing Dresden: no military advantage was anticipated; the advantage in view was purely political (weakening the will of the populace at large and inducing the political leadership to surrender). The method was by acting in a way intended to instil fear. The combination of those two facts makes the acts ones of genuine terrorism, on the definition here in view.[41]

To the objection that on that definition all war is terroristic, then, there are thus two possible lines of response. The pacifist would reply, 'Quite so!' The non-pacifist embracing my definition of 'terrorism' would try to draw a sharp distinction between 'military' and 'political' objectives. Any more general discussion of the moral merits of pacifism would clearly take us far afield; so here I shall simply leave that as an open choice between those two responses.

* * * * * *

Finally, note that states can terrorize the people of other states not only in the course of a war but also with the threat of war.

Just recall the old description of the nuclear standoff between the US and USSR as a 'balance of terror'. And recall that that phrase described not only the result of that state of affairs but also the intentions of each side in producing it. Under the strategic doctrine of 'mutually assured destruction', the aim was to prevent one's own country from being attacked by having a sufficiently large and secure stockpile of retaliatory weapons to withstand a first strike and still annihilate the enemy. Under the MAD doctrine, it would thus be suicidal for either side to attack the other: destruction would be mutual; and it would be assured.[42]

That terrifying prospect held the nuclear superpowers in balance throughout the Cold War. And it is of course a very good thing that it did so. Still, there is no denying that it was a case of two states terrorizing one another. And, equally undeniably, it would have been far better in ever so many ways if, somehow, the same result (no nuclear war) could have been achieved through other less terrifying means (mutual disarmament, for example).

States terrorizing their own people

Discussions of 'state terror' nowadays often focus on cases like that, of states terrorizing populations of *other* countries. But states can of course terrorize their own population.[43]

The political use of the term 'terror' had its origins, after all, in the Reign of Terror practised against the French by their post-Revolutionary Jacobin rulers.[44] Responding to demands by its Committee of Public Safety, the revolutionary Convention enacted a Law of Suspects in 1793 under which local revolutionary committees were empowered to arrest 'those who by their conduct, relations or language spoken or written, have shown themselves partisans of tyranny . . . and enemies of liberty.' Over the ensuing two years, more than 200,000 French citizens were detained under this law, of whom some 10,000 perished without trial and another 17,000 were executed.[45]

Contemporary regimes of terror – Stalin's Russia, Pol Pot's Cambodia, the military junta of Argentina – are clear successors. All provide undeniable instances of 'state terrorism . . . used

by authoritarian and totalitarian governments against their own people, to spread fear and make political opposition impossible'.[46]
Consider these plain facts, culled from the *Encyclopedia Britannica*:

• Beginning with the Great Purge show trials of the 1930s condemning potential political opponents as 'traitors', between 7 million and 15 million Soviets were confined to the forced-labour camps that constituted Stalin's Gulag. On one estimate, as many as 20 million died as a result of labour camps, forced collectivization, famine and executions; and another 20 million were subjected to imprisonment, exile or forced relocation.[47]

• In its four years of rule, from 1975 to 1979, Pol Pot's Khmer Rouge presided over the death (through forced labour, starvation, disease, torture and execution) of between 1 and 1.5 million Cambodians in its campaign against the country's professional and technical elites.[48]

• Between 1976 and 1983, the military dictatorship ruling Argentina conducted a 'dirty war' against political opponents, leading to the 'disappearance' (clandestine capture, imprisonment and usually murder) of at least 10,000 Argentinians suspected of 'subversion'.[49]

The logic of state terror is effectively set out by a 'Document on Terror' ostensibly produced by the NKVD – the precursor of the KGB – during the Stalinist terror. Although not the 'universal solution for all problems and difficulties, . . . amazing results . . . can be achieved with terror. . . . The aim of any action in the system of enlightened terror is to evoke a psychological process and implant and amplify its effects in the consciousness of the resonant mass.'[50]

* * * * * * * *

Purely pragmatically, that might be a bad policy for a government. *Random* acts (of violence or anything else) cannot, in general, be expected to evoke the sort of *systematic* compliance that governors want to evoke from the populace.[51]

The pragmatic arguments for adhering to the 'rule of law' tell equally against governing through a regime of random terror. Whether you think of human behaviour in psychological stimulus–response terms or whether you think of it in rationally intentional terms, regularity and consistency on the input side are usually the best ways to evoke the systematic results you desire on the output side.[52]

Random state terror can have its practical political uses, to be sure. Suppose the government wants to make people over-internalize its edicts, doing nothing that might remotely be conceived as a breach incurring the governor's wrath. Then wild, random over-responses to breaches might be a prudent plan. Many who have been subject to its random audits think that that is the strategy of the US Internal Revenue Service, for example.

It may not be a plan that works for long, however, when it comes to random violence against political opponents. Analysis of reactions to government use of 'death squads' against their opponents in El Salvador, for example, suggests that

> carefully targeted repressive violence may . . . reduce the level of active popular support for the opposition . . . [at least] temporarily. However, as the level of repressive violence escalates and its application becomes more indiscriminate, it may in fact produce increases in active support for the opposition because non-elites can no longer assure themselves of immunity from repression by simply remaining politically inert. Thus, they turn to the rebels in search of protection from indiscriminate violence by the state.[53]

Be those strategic calculations as they may, remember that the more fundamental issue here is conceptual. The fact that state officials are *conceptually capable* of terrorizing their own population seems undeniable.

Random kidnappings and killings, after the fashion of Pol Pot or Argentina's military government or El Salvador's death squads, surely count as instances of that. The only question (to which I shall be turning in chapter 5) is whether something substantially short of that might qualify as well.

* * * * * * * * * *

In defining 'terrorism' as 'acting with the intent of instilling fear in people for socio-political advantage', we earlier ran into a problem with war: much that a state does in the course of war might thereby qualify as terrorism. We face an analogous problem on the domestic side. Much that the state does to its own people, in the course of ordinary law enforcement, might on that definition also qualify as 'terrorism'.[54]

Of course *some* instances of particularly aggressive law enforcement clearly should count as terroristic (assuming officials of the state are conceptually capable of engaging in terrorist acts at all, as I have argued above that they are). 'Death squads' would be no less terroristic for being staffed by officers in police uniforms. The problem is that, on the definition here in view, all criminal laws and all activities enforcing those laws designed to 'deter' people from committing crime might similarly count as 'terroristic'. (People will be 'deterred' only if they have something to fear from non-compliance, after all.) While it certainly seems right that some instances of particularly aggressive law enforcement should count as terrorism, it does not seem right that all law enforcement should, necessarily.[55]

Let us begin by noticing a raft of things that we cannot say in response to this concern. We cannot say that law-enforcement officers – as legitimate officers of a legitimate state – are conceptually precluded from being terrorists, either ever or anyway so long as they are acting within their legal authority. That amounts to the definitional ploy dismissed at the beginning of this chapter. Nor can we say that law-enforcement officers are 'just doing their job' or 'just following orders'. That is the 'Nuremberg defence', which has been decisively dismissed in war-crime connections and ought for identical reasons be likewise disdained in connection with terrorism. And, in any case, the Nuremberg defence could only ever succeed in getting foot-soldiers and beat cops off the hook by putting people higher up the chain of command in their place: it does not exonerate the state from charges of terrorizing its own citizens; it only raises questions about which official to name as respondent on the charge sheet.

As in the international 'war' connection, so too in the domestic 'law-enforcement' connection: there are two possible responses that might seem more promising. One response is the anarchist's. Just as the pacifist would be happy to characterize all war as terroristic, so too the anarchist would be happy to characterize all coercive enforcement of state law as terroristic.[56]

Again, that would not necessarily preclude anarchists from conceding that some laws and some modes of law enforcement are morally worse than others. Modest fines imposed in accordance with norms of due process may well be less offensive, even to anarchist principles, than arbitrary summary executions (even if both are still beyond the bounds of what the anarchist is morally prepared to accept). Still, even acknowledging that some modes of law enforcement are morally worse than others, to the anarchist's way of thinking it is perfectly right that both law enforcement and terrorism should be morally condemned, in just the same way and for just the same reason.

The second broad line of response, here as in the international 'war' case, would be to try to find some way of distinguishing 'terroristic' forms of law enforcement from other forms of law enforcement.

One way might be through an adaptation of 'just-war' standards to the domestic context. We might say, for example, that law enforcement is not terroristic when it targets the guilty and only the guilty; and it is terroristic where it targets the population as a whole. But this does not seem a very promising approach, for at least two reasons. First of all, on the analysis just sketched, terrorism could be practised by law-enforcement officers only against the innocent; nothing they did to the guilty, however horrific, could ever count as 'terrorism'. That surely is not right.[57] Second, and more importantly, when trying to deter crime through the threats of sanctions, those threats are addressed to, and fear of those sanctions is intended to be instilled in, the population at large. True, the sanctions themselves will, hopefully, be brought to bear on the guilty and only the guilty. But the threats, and fear, are intended to be felt by everyone.

Another more promising analysis along these lines might build on the just-war standard of 'proportionality' rather than (or in addition to) 'innocence'. *Jus in bello* requires that violence be proportional to the ends that it legitimately serves. Perhaps just law enforcement ought be governed by similar standards; and perhaps the distinctive feature of 'terroristic' law enforcement is not (or not merely) its failure to discriminate between the innocent and the non-innocent but (instead, or perhaps in addition) the disproportionately harsh means that it employs. On that analysis, law enforcement becomes 'terroristic' when it overreacts especially badly.

There certainly seems to be something to that line of analysis. Only heavy-handed law enforcement will ever qualify as 'terroristic'. But is it really the case that *any* heavy-handed law enforcement should be seen as terroristic? Much though we might disapprove of the strict enforcement of a legal code that chops off the hands of convicted thieves, I do not think we would say that it is 'terroristic', exactly. Cruel. Barbaric. Inhumane. Terrifying, even. But it does not exactly seem to amount to 'terrorism', somehow.

A better way to make a distinction between terroristic and non-terroristic law enforcement is, I think, in terms of my definition of 'terrorism' as 'acting with the intention of instilling fear for some socio-political advantage'. Certainly, we may agree, enforcement of the criminal law threatens people with some truly frightening sanctions, and intentionally so. But enforcers of the criminal law do not ordinarily act for any 'socio-political advantage'. That ordinarily forms no part of their intentions in acting to enforce the law. And that is why we might be tempted to think that law enforcement, however frightening the threatened sanctions, does not ordinarily amount to terrorism.

What distinguishes those cases where law enforcement *does* seem terroristic is that, there, the officers of the state have indeed been pressed into the service of some partisan political cause. There, law-enforcement officials have become the agents of one part of society in its war on some other segment of society: against leftists and trade unionists in Argentina and Chile; against the bourgeoisie in Cambodia; against revisionists in Stalin's Soviet Union. It is precisely when the internal security forces have been co-opted to serve some blatantly political cause in brutal fashion that we are tempted to call their behaviour 'terroristic'.

Just as military campaigns always ultimately have some political purpose, so too does the criminal law always reflect the outcome of some political process and represent the victory of some over others in that process. And just as the seeking of military advantage always has larger political consequences, so too does the firm-but-fair enforcement of the laws found on the statute books. The crucial question would, on this analysis, be whether those further political consequences figured in the intentions of the agents in acting. If so, then their acting with the intention of instilling fear in the course of war or of law enforcement counts as terroristic; if not, then not.

Even if the intentions of officials in enforcing the law are not 'political', the law being enforced definitely is. Anarchists make much of that fact. 'Property is theft', for Kropotkin: any official of the state helping to enforce property title is aiding and abetting in that theft; and any official threatening to impose fearful sanctions for violation of property rights is indeed engaged in something anarchists such as Kropotkin would recognize as 'terrorism'. For them, what matters is that the official's actions are political in their effects, even if that was not that official's own intention.

A full assessment of anarchism would also take us too far afield, however. So, once again, I shall not attempt to adjudicate between those two possible responses. Suffice it to say, here, that it is clear that state officials can indeed sometimes terrorize their own citizens, and there are at least these two ways of making good analytic sense of that fact within the terms of the definition of terrorism that I have here offered.

State-sponsored terror and crimes of complicity

States might engage in terrorism in one last way. In addition to terrorizing citizens of other states or their own states directly, states can also terrorize people (either at home or abroad) at arm's length, by colluding with terrorist groups. By aiding and abetting terrorist groups, states might thus indirectly engage in terrorism themselves.

* * * * * * * *

The US has long been fixated on state-sponsored terror. US law requires that the State Department provide Congress with 'a full and complete annual report on terrorism for those countries and groups' that 'repeatedly support international terrorism'.[58] Under US law, severe consequences follow from a country's being placed on this 'terrorism list': a ban on arms-related exports and sales to that country, along with controls on the export of dual-use items; prohibitions on economic assistance to that country; and various other financial restrictions (including a requirement that the US oppose loans to that country by the World Bank and other international financial institutions).[59]

Historically, when the US talked about 'state-sponsored terrorism' it was referring principally to the activities of President Reagan's Evil Empire – the USSR and its client states – in fomenting armed insurrection around the world.[60] But there have always been issues with 'rogue states', too: not least Libya in the 1970s. And, with the collapse of communism, attention shifted decisively in the latter direction, most especially to the disparate set of states united in President George W. Bush's 'Axis of Evil'.[61] Countries on the State Department's official list of state sponsors of terrorism have, in recent years, included Cuba, Iran, Iraq, Libya, North Korea, Sudan and Syria.[62]

Although the identity of the accused has varied over the years, the US analysis of the problem of state-sponsored terrorism has remained remarkably constant:

> State sponsors of terrorism impede the efforts of the United States and the international community to fight terrorism. These countries provide a critical foundation for terrorist groups. Without state sponsors, terrorist groups would have a much more difficult time obtaining the funds, weapons, materials and secure areas they require to plan and conduct operations. The United States will continue to insist that these countries end the support they give to terrorist groups.[63]

* * * * * * * *

These themes have gained particular resonance after the September 11 attacks. In the wake of those attacks, the Bush administration repeatedly insisted that states that harbour terrorists, or aid and abet them, are themselves *ipso facto* terrorist states.

As President Bush said in his address to the US Congress immediately after the September 11 attacks,

> [T]onight, the United States of America makes the following demands on the Taliban: Deliver to United States authorities all the leaders of Al Qaeda who hide in your land. (Applause.) . . . Close immediately and permanently every terrorist training camp in Afghanistan, and hand over every terrorist, and every person in their support structure to appropriate authorities. (Applause.) Give the United States full access to terrorist training camps, so we can make sure they are no longer operating.
>
> These demands are not open to negotiation or discussion. (Applause.) The Taliban must act, and act immediately. They will hand over the terrorists, or they will share in their fate.[64]

In a radio address a fortnight later, President Bush re-emphasized that:

> Every nation has a choice to make. In this conflict there is no neutral ground. If a government sponsors the outlaws and killers of

innocents, they have become outlaws and murderers, themselves. And they will take that lonely path at their own peril.[65]

To the UN shortly after that, he stated plainly:

> For every regime that sponsors terror, there is a price to be paid. . . . The allies of terror are equally guilty of murder and equally accountable to justice.[66]

True to his words, President Bush took the US to war, first against Afghanistan and then against Iraq, in response to their alleged sponsorship of terrorism.

* * * * * *

While the US has a particular fixation on state sponsorship of terrorism, the international community as a whole certainly acknowledges that that phenomenon can indeed occur, and that it ought be firmly discouraged.

As early as 1970 the UN General Assembly had proclaimed, in its Declaration on Principles of International Law concerning Friendly Relations and Co-operation among States in Accordance with the Charter of the United Nations, that:

> Every State has the duty to refrain from organizing, instigating, assisting or participating in acts of civil strife or terrorist acts in another State or acquiescing in organized activities within its territory directed towards the commission of such acts, when the acts referred to . . . involve a threat or use of force.[67]

This language is echoed in the preambles to most international agreements on terrorism, figuring particularly prominently in, for example, the UN General Assembly's Resolution on Measures to Eliminate International Terrorism.[68]

* * * * * * *

While the phenomenon of 'state-sponsored terrorism' is most frequently discussed in international connections, where one state aids and abets terrorists in another state's territory, the same phenomenon also sometimes occurs domestically. States sometimes 'sponsor' – aid, abet and condone – terrorist groups acting within their own territory.

Consider the case of the Ku Klux Klan. The governments of many of the states of the old Confederacy were broadly in sympathy with the racist philosophy of the Klan and enforced by it through terroristic campaigns of lynchings, beatings and bombings. The states themselves could not pursue those aims openly and directly: the US federal government would have intervened to stop them. But they could, and did, turn a blind eye (at the very least) to terrorist acts of the Klan in pursuit of those objectives.[69]

* * * * * * * *

The phenomenon of 'state-sponsored terrorism' can be subsumed under the more general category of 'complicity with terrorism', which ought also be regarded as a terrorist offence. That is the crime that is committed by states in the case of states 'sponsoring' terrorism. But it is a crime that is more general in form, and that can be committed by individuals as well.

The UN's Convention for the Suppression of Terrorist Bombing states that:

Any person also commits an offence if that person:

(a) Participates as an accomplice in an offence as set forth in paragraph 1 or 2 of the present article [a terrorist bombing or attempted bombing]; or

(b) Organizes or directs others to commit an offence as set forth in paragraph 1 or 2 of the present article; or

(c) In any other way contributes to the commission of one or more offences as set forth in paragraph 1 or 2 of the present article by a group of persons acting with a common purpose; such contribution shall be intentional and either be made with the aim of furthering the general criminal activity or purpose

of the group or be made in the knowledge of the intention of
the group to commit the offence or offences concerned.[70]

* * * * * * * *

In conclusion: states and state officials can practise terrorism,
too. There is nothing in the concept itself to preclude that possibility. And there is much in the historical record to demonstrate that the possibility is a real one. States have practised
terror both against citizens of other states in time of war and
against their own people. Furthermore, states and state officials
have been complicit in the terrorism of others, by aiding and
abetting terrorist groups. Complicity with terrorism is a form
of terrorism, too. All these are important conclusions to carry
forward to the next chapter.

5

Warnings Can Be
Terroristic, Too: Profiting
Politically from Fear

The argument of the previous chapters has been that the best way of characterizing 'terrorism', both conceptually and empirically, is as 'acting with the intention of instilling fear for sociopolitical purposes'. For short: 'frightening people for political advantage'. Despite the great variety of ends for which such tactics have been deployed, that is the feature by virtue of which all of them seem truly to qualify as acts of terrorism at all. Moreover, as the last chapter has shown, public officials can deploy such tactics, too: and when they do, they are guilty of terrorism, as well.

This chapter focuses upon the issue of duly elected public officials profiting, politically, from the fear that terrorists engender. To some extent, of course, it is both politically inevitable and ethically unproblematic that they should do so. Whenever any country comes under attack, the government of the day almost always benefits from the tendency to 'rally around the flag'. Furthermore, the government is responsible for acting on behalf of the country in response to the attacks; and insofar as the government of the day is perceived to have 'responded well', then that is another morally unexceptionable way in which elected officials might profit, politically, from terrorist incidents.

There are other ways, however, to which we might indeed take moral exception. One obvious example would be if the politicians themselves had actually instigated the terrorist incidents: Hitler's henchmen burned the Reichstag in 1933, blaming the blaze on communists; and Hitler used that as a pretext for declaring a state of emergency and seizing complete power. Another example, only a little less odious, would be if politicians knowingly exaggerated the terrorist threat, fabricating false information to induce widespread fear from which they expected to profit politically. The 'Red Scares' in the US in the 1920s and the 1950s were pretty clearly incidents of that.[1] We would have little hesitation, I presume, in saying that Hitler, Palmer and McCarthy were guilty of 'terrorizing innocent civilians' in all those ways.

Certain aspects of the contemporary War on Terror might be relevantly similar. Consider the 'weapons of mass destruction' that the US and UK governments alleged that Iraq possessed and was disposed to use or to allow terrorists to use. Those allegations have since proven false: the weapons in question had been destroyed long ago. Just how much blame US and UK governments bear for 'terrorizing' their citizens by promulgating those frightening falsehoods depends, of course, on who knew (or could and should have known) what when. But insofar as the faulty intelligence was indeed politically influenced, those governments may well be guilty of moral crimes akin to those of Palmer and McCarthy. Knowingly telling people frightening lies, intending to profit politically thereby, would surely count as terrorism, of a sort.

Those, I take it, are easy cases. I shall say no more of them here (although I will return to aspects of them in chapter 6). In this chapter, I focus instead on harder cases. Those are ones in which politicians do no more than 'merely warn' people of risks that they genuinely, and on good grounds, believe to be posed by the terrorist activities of others. Are there any circumstances under which mere warnings of terrorism could themselves count as terroristic?

Clearly warnings can sometimes be acts of terrorism in their own right. When the IRA calls in a warning about a bomb it has planted, that is not just a 'warning of terrorism' – it is a 'terrorist warning'. That very warning counts as an (additional) act of terrorism, in and of itself. With rare exceptions (Hitler being one), politicians are ordinarily in a different position from that – the bombs of which they warn having been planted by others, not their own henchmen. But, I shall be arguing, their warnings of the terrorist threat posed by others can sometimes count as acts of terrorism themselves.

It all depends, I shall argue, on the intentions with which the warnings are issued. Remember, what made the 9/11 terrorist pilots' behaviour not merely 'murder' but also 'terrorism' was that they acted with the intention of instilling fear in people for their own political advantage. That is the distinctive feature that makes 'terrorist murderers' not merely 'murderers' but also 'terrorists'. And that – 'acting with the intention of instilling fear in people for their own political advantage' – is a feature that is shared both by the behaviour of murderous terrorist pilots and by the behaviour of politicians who commit no further moral offences beyond merely frightening people for political advantage.

As I shall go on to say at the end of this chapter, it is better that we be warned of terrorist bombs, even by terrorists themselves, than not be warned of the bombs at all. But it would be better yet again if the warnings were issued with purely humanitarian intentions, and in ways that do not deliberately stoke people's fears still further.

Threats and warnings

One important distinction that political philosophers traditionally draw in this vicinity is between 'threats' and 'warnings'.[2]

Of course, in a more colloquial sense, a threat is a warning as well: a warning of something that the threatener is resolved to do, unless the person threatened complies with the threatener's demands. A Mafioso might call it 'a friendly warning', and perhaps there is even some colloquial sense in which a threat gives 'fair warning'. Still, a threat is not, strictly speaking, a (mere) warning.[3]

* * * * * *

Threats clearly seem importantly different from warnings, in some morally significant respect. But the exact nature of the difference proves elusive.

Here is one way we might attempt to draw the distinction. A (mere) warning, we might say, is of something that is outside the volitional control of the warner, whereas a threat is of something that is within the volitional control of the threatener. That of which you merely warn is something that will or will not happen, regardless of whatever you (the 'mere warner') subsequently do. That which you threaten is something that will happen or will not happen only in consequence of something that you (the 'threatener') subsequently do. In short: we warn of others' doings, we make threats concerning our own.[4]

But that is not quite right. Suppose I am the official in charge of a major dam. Suppose that the dam is already at 100 per cent capacity, and the meteorologists are predicting heavy rain, so heavy as to pose a risk of the dam collapsing and thousands of lives and homes downstream being destroyed. Further suppose that, if the predicted rains come, the only way to avert that catastrophe would be to open the sluice gates fully. Doing so would destroy a hundred or so homes along the riverbank, but at least it would avert the much greater catastrophe that would ensue if the dam collapsed altogether. Accordingly, as the official responsible, I issue a public warning to people living along the riverbank that I might have to do that, advising them to evacuate their homes in good time.

Is that a threat or a warning? Well, the act in question is under my volitional control. It is something I intend to do, if certain circumstances arise; and it is also something which I could refrain from doing, if I chose otherwise. On the definition sketched above, therefore, it looks like a threat. But I think most of us would regard it as a genuine warning, instead.

Problems for this analysis arise from the opposite direction as well. Things that intuitively seem to be threats can come out looking like mere warnings on that analysis.

Nuclear strategists in the Cold War used to talk of 'Dooms-day Machines'. Mutually assured destruction would be all the stronger as a deterrent threat if, once you were attacked, you were powerless to call off your forces' devastating counter-attack. (The deep-sea submarine fleet came to be seen in that light, once it was appreciated that the command-control-communications infrastructure would be the first thing to be destroyed in any all-out nuclear assault: the submariners would indeed be on 'auto-pilot' after a devastating first strike on their homeland; no one would be able to countermand their 'stand-ing orders' concerning what to do in the case that they lost contact with headquarters.)[5]

Once the Doomsday Machine's settings have been locked in, they are *ex hypothesi* beyond the power of anyone to alter. At that point, its workings are beyond the volitional power of anyone – including the person issuing the threat/warning – to alter. So, at that point, someone warning of what her own Doomsday Machine will do is (on the definition in view) offer-ing a genuine warning rather than issuing a threat.

But that does not seem right. In the terminology of nuclear strategists, a Doomsday Machine would have constituted a 'deterrent threat' both before and after it was irrevocably armed. The machine poses a 'threat', even though (obviously) it has no volitional power over itself and (once armed) its maker has no control over it either. If its maker were guilty of some moral wrong in making such a device, we would be inclined to describe that wrong in terms of 'creating the threat' of mass annihilation: and we would persist in that description, I think, even (indeed, especially) after the device had been irrevocably armed.

Thus it seems that the degree of moral opprobrium attach-ing to threatening/warnings does not necessarily track the degree of volitional control one has over prospective events being threatened/warned about. Sometimes we morally blame people for making what on that analysis seem to be mere 'warnings' about things over which they (no longer) have any volitional control, as if they were 'threats'. And sometimes we morally exonerate people from making 'warnings' about things over which they do; they do not really seem to carry the oppro-brium of 'threats', even though the person making them does indeed possess such volitional control.

* * * * * * * *

Another way to cast the difference between threats and warn-ings is this: receiving a threat makes people worse off, whereas receiving a warning makes them better off (at least ordinarily; at least potentially).[6]

But the latter is true only if there is something recipients can do in response to the warning that makes them better off than they would have been had they not received the warning. In the limiting case, a warning about something you literally cannot do anything at all about is of no practical use to you; it might even make you worse off, causing dread or worry that is pragmatically pointless. So too in cases well short of that: a warning about something you cannot do very much about might similarly make you worse off, on balance.

* * * * * * * *

Yet another way to cash out the intuitive moral difference between threateners and warners is not in terms of the effects of their actions but rather in terms of the intentions lying behind them. Warners – pure warners – issue their warnings in hopes of averting the harmful outcomes of which they warn. The intention of threateners, in contrast, is – if not exactly to cause the harmful outcomes that they threaten – at least to do so conditionally, i.e., if their demands are not met.

That seems both true and important. The threatener clearly is a morally worse person than the mere warner, by virtue of that conditional intention to cause wrongful harm.[7] And the threatener is morally worse, yet again, if she goes on to act on the threat and cause the threatened harm.

But notice that there is another intention in play here: the threatener's intention in *issuing* the threat. You announce, 'I will blow up this building unless I am paid £100,000!' That is clearly a threat. It clearly announces your conditional intention to blow up the building if the £100,000 is not paid. But what was your intention in making that announcement itself? To get £100,000 and be released from having to carry through on that threat, of course.

Thus, the threatener's intention in making the threat is importantly different from her other (conditional) intention to act on the threat. Indeed, the first is typically in tension with the second, in that the intention lying behind the issuing of the threat is precisely to prevent the condition from arising in which that other intention (the evil threatened) would be acted upon. The threatener issues the threat in hopes of having the demands met – of getting the £100,000 – *rather* than blowing up the building. For the threatener, *qua* threatener, detonating the bomb would be a mark of failure in achieving her primary intention.

That fact, in turn, puts the threatener perfectly on a par with the mere warner, in precisely the respect in which we earlier hypothesized they might crucially differ. The distinctive feature of the warner, we had hypothesized, was that he issues his warning in hopes of averting the harmful outcome envisaged in his warning. But on closer inspection that turns out to be true of the threatener's intentions, as well. Just like the warner, her whole point in issuing her threat was to avert the outcomes she threatens – her intention was to 'get the £100,000, and not detonate the bomb' rather than 'not get £100,000 and detonate the bomb'.

* * * * * * * *

There remains one crucial difference between the warner and threatener, however. Mere warners issue warnings *purely* in hopes of averting the harmful events of which they warn.[8] Threateners, in contrast, issue threats partly in hopes of averting the harmful events they threaten; but they also do so partly in hopes of achieving the other objectives embodied in their demands. That *mixture of intentions* (the 'other objectives' also being pursued) seems to be what sets threateners apart from 'pure warners', morally speaking.[9]

Note that the 'other objectives' need not be 'things which would [themselves] be immoral' in order for the threat to qualify as a threat. When I threaten my travel agent that I will take my business elsewhere unless she finds me a better fare, I doubtless am making a threat, even though the action I foreshadow would be entirely within my rights both morally and legally. That may make the threat morally permissible, but it does not make the threat any less a threat.

* * * * * * * * * *

Intuitively there seems to be an important moral difference between those who threaten to commit frightful acts themselves and those who merely warn that such acts may (or will) occur by someone else's hand. But what exactly is that difference?

On the analysis I have here been offering, it is not the difference between someone else's doings (of which I merely warn) and my own (which I genuinely threaten). Neither is it simply the difference between doing something that makes others worse off (threatening them) versus better off (warning them).

Instead, the difference has crucially to do with the differing intentions with which threats and warnings are issued. Warnings are issued purely with the intention of averting the harms of which they warn. Threats are issued partly with that intention, but partly too in pursuit of some other objective of the threatener.

Impure warnings: 'terrorist warnings' versus 'warnings of terrorism'

Thus, the paradigm case of a 'pure warning' seems to be one in which the warning is issued purely with the intention of averting the harm of which it warns. That is what makes warnings, in that pure case, not just morally permissible but morally laudable. But there are other sorts of warnings made with less pure intentions. Those 'impure warnings' can be morally tainted by the other intentions thus intermixed with the intention (which often coexists, at least in part) to avert the harms of which they warn.

Exactly what sort of (maybe modest) moral wrong 'impure warnings' might constitute depends upon the exact nature of those 'other intentions'. Consider, as a variation on the 'threatener' scenario above, the case of a 'mere warner' who knows where a bomb is planted and offers to reveal its location in exchange for the same £100,000 the bomb-planter has demanded. The 'warner' then is not a 'pure warner', issuing the warning purely with the intention of averting the harm being warned of. The 'warner' acts in part with other intentions – an identical intention (securing £100,000) as the bomb-planter herself. No doubt this 'impure warner' is guilty of a lesser moral offence than the bomb-planter herself, in such circumstances. (After all, the merely 'impure warner' did not herself plant any bomb.) Still, there is no doubt, either, that the 'impure warner' is morally tainted by having acted with the same venal intentions as the bomb-planter herself in issuing her impure warning.

Now let us apply those lessons to cases of terrorism itself. An important distinction ought be drawn (and colloquially often is, if not always with any great precision) between 'terroristic warnings' and 'warnings of terrorism'. The latter term I will be using to refer to a 'pure warning', issued purely with the intent of averting the harm being warned of. The former term I will be using to refer to the case in which the warning is issued in (substantial) part with the characteristically 'terrorist' intent of instilling fear to further some socio-political ends. The very act of issuing the warning for such purposes would then qualify, under my definition, as an act of terrorism in and of itself.

* * * * * * * * *

The following set of cases together suggest that at least certain sorts of politically motivated warnings, even if they concern the acts of others, might reasonably be deemed terroristic.

These cases are all very similar in very many respects. All involve an IRA terrorist planting a bomb that will, unless defused, destroy much property and kill many people. All involve someone telephoning a warning to the police. The question will be in which cases that warning itself constitutes a terrorist act, and in which cases it does not. The purpose in holding as much else as constant as possible is to probe precisely which of these small variations transforms the act from one of a mere 'warning of terrorism' to one of a 'terrorist warning'.

Consider, then, the following people:

- *Kevin* is the IRA member who planted the bomb. But having armed it, Kevin is incapable of disarming the bomb himself (only the police can do that, at this point). Kevin rings the police, warning them of the bomb. He does so partly in hopes of avoiding death and destruction (he wants to frighten people, not to kill them). But he does so also largely in hopes that people will be frightened that a bomb has been planted, and that their being frightened will help to further the IRA's political aim of forcing the British to withdraw from Ulster.
- *Linda* is a member of the same IRA cell as Kevin. She helped to plan the planting of the bomb, and she has been assigned the job of ringing through the warning once the bomb is in place. She does so partly in hopes of avoiding death and destruction (like Kevin, she wants to frighten people, not to kill them). But she does so also largely in hopes that people will be frightened that a bomb has been planted, and that their being frightened will help to further the IRA's political aim of forcing the British to withdraw from Ulster.

- *Michael* is a member of the IRA but in a different cell altogether. He took no part in planning the planting of the bomb. But when he finds the bomb hidden among some rubbish, he knows immediately what it is. He rings the police with a warning. He does so partly in hopes of avoiding death and destruction (like Kevin and Linda, he wants his organization to frighten people, not to kill them). But he does so also largely in hopes that people will be frightened in ways that will help to further the IRA's political aim of forcing the British to withdraw from Ulster.

- *Nell* is not a member of the IRA, but she sympathizes with their aims. She finds the bomb hidden among some rubbish. She rings the police with a warning. She does so partly in hopes of avoiding death and destruction. But she does so also largely in hopes that people will be frightened in ways that will help to further the IRA's political aim of forcing the British to withdraw from Ulster.

- *Oran* is a member of the UVF, a militant Protestant Unionist group. He finds the bomb hidden among rubbish, and rings the police with a warning. He does so partly in hopes of avoiding death and destruction. But he does so also largely in hopes that people will be frightened in ways that rebound against the IRA and thus help to further the UVF's political goal of preventing the withdrawal of the British from Ulster.

- *Pat* is not a member of the UVF, but she sympathizes with their aims. She finds the bomb hidden among some rubbish. She rings the police with a warning. She does so partly in hopes of avoiding death and destruction. But she does so also largely in hopes that people will be frightened in ways that rebound against the IRA and thus help to further the UVF's political goal of preventing the withdrawal of the British from Ulster.

- *Quinn* is politically indifferent. He finds the bomb hidden among rubbish, and rings the police with a warning, purely in hopes of avoiding death and destruction.

* * * * * * *

What should we make of each of those cases? Which of those people were 'warning of terrorism', and which were themselves engaging in a form of terrorism by making a 'terrorist warning'?

Quinn presents one clear case. He rings the police with a 'pure warning' – one issued purely with the intent of averting harm to prospective victims of the bomb, and with no further political intent. Clearly, therefore, Quinn is no terrorist.

It is equally clear that people like Kevin and Linda who conspire to plant the bomb are terrorists. Indeed, they count as terrorists twice over, firstly in planting the bomb and secondly in ringing the authorities, warning of the bomb. Both acts were done with the 'intention of instilling fear in people for political advantage'. Both are terrorist acts. But they are separate terrorist acts.

On the scale of moral evils, planting a bomb must definitely count as a greater evil than merely warning of a bomb, even if the latter was done with clear terrorist intentions. The latter is clearly the lesser of the two moral offences committed by terrorists Kevin and Linda. I do not dispute that in the least. I merely want to point out that that lesser terrorist offence (issuing a terrorist warning) is an act of terrorism, as well.

* * * * * * *

Next I want to ask whether other people on that list, besides easy cases like those of Kevin and Linda, might be similarly guilty of that second and lesser terrorist offence.

More interesting are the cases of Michael and Oran. Neither had any role in planting the bomb; they are in no way guilty of *that* terrorist offence.[10] But – to fix the focus firmly on the question before us – are they guilty of a different (and lesser) act of terrorism, in ringing the authorities to warn of the bomb?

It all depends on their intentions in so doing. In the stories as told, both did so largely (let's assume each as largely as the other) in order to instil terror in the population as a means of furthering their (differing) political ends. Certainly by the definition I have offered, both Michael's and Oran's warnings would count as terrorist acts.

Indeed, on any credible definition, if one of those warnings counts as a terrorist act then surely the other must also. Neither Michael nor Oran took any part in planting the bomb; both were merely warning, under otherwise identical circumstances, about something that other people had done. Surely then it cannot matter whether the bomb had been planted by 'our side' or 'theirs'. Warning about the consequences of 'their' acts, if done with identical intent to instil identical fear for strictly analogous political purposes, is surely morally on a par with warning about the consequences of acts performed (without any complicity on my part) by people on 'my own side' of politics.

* * * * * *

That is my main point in introducing these examples. But, just for the sake of completeness, consider the remaining pair of 'mere sympathizers', Nell and Pat.

We might at first brush be inclined to judge Nell (who merely sympathizes with the IRA) less harshly than Michael (who is actually a member, albeit of some other cell not responsible for this bomb). We might be so inclined for several reasons. One reason might be the thought that a mere sympathizer is less committed to the cause than an actual member; and hence Nell's telephone call to the police was (we might be inclined to suppose) motivated more purely by a desire to avoid death and destruction, and less by a desire to frighten people for the IRA's political ends, than was Michael's.

Empirically, that may well be a fair generalization. But for purposes of the example let's hold that factor constant as well. Let's assume that the mix of intentions was identical for both Nell and Michael; and let's assume that, for both of them, furthering the IRA's political goals was much the stronger intention than just protecting the public from harm. Then I think we should say that Nell's act was every bit as much one of terrorism as Michael's. What determines whether the warning counts as terrorism is one's motives, not one's memberships or affiliations.[11]

And, for the same reasons we should judge the cases of Michael and Oran symmetrically, we should judge the cases of Nell and Pat symmetrically. In the case of Michael and Oran, who warn of the bomb primarily to advance the political goals of their side of politics, I argued that if one's warning should count as a 'terrorist warning' so too should the other's: it should make no difference whether the bomb was planted by 'our side' (in a way that does not at all involve Michael) or 'theirs'. So too in the case of 'mere sympathizers' rather than actual members of the groups in question: it should make no difference whether the bomb was planted by 'our side' or 'theirs'; if Nell's warning counts as a 'terrorist warning', so too should Pat's.

* * * * * * *

The analysis I have been developing here says that, to count as a terrorist, you do not need to plant the bomb yourself. The person who planted the bomb is a terrorist too, of course, and is undeniably guilty of more and much worse offences. But someone who merely warns others of the bomb, purely for her own political ends, could reasonably be regarded as having committed a terrorist act as well.

Furthermore, issuing warnings intended to frighten people, primarily for one's own political advantage, counts equally as an act of terrorism, regardless of whether those issuing the warnings are acting in sympathy with or in opposition to the actions of the group about whom the warnings are issued. In the above examples, the moral wrong that Oran has committed seems morally on a par with that of Michael and Nell in turn.

Politicians' intentions matter, too

At the outset of this chapter, we saw the crucial role that intentions play in distinguishing what we ordinarily regard as morally permissible (even laudatory) warnings from what we ordinarily regard as morally impermissible threats. What we have just seen through that suite of IRA bombing examples is that, depending again on the intentions underlying them, warnings of terrorism might in and of themselves count as terrorist acts. Morally, a terrorist warning of a bomb is much less bad than is a terrorist planting the bomb; but both are forms of terrorism, and both are bad (to differing degrees) for that reason.

In the IRA bombing examples above, one thing that was held constant across all those cases was that the person ringing in the warning was always a private individual. Let us now transpose the lessons from those cases about the crucial role of intentions in distinguishing between 'warnings of terrorism' and 'terrorist warnings' to the case of *public* officials.

* * * * * * *

Let us begin our exploration of those issues by extending our suite of IRA bomb examples. In all these cases, as in all the previous ones, a bomb has been planted by the IRA. In the following examples, all of the individuals will be public officials who issue warnings about that bomb. The question, as before, is which of those warnings count as 'terrorist warnings' – acts of terrorism in and of themselves – and which as mere 'warnings of terrorism'.

Consider, then, the following cases.

- *Ruth*, who is not a member of the IRA but sympathizes with their aims, is Minister of Agriculture in a power-sharing government in Northern Ireland. She receives a report of a bomb hidden among some rubbish, and she issues a public warning to evacuate the area. She does so partly in hopes of avoiding death and destruction. But she does so also largely in hopes that people will be frightened in ways that will help to further the IRA's political aim of forcing the British to withdraw from Ulster.
- *Stan*, who is not a member of the UVF but sympathizes with their aims, is Minister of Agriculture in a power-sharing government in Northern Ireland. He receives a

report of a bomb hidden among some rubbish, and he issues a public warning to evacuate the area. He does so partly in hopes of avoiding death and destruction. But he does so also largely in hopes that people will be frightened in ways that rebound against the IRA and thus help to further the UVF's political goal of preventing the withdrawal of the British from Ulster.

- *Theresa*, who is not a member of the IRA but sympathizes with their aims, is Minister of Information in a power-sharing government in Northern Ireland. She receives a report of a bomb hidden among some rubbish, and she issues a public warning to evacuate the area. She does so partly in hopes of avoiding death and destruction. But she does so also largely in hopes that people will be frightened in ways that will help to further the IRA's political aim of forcing the British to withdraw from Ulster.

- *Ulee*, who is not a member of the UVF but sympathizes with their aims, is Minister of Information in a power-sharing government in Northern Ireland. He receives a report of a bomb hidden among some rubbish, and he issues a public warning to evacuate the area. He does so partly in hopes of avoiding death and destruction. But he does so also largely in hopes that people will be frightened in ways that rebound against the IRA and thus help to further the UVF's political goal of preventing the withdrawal of the British from Ulster.

- *Vanessa*, who is Minister of Agriculture in a power-sharing government in Northern Ireland, is completely indifferent as between the political objectives of the IRA and UVF. She receives a report of a bomb hidden among some rubbish, and she issues a public warning to evacuate the area. She does so partly in hopes of avoiding death and destruction. But she does so also largely in hopes that people will be frightened in ways that rebound to her personal political advancement.

- *William*, who is Minister of Information in a power-sharing government in Northern Ireland, is completely indifferent as between the political objectives of the IRA and UVF. He receives a report of a bomb hidden among some rubbish, and he issues a public warning to evacuate the area. He does so partly in hopes of avoiding death and destruction. But he does so also largely in hopes that people will be frightened in ways that rebound to his personal political advancement.

- *Xena*, who is Minister of Information in a power-sharing government in Northern Ireland, is completely indifferent as between the political objectives of the IRA and UVF. She receives a report of a bomb hidden among some rubbish, and she issues a public warning to evacuate the area, purely in hopes of avoiding death and destruction.

* * * * * * * * *

Xena, clearly, is no terrorist. Like Quinn in the previous suite of cases, Xena issues the warning purely with a view to avoiding death and destruction. That being the only intention behind her act, it clearly counts as a 'warning of terrorism' rather than as a 'terrorist warning'.

The cases of Ruth and Stan, Theresa and Ulee are trickier in various ways I shall go on to discuss shortly. But I think we can say one thing with confidence from the start. If the warning from the first member of each of those pairs counts as a 'terrorist warning' then so too should that from the second; if Ruth's is a 'terrorist warning' then so too is Stan's, and if Theresa's is then so too is Ulee's. As in the cases of Michael and Oran, likewise in these cases: whether or not the issuing of the warning itself constitutes an act of terrorism should turn on the intentions of the person issuing the warning, not on whether the bomb had been planted by people on one's own side of politics or the other's.

The difference between those two pairs of cases lies in which portfolio the politician in question holds. Ruth and Stan are Ministers of Agriculture. Issuing warnings of terrorist bombings is in no way part of their portfolio responsibilities. Of course, in some larger sense anyone who knows of a danger to the public should warn of it, especially perhaps anyone in a position of public responsibility. But the point remains that Ruth and Stan will be going out of their way – going outside their portfolio responsibilities – to issue the warnings. Theresa and Ulee, in contrast, as Ministers of Information, are charged with responsibility for issuing precisely such warnings as a core part of their jobs.

What all of those cases nonetheless have in common is that the warnings are being issued largely with the intention of instilling fear in the populace in ways that will further the political aims of the IRA or UVF. And that, I argue, is crucial.

Compare the cases of Nell and Ruth. Both are IRA sympathizers. Both issue their warnings largely with the intention of instilling fear in the populace that will further the political aims of the IRA. The only difference is that Nell is a private citizen and Ruth a public official, albeit in a ministry not actually responsible for issuing warnings of terrorism. When Ruth steps outside her portfolio responsibilities to issue the warning, what grounds have we for regarding her warning as any different from that of a private citizen such as Nell? If we regard Nell's act as a 'terrorist warning', by virtue of the fact that it was motivated primarily by a desire to further the IRA's political aims, then so too should we regard Ruth's as a 'terrorist warning'.

And, as I have said, if we so regard Ruth's, then, as I have said, we should similarly regard Stan's. He too steps outside of his portfolio responsibilities gratuitously to warn of the IRA's bomb and thereby further his own political ends. He acts not to further the IRA's political aims but rather to frustrate them, thus furthering the aims of the UVF, which he supports. But surely which side of politics one is on should not matter in determining whether otherwise identical acts count as 'acts of terrorism'. If Ruth's warning counts as a 'terrorist warning' in support of the IRA's aims, so too should Stan's count as a 'terrorist warning' in support of the UVF's.

* * * * * * * *

What then of Theresa and Ulee? They are both Ministers of Information. It is their job to warn of terrorist acts. We cannot complain that they are 'going out of their way' or 'stepping outside their portfolio' to do so, as we did of Ruth and Stan.

Here, however, intentions surely still bite. If, in issuing the warning, Theresa and Ulee had been acting purely or even primarily with the intention of 'doing their job' or 'protecting the public' (which is surely the key element in that part of their job description), then we would have no grounds for calling their acts ones of 'terrorism'. It may be that the warnings rebound to the advantage of their favourite political cause; it may be that Theresa and Ulee could foresee that at the time they issued the warnings. But if that was not their primary intention in issuing them, only an incidental by-product, then on chapter 3's intention-based definition of 'terrorism' they would not count as 'terrorist warnings'.

But that is not the case in the stories as told. In both cases, Theresa and Ulee issue their warnings largely with the intention of instilling fear that will further the political aims of the IRA and UVF respectively. That distinctively 'terrorist' intention turns 'warnings of terrorism' that could, on that alternative scenario, have been merely 'part of their jobs' into 'terrorist warnings', which are acts of terrorism in and of themselves.

* * * * * * * *

Consider now the more marginal cases of Vanessa and William. Neither has any sympathy for either the IRA or the UVF. But neither is either of them acting purely or principally to 'protect the public' in issuing their warnings. Instead, their warnings are motivated largely by a desire to promote their own political careers. Being seen as responsible for issuing the warnings will increase their vote share, perhaps; perhaps they will even become prime minister in consequence.

Perhaps 'terrorist' seems to be too big a word to apply to cases like that. Vanessa's and William's behaviour might have been many things: cynical, opportunist, manipulative even. But terroristic? 'Terrorism', by chapter 3's definition, has to involve 'acting with the intention of instilling fear for some *socio-political* purpose' – and the 'purpose' underlying Vanessa's and

William's purely careerist acts was not 'political', in the right sort of way.

Both of them were frightening people largely with the intention of furthering their own political careers, to be sure. But, we might suppose, 'career' – even a political career – is not the same as a 'cause'. The person who threatens to blow up a building unless she is given £100,000 is clearly a 'threatener'. If however it is merely the money she is after, she is not a 'terrorist' but merely an 'extortionist'. Neither does someone qualify as a 'terrorist' merely by making frightening threats against a bank manager's family unless he gives her a job. Why ought we regard 'jobs in politics' any differently than 'jobs in banks', here?

Well, were it merely a job – the postmastership of some small town, say – then that reply would have much merit. The fact that it is a political appointment is not sufficient to make it 'political' in the right sort of way. The job may be one that is dispensed by politicians; but the processing of the mails is itself an apolitical process. It makes no political (which is to say, 'policy') difference who occupies the position.

The same obviously cannot be said about the post of prime minister, or even minister of state or 'government of the day'. There, it does make a political difference – a policy difference – who gets the job. Control over the actions and policies of government is precisely what terrorists of the classic sort seek; and it is precisely that intention that marks them off from ordinary murderers, kidnappers and extortionists. A politician standing for office, who proceeds to act with the intention of frightening people for the same objectives (control of government and its policies), might well therefore be regarded as a terrorist in the same way and for the same reason as would be a political actor doing the same thing outside the electoral process.

* * * * * * * *

There is one interesting wrinkle in the story to note here. What I have just said applies basically just to policy-oriented politicians. Suppose Vanessa and William were pure careerists. They want the job, and that is all they want. They might have to make policy promises in order to get the job; they might have to act on those promises, once elected, to keep the job. But their intentions were purely to get the job, and implementing policies is purely a by-product (like the death of innocent civilians, say, in the double-effect justification of bombing military targets in city centres).[12]

Now suppose such a politician engages in the sort of behaviour associated with Vanessa and William. The politician issues frightening warnings, and she does so with the intention of instilling fear in people for the purpose of increasing her chances of being elected. It is not quite the same as the case of the postmaster: it will, let us assume, make some policy difference if she is elected instead of her opponent. But her intention in issuing the frightening warnings, let us assume, is not to make any difference to policy but merely to obtain the job.

If the job were all (or even just 'mostly all') she were after in issuing frightening warnings, then it seems her purposes would indeed not be 'political' in the way that we would require to count her warnings as 'terrorist'. It may still be wrong to frighten people into giving you a good job; it may still be wrong to do so if what you tell them, although frightening, is perfectly true. (That is to say, it may be that you should give people 'reasons' for giving you a job, and 'frights' are not 'reasons'.) But those wrongs, if wrongs they be, would not be regarded as 'terrorist' wrongs under my definition. Purely or almost purely careerist politicians cannot count as 'terrorists' – which in itself is, in some sense, actually to their discredit.

* * * * * * *

On the face of it, it might have seemed implausible to regard public officials who do nothing more than make accurate warnings of a terrorist attack as themselves having committed an act remotely akin to terrorism. But I hope that this extended suite of IRA bomb examples has served to demonstrate that

that conclusion is not at all implausible, at least under certain circumstances.

Acting with the intention of instilling fear for socio-political purposes can plausibly count as 'terrorism', regardless of who commits the act. And 'issuing warnings' can be among the acts that can be 'terrorist' in that way.

The *Oxford English Dictionary*, incidentally, agrees. Note its second definition of 'terrorist': 'One who entertains, professes, or tries to awaken or spread a feeling of terror or alarm; an alarmist, a scaremonger'. So insofar as politicians' warnings count as 'alarmist', they would indeed meet the dictionary's definition of 'terrorist'. Certainly the warnings would count as 'alarmist', and hence 'terrorist', if they were overstated (which *ex hypothesi* in the IRA case they were not). But even beyond that, the OED offers other subsidiary definitions, both of 'terrorist' and 'alarmist', on which warnings would clearly count as that even if they involved no exaggeration: on those definitions, merely an intent to spread panic and alarm would suffice to qualify someone as a 'terrorist'.[13]

Dictionary definitions merely track 'ordinary usage', of course, and morally speaking that proves nothing. But in searching for moral rather than merely lexicographic grounds for the conclusions that I am here urging, we need only recall the distinction emphasized throughout this chapter between 'terrorist warnings' and 'warnings of terrorism'.

What I have continually said, and what the IRA bomb examples illustrate, is that warnings can count as 'terrorism', in and of themselves, insofar as the warnings were issued with the intention of instilling fear for some partisan political purpose. Terrorists of the classic sort thus commit two acts of terrorism: one in planting the bomb, the other in issuing the warning. Within terrorist cells, recall, there is often one person whose job is to plant the bomb, another whose job is to ring in the warning. Both, clearly, are guilty of terrorist offences. They are not guilty of the same offence, to be sure: planting a bomb and phoning the police are different acts. Nor are they guilty of equally bad offences: planting the bomb is clearly worse than merely warning of it, even with the same intentions. Still, both are clearly guilty of an act of terrorism (albeit a different act of terrorism).

The point is just this: people who do nothing more than issue warnings with the intention of instilling fear are in those other connections deemed 'terrorists', provided they issue those warnings purely or predominantly for political purposes. Why not say the same of the public officials who do just the same?

Terrorism as an aggravated wrong: is 'violence' required?

Can people who commit no further moral offences, beyond frightening people for political advantage, truly count as terrorists?

There is a temptation to restrict the definition of 'terrorism' to cases of people who 'commit some (other) *serious moral offence* with the intention of instilling fear in people for their own political advantage'.[14]

Defining 'terrorism' in that way would have two consequences. One would be to ensure that 'terrorism' is always morally wrong (at least *prima facie*).[15] The other would be to ensure that *only* people also committing 'some other serious moral offences' (such as killing people) could count as terrorists – thus exempting people such as politicians who do nothing more than merely 'frighten people for political advantage' from charges of 'terrorism'.

The suggestion here is that we might think of 'terrorism' as being akin to the crime of 'aggravated assault'. Just as there can be no 'aggravated assault' without an assault, there can be no 'terrorist murder' without a 'murder'. So, too, perhaps there can be no 'terrorism' (seeing it as akin to 'aggravation' in the 'aggravated assault' analogy) without some other 'serious moral offence' which it aggravates. Simply 'acting with the intention of inducing fear for political ends' would not then be terrorism, when the acts in question are not themselves immoral and no other immoral acts are committed.[16]

* * * * * * * *

Chapter 4 opened with a critique of a 'definitional ploy' confining the term 'terrorism' to 'non-state actors'. One can easily see why the US State Department and CIA favour such a definition: it exempts states and their agencies from ever counting as 'terrorists', whatever they do.

There is an analogous (if almost certainly less deliberate) definitional ploy involved in the present proposal. *If* we restrict the term 'terrorist' to 'people who commit some serious moral offence with the intention of instilling fear in people for their own political advantage', and *if* we suppose that issuing (accurate) warnings about terrorism can never be a 'serious moral offence' no matter what the intentions behind the warnings, then people giving warnings of terrorism (whatever their reasons for doing so) can never – by definition – count as 'terrorists'.

Of course, if there were independent reasons for thinking that that is the right way to define 'terrorism', then that would indeed be the correct conclusion. But the structure of the argument – conferring 'immunity, by definition' on privileged and powerful actors – ought at least arouse suspicions and invite careful investigation.

* * * * * * * *

The first thing we notice, upon that further reflection, is that the middle 'if' in the formulation two paragraphs back is not correct. Surely we do *not* suppose that issuing (accurate) warnings about terrorism can never be a 'serious moral offence' no matter what the intentions behind the warnings. Think back to the IRA bomb cases. When the IRA member who himself planted the bomb then also phones in a warning about it, we deem that a 'terrorist warning' – a second act of terrorism in and of itself, different from and additional to the act of terrorism involved in planting the bomb. True, it would be even more wrong, once the bomb is ticking, not to warn than it is to warn. But both are wrongs, wrongful acts of terrorism.

What makes those warnings wrongful acts of terrorism is precisely the intention lying behind the acts, the intention to instil fear for political advantage. And, as I argued above, that is a feature that duly elected politicians' warnings can, in certain circumstances, share. If so, they would be wrong in the same way and for the same reasons as the terrorists' own.

So that one key step in the 'definitional ploy' to immunize those who themselves do nothing more than warn of terrorism from counting as 'terrorists' fails. And it does so for reasons that have already been analysed.

* * * * * * * *

Defining 'terrorism' so that it necessarily also involves some other 'serious moral offence' would enable us to draw a sharp distinction between the 9/11 pilots (who clearly count as terrorists in those terms) and politicians reacting to them (who would not, or anyway not usually).

It might do so, however, at the cost of forcing this absurdity. Imagine, if you can, a reign of terror that is so successful that its objects are completely cowed. No threats ever need to be made, much less carried out; no moral wrongs ever need to be done to the cowed population. (Domestic abuse, of a purely non-physical form, is sometimes said to be like that.) On the analysis here in view, that would therefore fail to qualify as a case of 'terrorism' at all. But surely it would be absurd to treat really successful cases of terrorization as not involving terrorism at all.[17]

* * * * * * *

In suggesting that to count as 'terrorists' people have to 'commit some other serious moral offence', the 'other serious moral offence' in view typically involves 'violence'. That is typically construed, implicitly or explicitly, as 'wrongful violence' (so a public executioner discharging his official duties, however gruesomely, would not count as a 'terrorist'). Most typically, it is construed as 'violence against innocents'.

The latter formulation, of course, takes us back to the just-war version of the argument that I have already queried at length in chapter 2. So here I shall focus instead on the more general version of the argument, couched in terms merely of 'wrongful violence'.

The first thing to note is that, while reference to 'violence' is a common feature in definitions of 'terrorism', it is far from a universal one. Public agencies almost always include it, defining 'terrorism' as:

- 'the use of *violence* for political ends including the use of violence for the purpose of putting the public or any section of the public in fear' (UK Prevention of Terrorism Act, 1974);[18]
- 'pre-meditated, politically motivated *violence* perpetrated against non-combatants, targeted by sub-national groups or clandestine agents, usually intended to influence an audience' (US State Department and CIA);[19]
- '*unlawful* use of *force and violence* against persons or property to intimidate or coerce a government, the civilian population, or any segment thereof, in furtherance of political or social objectives' (FBI).[20]

And many scholars follow public agencies in that practice.[21] But, in the less politicized definitions found in dictionaries, such a restriction is generally absent. They equate 'terrorism' simply with 'intimidation' (*Webster's*) or 'the employment of methods of intimidation' (OED). They call it simply 'a policy intended to strike with terror those against whom it is adopted' (OED).[22]

On some extreme versions, 'wrongful violence designed to influence government policy' is the *sole* defining feature of terrorism, and any connection between 'terrorism' and the actual or intended production of 'terror' would be a purely contingent one (albeit an empirically common one).[23] That has been shown to be wrong in chapter 3 above.

It is the more moderate version of the politicized definition that is of particular interest here. On that proposal, there are *two* individually necessary and jointly sufficient conditions for an act to qualify as one of 'terrorism': first, it must be an act intended to instil fear in people for one's own political advantage (just as my chapter 3 definition would require); and, second, it must be an act of wrongful violence.

Whether terrorism always necessarily involves violence is debatable. The example offered above of a very successful reign of terror suggests not; and other examples might be adduced.[24] Still, even if only as a purely contingent fact, terrorism does often involve violence. Let us therefore concentrate on those common cases where the two are found together.

The central question I want to raise is this: even if we think that instances of 'terrorism' necessarily involve someone, somewhere, performing or threatening to perform acts of 'violence', do we have any grounds for thinking that only those people who are *themselves* engaged in those acts of violence count as 'terrorists'?

The IRA bombing examples suggest not. Perhaps, as the politicized definitions would have it, those examples only count as an instance of terrorism at all because an act of violence (planting a bomb) is involved somewhere in the story. But surely it would be wrong to suppose that the only terrorist in the above scenarios is Kevin, the person who actually committed the act of violence and planted the bomb.

Linda, his co-conspirator, is surely every bit as much a terrorist, even though she took no active part in planting the bomb. And, as I argued earlier, so too is Michael – the member of some other IRA cell – who is in no way implicated in the planting of this bomb but who is nonetheless delighted to further the IRA's ends by ringing through the warning. He is every bit as much a terrorist as the first two. So too is his UVF counterpart Oran, who is delighted to further the UVF's ends by ringing through the warning. Neither of those latter two, however, are actively or even passively implicated in the 'act of violence' that is constituted by planting the bomb.

Thus, even if we think that an instance of terrorism must involve an act of violence on the part of someone, somewhere, there is no reason to think that people who have not themselves been actively or even passively involved in that act of violence cannot count as 'terrorists' in the ensuing scenario. Michael and Oran clearly did, in the IRA example I have sketched. They did so, because they piggybacked on that act of violence in themselves 'acting with the intention of frightening people for their own political advantage'.

The same might also of course be true of Western political leaders trumpeting a War against Terror. Suppose they did not themselves engage in violence. Still, in issuing warnings of the violent intentions of others, for their own political advantage, they might thereby have engaged in (lesser) acts of terrorism themselves.

* * * * * * * *

In light of this discussion, perhaps we ought amend our chapter 3 definition to read as follows: 'terrorism is acting with the intention of instilling fear *of violence* for socio-political purposes'.

There are of course a great many different ways of defining violence. Must it be 'active' or can it also be 'passive'? Must it be physical, or can it take other forms? Must it be to people's bodies, or might it be to their interests? Must it be intentional?[25]

We can leave all those questions open, observing simply that what you will regard as 'terrorism' depends on what you regard as 'violence'. If you do not regard destroying a person's reputation as a form of 'violence', then you will not (and indeed ought not) regard threatening to do so a 'terrorist threat', either.[26]

Revising chapter 3's definition of 'terrorism' in this way might help us distinguish between two kinds of cases that might seem genuinely different. Contrast the case of the Ministers in the IRA bomb examples with the case of Abe, a Health Minister conducting a campaign to warn people of some horrible disease against which they ought take precautions. As before, let us suppose that the information is all perfectly true; the disease is genuinely frightful, and it is genuinely preventable by the measures being recommended. Furthermore, let us suppose, the information campaign if successful would rebound to Abe's political benefit, so that he would then be a great national hero and become prime minister.

Indeed, suppose Abe's case parallels perfectly that of William in the IRA bomb case. Like William, Abe has acted with the intention of instilling fear in people; like William, he has acted within the scope of his portfolio responsibilities. Let us further suppose that Abe does so largely with the intention of promoting his own political career. And finally, let us suppose that some policy consequences would follow from his successfully pursuing his political career (which for reasons given above is necessary to make William's case one of a 'terrorist warning'). Then, on chapter 3's definition, Abe would indeed be guilty of 'terrorizing' the population and not just 'terrifying' it.

There might however be one good reason not to call Abe's warning (unlike William's) 'terroristic', fear-inducing and politically motivated though it might have been.

The reason is just this: 'terrorist warnings' (warnings that themselves constitute an act of terrorism) are 'warnings of terrorism that are issued with terrorist intent'. So far, we have been focusing on the 'with terrorist intent' part of that formula. That, we have concluded, means that the warnings must have been 'issued with the intention of instilling fear in people for one's own socio-political purposes'. But we also need to recall that 'terrorist warnings' are a subspecies of 'warnings of terrorism'. Warnings, even with that feature, do not count as 'terrorist warnings' unless they are 'warnings *of terrorism*'. Warnings issued with that intent but concerning something else – a snowstorm, or an escaped convict – are not 'warnings of terrorism', or hence 'terrorist warnings' either.

In that respect, the case of health minister Abe really is different from information minister William's warning about the IRA bomb. Assuming the disease was naturally occurring, and not itself a case of biological terrorism, warning of it even with the single-minded intention of instilling fear in people for his own political advantage would not constitute terrorism, because the warning was not itself a warning of terrorism. What William was warning of was an impending act of terrorism, an IRA bombing; and a warning of such an act of terrorism can (provided certain conditions are met) be seen as a 'terrorist warning', an act of terrorism in its own right.

* * * * * * * *

Finally, we might consider further amending the revised definition above as follows: 'terrorism is acting with the intention of instilling, for socio-political purposes, fear of violence for socio-political purposes'.

The phrase 'for socio-political purposes' appears twice in that formulation. Both appearances relate to the point made in chapter 3 and frequently repeated since: terrorism is defined in terms of its perpetrators' intentions and purposes, not their effects alone. A kidnapping is terrorist only if it is conducted for some socio-political purpose. If the intention is merely to secure ransom, with no political intent, then the kidnapping is not terrorist.

The first time the phrase appears, it specifies the intention of the person who is deliberately instilling the fear. That counts as an act of terrorism if and only if the person performs that act intending by it to further some socio-political aim. That has been discussed already.

The second time the phrase appears, it specifies the intention of the person responsible for the 'violence' that, on this revised definition, must be the object of the fear being instilled. The reformulated definition above says that the violence must also be oriented towards some socio-political aim, in order for instilling fear of it to count as terrorism.

Suppose the Ministers in the above examples were warning of bombs planted not by the IRA but rather by extortionists motivated purely by considerations of financial gain. A Minister warning of IRA terrorist bombs for her own political advancement might (in certain circumstances elaborated above) be said to be issuing a 'terrorist warning', a warning about terrorists that was itself an act of terrorism. But if the Minister were making the same warning for the same reason about bombers who were not themselves terrorists, but merely extortionists, then the Minister's warning could not itself count as terrorist either.

* * * * * * * *

Not much hinges on these refinements for the larger issue at hand, so I will not explore them further.

The larger issue before us, here, is how to regard political leaders, not themselves in league with terrorists, who issue warnings of terrorism largely for their own political purposes. The argument of this chapter has been that such political leaders are doing something that we would in other contexts regard as an act of terrorism in and of itself, and that we should say the same thing in their case as well.

Better 'terrorist warnings' than none at all?

There might be one final source of hesitation in condemning the public officials who issue warnings of terrorism, even for discreditable purposes.

That reason is just this: whatever their purposes, the public officials ended up performing an important public service. The IRA bomb really was there, and really would explode and kill lots of people unless they were warned. There was indeed something the public could do to protect itself against those horrors, if warned. Whatever the public officials' own private intentions in issuing the warning, it was on balance good for those warnings to have been issued.

But, the objection would go, acts of 'terrorism' are always at least *prima facie* wrong. So to say that the Ministers are guilty of having 'terrorized' the population seems to imply that they have committed what is, at least *prima facie*, a moral wrong. Yet we have just agreed that it was, on balance, good that the warnings were issued.

* * * * * * *

One response is of course just to point out the difference between *prima facie* and 'on balance' moral assessments. The former just say that, 'morally speaking, there is something to be said against it': something that would be decisive in the absence of any countervailing considerations. But once we weigh in the countervailing considerations involved in these cases, it is 'on balance' better that those morally tainted warnings be issued so as to avert those greater evils. Take the case of classic terrorist calls: even accepting that 'terrorist warnings' are themselves a form of terrorism, and *prima facie* wrong on that account, surely we agree that 'on balance' it is better the police receive the call and evacuate the building before the bomb goes off. A terrorist who does not issue warnings is worse than one who does, at least once the bomb is ticking and beyond her present power to defuse.

* * * * * * * *

A second response would be this: saying that the warnings should not have been issued *in that way* (by those people; with those intentions) is not to say that the warnings should not have been issued *at all*. The issue simply concerns how the warnings should have been handled: who should have issued them, and for what purposes.

Consider this example.[27] Suppose the intelligence services provide precise and credible evidence of an impending terrorist bombing, and that the best way to avert substantial loss of life is by making a public announcement that people should avoid the target area. Suppose furthermore that such episodes are unfortunately common in the jurisdiction in question, and that clear routines have been established for dealing with them. Ordinarily, suppose, it would be the chief of police who makes such an announcement. But now suppose that an election is only days away, and the mayor chooses to make the announcement herself, in the expectation that doing so will win her votes.

In such a case, I think it would be reasonable to accuse the mayor of terrorizing her city. Assume, here, that the warning would have been equally efficacious if made by the police chief in the routine way, and that the only difference that it makes (or, more to the point, that the mayor believes it will make) for her to issue the announcement herself is to increase her share of the vote. Then I think we would say that the mayor's warning is more like a 'terrorist warning' – a warning that is itself terroristic – whereas the police chief's would not have been.

* * * * * * * * * * *

Consider one final variation on these scenarios. Suppose that (for some reason or another) the mayor was the only person who *could* make the announcement. Or, perhaps more realistically, suppose that the warning would be vastly more efficacious if made by the mayor than by the police chief. (Suppose, perhaps, that the police chief has a reputation for issuing false alarms, and the only way to get people to take this warning seriously is for the mayor herself to make the announcement.)

Would it then be wrong for the mayor to issue the announcement? 'Surely not', we are strongly inclined to say. And that seems to be the right response.

But we must be careful in describing what that example goes to show. The proper conclusion is not that 'there is not anything morally bad about the mayor's making the announcement primarily for her own political purposes'. The proper conclusion is instead that 'the mayor's doing so is not morally bad, all things considered'. The fact remains that it is morally bad ('terroristic') for the mayor to make the announcement; it would merely be morally worse for her not to do so, and risk hundreds of people dying needlessly. Lesser evils are nonetheless evil.

6

Warnings Bound to Be Misheard

The argument of the previous chapter has been that a sheer warning of terrorism can in and of itself constitute an act of terrorism, depending on the intentions behind it. If made with the intention of instilling fear in people for some socio-political purpose, that warning ought be seen as itself constituting an act of terrorism. We recognize that already, when confronted with a 'terrorist warning' rung in to the police by the bomber's accomplice. The argument of the previous chapter was that we ought similarly regard a politician's warning of the terrorist acts to be committed by others, when that warning is issued with similar intentions of frightening people for the politician's own political purposes.

Clearly we ought regard the politician's warning that way, if it is exaggerated or unduly 'alarmist'. (That is one of the dictionary definitions of a 'terrorist', after all.) The previous discussion, however, concentrated on cases where the warnings were entirely accurate and not at all exaggerated. Even those, I argued, can – depending on the intent behind them – rightly be regarded as 'terrorist warnings', in themselves acts of terrorism.

Next I want to turn to questions of how even accurate messages can be knowingly and deliberately misleading, given what we know about how the messages will be received. Suppose you know someone has a pathological fear of snakes. Then when commenting to her, 'You know, I saw a snake on this trail a couple of years ago', you ought realize that that will be heard by her as communicating a much higher probability than there really is of encountering another snake on the trail today. She will hear 'snake' much more loudly than she will 'a couple of years ago' (and, by implication, 'not since').

In this chapter, I recall familiar facts – some about the psychology of risk perception, others about the sociology of the newsroom – concerning how certain sorts of information are inevitably miscommunicated and misperceived. Information about terrorism in general, and about weapons of mass destruction in particular, falls into those familiar categories. Information about the dangers of terrorism or weapons of mass destruction, even if it is factually accurate, will inevitably be received in an exaggerated way.

That forms the basis for my second complaint against politicians issuing even accurate warnings of terrorist risks. Insofar as these socio-psychological mechanisms are known to them – and they certainly will be to their media consultants, at least – politicians issuing warnings about terrorism and weapons of mass destruction ought know that they are sending messages that will be received in an 'alarmist' way. They will be received as conveying an exaggerated sense of the real dangers. Politicians sending messages that they know will be received in an alarmist way itself counts as 'alarmist', and hence 'terroristic' – even if on the face it their messages seem cool, measured and factually accurate.

Much of this chapter will thus be concerned with the gap between 'objective facts' and 'subjective perceptions'. In the sociological and psychometric studies upon which I will be drawing, subjective misperceptions stand out because the objective facts of the matter (the probability of dying from a heart attack, etc.) can be independently established. In dealing with the risks of terrorism, the objective probabilities are less clear-cut. We cannot say with nearly such confidence that people are 'overreacting', because we cannot say with nearly such confidence what an accurate perception and appropriate response would be.

That is largely true, and its truth constitutes a good reason for prudently risk-averse policy-makers to take some (but not any and all possible) extra precautions against terrorist attack. Still, there are some things that *can* reasonably be said to help us get a better fix on the real risks posed by terrorism.

One thing that can be done, for example, is to put the deaths of 9/11 into statistical perspective. Michael Ignatieff quite properly pleads with us to 'distinguish clearly moral condemnation from threat assessment'; I echo that plea.[1] Accordingly, I begin this chapter by showing that, awful though the events of that day were for those touched by them, from a larger statistical perspective they were much less significant than is ordinarily supposed. There are more imponderables surrounding the probable frequency and possible magnitude of large-scale terrorist attacks recurring. But even there, some evidence can be brought to bear suggesting that the real risks are objectively much more modest than commonly supposed.

In short, the gap that psychological studies tell us to expect between 'subjective perception' and 'objective fact' about risks of this sort does indeed seem to be present in popular perceptions of the likelihood and probable costs of terrorist attacks. Politicians playing on those familiar mechanisms of misperception, for socio-political purposes of their own, are committing a political wrong that is once again akin to an act of terrorism in itself.

Maybe there is literally no way for politicians to send a modulated message about the risks of terrorism. Maybe, given the way people are bound to react, politicians inevitably face the stark choice either of sending a warning that will be received in an exaggerated way or of sending no warning at all. Does it then follow that they ought issue the warning, even though it is bound to be misheard? Not necessarily. Everything depends on how much good and how much harm would be done by that sort of message. The UK practice of alerting security services but not stirring up the public unduly, which I discuss below, constitutes an important counterpoint to the US system of highly public and inevitably alarmist 'terrorism alerts'.

How big a deal is terrorism?

Objectively, how big a deal is terrorism? Let's start by asking that question of the most dramatic act of terrorism of modern times. How big a deal was 9/11?

Well, it depends on how you look at it. Here I shall suggest several alternative ways of looking at the events of 9/11, and the risks that their recurrence would pose.

* * * * * * *

On the standard way of looking at them, the events of 9/11 are a very big deal indeed. Here is one classic representation, contained in the US 9/11 Commission's *Report*:

> On September 11, the nation suffered the largest loss of life – 2973
> – on its soil as a result of hostile attack in its history. The Fire
> Department of New York suffered 343 fatalities – the largest loss
> of life of any emergency response agency in history. The Port
> Authority Police Department suffered 37 fatalities – the largest loss
> of life of any police force in history. The New York Police Depart-
> ment suffered 23 fatalities – the second largest loss of life of any
> police force in history, exceeded only by the number of PAPD
> officers lost the same day.[2]

* * * * * * *

Here is another way of looking at the magnitude of 9/11 deaths that once again makes that act of terrorism seem like a pretty big deal.

In terms of the loss of 'innocent' lives, the 9/11 death toll was equivalent to twenty-seven years of The Troubles in North-ern Ireland.[3] Thinking within the frame of 'terrorist problems', The Troubles in Northern Ireland are definitely a major problem; and anything that condenses the horror of so many of Ulster's problematic years into a single day seems, by exten-sion, a very big deal indeed.

Everything depends on your point of comparison, however, even thinking within the frame of 'terrorist problems'. The

Tamil Tigers have killed more than 100,000 people so far.[4] The loss of life in the 9/11 attacks was only 3 per cent of that. Or, again, the loss of life in the 9/11 air attacks and ensuing fires was only a little over a tenth that in the fire-bombing of Dresden on the night of 13 February 1945.

* * * * * * * *

'Some concepts', psychologists report, 'are inherently difficult to communicate.' Pre-eminent among them 'is giving a feeling for very low probabilities. We have 285 million people in the denominator, when thinking about the risk of terror for an individual in the US. However, our perception of these risks may be unduly influenced by a relatively small number of very salient incidents in the numerator.'[5]

So here is yet another way of framing 9/11. Think in terms of the increase brought about by those attacks to the probability of dying in the US in the ways that claimed 9/11's victims:

- How much did the 9/11 attacks increase your chances of dying by homicide in the US in 2001? By 16 per cent that year.[6]
- How much did the 9/11 attacks increase your chances of dying in an air crash in 2001? By a little over a third.[7]
- How much did the 9/11 attacks increase your chances of dying from an accidental or intentional injury at work in 2001? By around a third, once again.[8]

Put that way, those sound like modest increases – significant, but certainly far less than the doubling or trebling that the tone of post-9/11 rhetoric would suggest. And, as I shall go on to show below, those increases might be even less consequential than that way of putting them makes them seem. But, before turning to those discussions, notice that there is another way of describing those risks that make them seem truly trivial:

- How much did the 9/11 attacks increase your chances of dying by homicide in the US in 2001? From a probability of 0.0000607 to a probability of 0.0000711.[9]
- How much did the 9/11 attacks increase your chances of dying in an air crash in 2001? From a probability of 0.0000024 to a probability of 0.0000128.
- How much did the 9/11 attacks increase your chances of dying from an accidental or intentional injury at work in 2001? From a probability of 0.0000291 to a probability of 0.0000395.

In other words, the chances of dying in each of those ways remained *utterly minuscule* – substantially less than 1 in 10,000 – even after the effects of 9/11 were added.

* * * * * * * *

Next let us compare the probabilities of various other ways people might have died in the US in 2001. Again, all those ways of dying along with 9/11's contribution to them pale considerably.

Confining ourselves just to ways of death that are in some sense or another 'preventable', note that in 2001 people in the US were:

- fifteen times more likely to die in a motor vehicle accident than in the 9/11 attacks;
- ten times more likely to be killed by firearms (including being a third as likely to be killed by accidental discharge of firearms);
- seven times more likely to die of alcohol-related causes, and eight times more likely to die of drug-induced ones;
- five times more likely to die of accidental poisoning or exposure to noxious substances;
- five times more likely to die of HIV.[10]

And, again, if we looked at the 9/11 deaths from a broader geographical perspective, we would note that almost eighty times as many people died in the tsunami on Boxing Day 2004, a great many of which deaths would also have been preventable had tsunami-warning systems been in place. And, as the British prime minister reminded the world in the wake of that disaster, 'There is the equivalent of a man-made preventable tsunami every week in Africa.'[11]

* * * * * * *

But let's stick with the US for the moment; and let's concentrate just on the increased risk of being murdered.

As I said, the 9/11 attacks increased your chances of being murdered in the US by something like 16 per cent over what it would otherwise have been in 2001. But note that the homicide rate in the US varies dramatically, both from year to year and from state to state. The 16 per cent difference attributable to the events of 9/11 falls well within the range of 'normal variation' in the US, in both dimensions.

Thanks in part to the 9/11 attacks, the 2001 US homicide rate was 7.1 per 100,000 population. That was up from 5.9 the previous year. But over the decade 1992–2001, the US homicide rate had fluctuated between 5.9 and 9.8; and it had been above 2001's rate in six of those ten years.[12] The 9/11 attacks made the US a less safe place than it would otherwise have been in 2001, undoubtedly. But it did not make it an appreciably less safe place than it had always been, taking account of year-to-year fluctuations in the murder rate.

There is even greater variability in homicide rates across the states of the US. In 2001, the homicide rate varied from a high of 14.8 per 100,000 population in New York State to a low of 1.6 in Maine. Averaged across the whole country, the 9/11 attacks increased an American's probability of dying by homicide less than that probability would have increased for someone moving in that year from Indiana to Illinois, or from Kansas to Missouri.[13]

* * * * * * * *

Such calculations suggest that even dramatic acts of terrorism such as 9/11 – awful though they are by those who directly experience them – are not so necessarily a very big deal from the point of view of the population at large. Or anyway, they ought not be. They do not objectively make all that much difference to the life prospects of people in general in the country. Or anyway they do not unless such episodes recur frequently.

Calibrating risks

That is to say, the question in part is 'how bad is any given incident of terrorism?' and also in part 'how likely is it to recur?' How big a deal we should regard 9/11 as being depends, in part, on how often that sort of thing is going to happen.

If something like 9/11 happened literally every day, then that would be a very big deal indeed: that would involve a death rate ten times that caused by the Tamil Tigers or nearly five times that caused by the 2004 tsunami. If something like 9/11 happened once every year, then that would be a moderately big deal: it would involve a permanent increase in the chances of being murdered in the US by something like 16 per cent, and of dying in an air crash or in a violent or accidental injury at work of twice that. If something like 9/11 happened only once every few years, however, it is not really such a big deal at all. The rise in the murder rate in the years that it happens falls within the range of 'normal variation' from year to year, as I have just observed.

* * * * * * * *

In trying to calibrate the frequency with which terrorist attacks such as the US experienced on 9/11 might recur, we inevitably enter a world of imponderables. Risks, by their nature, refer to possibilities (or probabilities) that have not yet been actualized. Still, we must try to estimate them, somehow.

Table 6.1   Possible scale of terrorist attacks

Type of attack	Possible fatalities	Estimated likelihood
Efficient biological attack (e.g., clandestine wide dispersal of a contagious agent such as ebola, smallpox or anthrax)	1,000,000	Extremely low
Atomic bomb detonated in major US city	100,000	Very low
Successful attack on nuclear or toxic chemical plant	10,000	Very low
Simple, relatively inefficient biological or chemical attack in one skyscraper or stadium	1,000	Low
Conventional attack on a single train, aeroplane	250–500	Low
Suicide attack with explosives or firearms in a mall or crowded street	50–100	Modest

In 1993 the US Congress's Office of Technology Assessment produced an assessment of the probability and possible harm of various sorts of terrorist attack.[14] Their estimates are reproduced in table 6.1.

'Everything changed on September 11th', we are told. No doubt among the things changed would be official estimates of terrorist risks.[15] Notice, however, that the events of that day did not strictly speaking contradict any of those OTA estimates. Crashing fully fuelled aeroplanes into buildings is not among the scenarios envisaged in table 6.1.

That in itself highlights an important truism. The most successful terrorist attacks are likely to come in ways we did not, maybe could not, anticipate in advance – and in consequence could not protect against either.

* * * * * * * *

Which estimate of the magnitude of risks – the pre- or post-9/11 estimate – is more trustworthy? That is an open question that is, by its nature, difficult to answer. But here is one way to think about it.

In everyday life, we test our estimates of the probability of an event occurring by observing the frequency with which the event occurs, over a series of independent occasions on which we think it might have happened. Thus, for example, we suppose *ex ante* that the probability of a tossed coin coming up heads is 0.5. To test that we would toss the coin a couple of hundred times. If it comes up heads much more than half the time, we would have to revise our probability estimate (concluding that the coin was not a 'fair coin' but rather biased somehow in favour of landing on that side).

Testing claims about the probability of something by observing the frequency of its occurrence is not much use when it comes to low-probability events of which we have limited experience.[16] The fact that spring floods have not breached containment barriers in the past 200 years is not particularly strong evidence either for or against the engineers' claims that the probability of such a breach is 1 in 10,000; neither, come to that, is the fact that we have had two floods in the past ten years. Hence, if the probability of terrorist attacks is (as the OTA said) 'extremely low' or 'very low', then we cannot infer much about the probabilities just by observing the (in)frequency of such terrorist attacks actually occurring.

Post-9/11, of course, official estimates of further terrorist attacks increased dramatically. They ceased being treated as 'extremely low' or 'very low' probability events. Indeed, they ceased even to fall into OTA's category of 'modest' probability events, such as a suicide bomber in a crowded mall. In the run-up to the 2004 US presidential election, the Department of Homeland Security declared the 'threat level' at Code Orange, indicating 'a *high risk* of terrorist attacks'. The week after the election, the threat level was lowered to Code Yellow, still representing 'a *significant risk* of terrorist attacks'.[17]

Now, calling them 'significant' or 'high' risks implies that those are the sorts of things that ought be expected actually to happen relatively frequently. When it comes to the events that are judged to be that likely to occur, we should be able to make moderately strong inferences about probabilities from actual frequencies.[18]

Suppose the risk of a terrorist hijacking of any given commercial flight were 1 in 10,000.[19] Well, every year there are over 10 million scheduled airline flights in the US.[20] So on that assumption we ought statistically expect over 1000 hijackings a year, or over twenty a week (and some multiple of that, in terms of attempted but foiled hijackings). In the 200 weeks since 9/11 that probability estimate would have led us to expect 4000 successful hijackings and some multiple of that in terms of attempted but foiled hijackings. Instead, we have observed no successful hijackings and only one attempted attack (by the shoe-bomber, Richard Reid). That fact ought make us mightily wary of claims that the risk of terrorist attack was anything like that high.[21]

Curiously, it does not. In a study of over 1500 subjects in the six months following the 9/11 attacks, researchers found that (at least after the first month) there was no appreciable decline in people's perception of the risks of a future attack. On a scale of 0 to 1, people's perception of the risk remained stuck in the 0.70s for the full six months of the study – despite the passing of month after month with no recurrence of the 9/11 attacks.[22]

RAND's premier analyst of terrorism advised the US 9/11 Commission to 'measure our progress' in the War on Terrorism according to 'the passage of time without a major terrorist attack'.[23] Rationally we ought to take note of this. In practice, however, we seem not to do so. The ordinary updating of beliefs in light of experience (here, the experience of no subsequent attacks) is somehow blocked in the case of risks of terrorism. Psychological mechanisms that might explain that will be discussed below.

Certainly there is something here to justify Laurence Tribe's contemptuous commentary:

> The administration has taken to emphasizing the seriousness of the current crisis by gravely intoning that it is a virtual certainty that there will be another massive terrorist attack on our nation – an attack of *some* kind, at *some* point in time, conducted by *some* terrorist group. This 'warning', offered as 'news' and promulgated

through varying levels of warning codes displayed prominently at the bottom of news broadcast screens and internet web pages of almost every major news source in the country, is of course an inherently nonfalsifiable proposition. If an attack doesn't take place by any given point in time, that does not prove the prediction was wrong – it could still happen in the very next week, the next month, the next year, the next five years. And if it does, the government can grimly exclaim, 'We warned you!' ... One wonders what the great logician Karl Popper would have said about that kind of 'heads we win, tails you lose' proposition![24]

* * * * * * * * *

Before turning to psychological explanations for why so many people are taken in by such empty warnings, however, we ought consider one other more rational one. Perhaps there *would* have been many more attacks, had it not been for the extra security measures undertaken. As Tony Giddens put it in the House of Lords debate on the Prevention of Terrorism Bill:

> In order to manage risk, you must scare people, because you must alert them to the reality of the risk that they face ... But if you scare them and action is taken to minimize the risk and reduce its potential impact such that nothing happens over a certain period, people will say, 'Why were you scaring us in the first place?'[25]

That sort of riposte – that there would have been far more attacks had it not been for the warnings – would be rather more credible if we could point to any appreciable number of 'foiled attempts'. But (one lone shoe-bomber apart) we cannot.[26]

Public officials might like us to think otherwise. In the UK, the Prime Minister and Metropolitan Police Commissioner talk of 'several hundred' people plotting attacks. But the fact of the matter is that, 'of the 701 people arrested under the Terrorism Act since September 11, half have been released without charge and only 17 convicted under the Act.'[27] Similarly, in the US, the president claims that, 'Since September the 11th, federal terrorism investigations have resulted in charges against more than 400 suspects, and more than half of those charged have been convicted.'[28] Re-inspecting those records, however, the *Washington Post* discovered that only '39 people – not 200, as officials have implied – were convicted of crimes related to terrorism or national security' and 'the median sentence was just 11 months.'[29] Furthermore, among the handful of people actually convicted of terrorism-related offences, only one – shoe-bomber Richard Reid – was literally foiled in the act of attempting to detonate a terrorist bomb.

It is a trivial analytical truism that no more terrorist bombings of aeroplanes can succeed than are attempted, and we know how many of those there have been since 11 September 2001 (exactly one). Maybe there would have been more such attempts, had would-be terrorists not been deterred by additional security measures. There is no way of testing that counterfactual proposition.

Still, at face value it seems unlikely that the long queues at metal detectors, for example, had much to do with the absence of further attacks on commercial airliners. A shard of broken glass, undetectable by metal detectors, would have served the 9/11 hijackers' purposes just as well as box-cutters did. And even the shoe-bomber had other, non-metallic ideas about how to destroy a plane. If terrorists have not hijacked more planes since 9/11, therefore, that probably has next to nothing to do with all the more rigorous metal detectors screening at airports around the world and much more to do with something else, whether terrorists' altered intentions or altered capabilities or something else yet again. The long queues there served other social functions – maybe reassuring the public, maybe reminding them of the terrorist threat, or maybe pure party-political advertising. Actually preventing terrorist hijackings seems unlikely to have been one of their major accomplishments.

Mechanisms of misperception

There is by now a substantial literature in social psychology, for which Daniel Kahneman was awarded the 2002 Nobel

Prize in Economics, concerning the ways in which information about risks is perceived and misperceived by even sophisticated experimental subjects.[30] (Many of these experiments are performed on university students, often in business schools where presumably they would have been taught to avoid precisely the errors to which these studies show they are nonetheless prone.) As US Supreme Court Justice Stephen Breyer summarizes them, these findings show that

> We simplify radically, we reason with the help of a few readily understandable examples; we categorize (events and other people) in simple ways that tend to create binary choices – yes/no, friend/ foe, eat/abstain, safe/dangerous, act/don't act – and may reflect deeply rooted aversions, such as fear of poisons.[31]

In what follows I shall survey three disparate bodies of work. All point in the same direction, however: towards a conclusion that the popular perception of the risk of terrorism almost certainly exaggerates the real risk. Although it is a central tenet of the liberal political faith that we ought respect people's preferences, even liberals ought demur where there are clearly demonstrable mechanisms at work that systematically mislead people into making choices that ill-serve their own purposes.[32]

The psychological evidence suggests, for example, that everyone thinks they are 'better than average' drivers. But, by the definition of 'average', they cannot all be.[33] This provides one good reason to make the wearing of seat belts legally compulsory: if it were left voluntary, people's propensity to overestimate their own skills and underestimate their real risk of crashing would clearly cost lives.

Here I will be making a related argument concerning risks of terrorism. Given familiar psychological mechanisms at work leading people to overestimate those risks, public policies ought not link to popular perceptions and preferences.

* * * * * * * * * *

Among the 'irrationalities' discovered by social psychologists studying public reactions to risks, one of the first uncovered was a tendency to overreact to 'collective risks'. That is to say, respondents seem to think it is much worse for 1000 people to die in the same event than it is for the same number of people to die in separate events.[34]

That clearly would feed into reactions to 9/11. An awful lot of people died as a result of a single event (or two or three or four, depending on how exactly you individuate them). And that, in the public mind, made those attacks an awful lot worse than a series of smaller events, the death toll of which added up to the same overall total.

Objectively, of course, it is utterly irrational to view the one differently from the other. If there are 1000 dead bodies at the end of the day, whether the deaths occurred in a single event or 1000 separate ones, why should one scenario be regarded as worse than the other?

Suppose you are a traffic-safety engineer, with a modest budget for reconstructing dangerous sections of some particular roadway. Suppose that your budget would allow you to rebuild only one of the following two dangerous stretches of road: Hairpin Turn, where around fifty single-fatality accidents occur every year; or Pile-up Bend, where once every year twenty people are killed in a single massive pile-up. Surely it would be irresponsible for the traffic-safety engineer to straighten Pile-up Bend rather than Hairpin Turn, thus saving fewer lives rather than more just because the latter are lost one at a time.

Here is one way in which we might try to rationalize aversion to 'collective risks' killing many people at once. Confronted with 1000 separate deaths, people assume (quite rightly) that they have a pretty clear idea of the probability of each of those events. They have evidence from well over $N = 1000$ independent events to go on, allowing them to judge with some confidence how common such occurrences will be in future. When confronted with 1000 deaths from a single episode, people have no clue how common or uncommon that episode is likely to be: $N = 1$ is not much to go on. Assuming they are risk-averse (and who wouldn't be, given such a large number of deaths) they strive to avoid courses of action that threaten to produce large-numbers-of-deaths-all-at-once.

That might be a good reason for responding as we do to unfamiliar, one-off events such as 9/11, of which we have inadequate past experience to form reliable probability estimates.[35] But that is not all, or even most, of what underlies the psychological tendency to overreact to 'collective risks' killing lots of people at once.

In the traffic-safety example, there was no uncertainty about how many people would die at each stretch of road. We know from sad experience over many years that the twenty-fatality crash at Pile-up Bend is a regular annual occurrence, as are the fifty single-fatality accidents at Hairpin Turn. If people are prone to regard the former 'collective risk' as worse than the latter – as the psychometric evidence suggests they are, even in stories that are told this way – then it cannot (just) be because of the greater uncertainty associated with the higher fatality, less frequent occurrences. There really is a separate psychological mechanism at work, leading people to overreact to the latter as such.

* * * * * * *

Another familiar psychological mechanism that distorts people's perceptions of the badness of risks such as terrorism is the so-called availability heuristic.[36]

That says that risks of events that are 'easily imaginable' are intuitively assigned an exaggerated probability of occurring. The probability of dramatic events occurring is overestimated, and of 'boring' ones underestimated, accordingly. The chances of dying from a mundane heart attack are underestimated, according to all the standard psychometric literature.[37] The chance of dying dramatically, from a bear attack in Yosemite or of snakebite, for example, is systematically overestimated.

This propensity to overestimate events that are vividly imaginable leads, for example, to opposition to proposals by environmentalists to reintroduce large predators into wilderness areas. Objectively, of course, 'the risk of being attacked by one of these beasts is tiny by comparison with almost any of the other hazards that we confront in daily life. In Canada, where bears occasionally prey on people, you are nonetheless 67 times more likely to be killed by a domestic dog, and 374 times more likely to be killed by lightning.'[38] Still, because dying in the jaws of a bear is so vividly imaginable, and hence psychologically 'available', people tend badly to overestimate its probability.[39]

So too the chances of dying from a terrorist attack. 'In the aftermath of a terrorist act, and for a period thereafter, that act is likely to be both available and salient, and thus to make people think that another such act is likely, whether or not it is in fact. One or two terrorist incidents will have a significant impact on ... exaggerated risk perceptions.'[40]

Psychological experiments confirm this speculation. The dramatic nature of 'dying at terrorists' hands' distorts people's judgement of the size of the risk and what it is worth to protect against it. In one experiment, for example, respondents were asked how much they would pay for two different flight insurance policies: Policy A would provide them with an extra US$100,000 of life insurance in case of death by 'any act of terrorism'; Policy B would pay the same sum in case of death by 'any reason'. Of course 'any reason' includes 'any act of terrorism'; so if people were thinking clearly, they ought be prepared to pay more for the more inclusive Policy B than for less inclusive Policy A. But, by pointedly mentioning 'terrorism' as a cause of death, Policy A evokes in the mind's eye a vivid set of circumstances in which one might claim against the insurance, and that led people to agree to pay on average 17 per cent more for that less inclusive policy ('any act of terrorism') than for the more inclusive one ('any reason').[41]

* * * * * * *

A third mechanism of misperception has to do with the notion of 'home' and the role it plays as a psychological anchor in our lives.

Psychologists and criminologists know this full well. So too do politicians.[42] One's home is one's castle, they say; and law-and-order politicians insist that people ought be allowed to defend it against intruders. As Michael Howard put it, in launching the Tories' 2005 pre-election anti-crime campaign,

> burglary is a serious crime. It destroys people's peace of mind. Once you've been the victim of burglary you feel violated – because your home is the centre of your life. . . . People deserve to feel safe in their own homes.[43]

Insecurities surrounding 'home and hearth' figure largely in the 'homeland security' themes in the War on Terror. Many commentators join President Bush in saying that 'everything changed' on 9/11.[44] The most plausible candidate for what exactly changed is 'Americans' sense of invulnerability, when working and traveling in their own homeland'.[45] However dangerous a place the world might be, Fortress America had long led Americans to suppose that at least they were safe at home. Post-9/11, 'we no longer feel secure, although we cannot measure the extent of the danger. Nothing is more important to us than reestablishing the reality and sense of security.'[46]

It is not quite true that the continental US had never come under attack from a foreign power. That is to forget that Washington was sacked and the White House burned by the British in 1814; and that is a singularly 'winner's perspective' on the War Between the States (the losers of which saw their country being sacked in the course of Sherman's march and occupied by foreign troops for decades to follow). But it is true, and perhaps important to the American psyche, that the continental US was immune from foreign attack throughout the twentieth century, its two world wars and its long Cold War (even if it was a close thing during the Cuban Missile Crisis).

The events of 9/11 changed that, making Americans feel vulnerable wherever they went. They no longer felt safe at home (especially in big cities), or travelling (especially by air), or at work (especially in high-rise offices or government buildings). As John Lewis Gaddis puts it,

> The images of terrified New Yorkers running through the streets of their city to escape great billowing clouds of ash, dust and building

fragments; or of the government in Washington forced to seek shelter; or of several days of skies devoid of the contrails we have come to expect aircraft to add to the atmosphere over our heads – these memories will remain in our minds just as vividly as the images, from six decades earlier, of American naval vessels aflame, sinking at their own docks, within an American naval base on American territory.[47]

The rhetoric of 'homeland security' plays on those fears. It evokes images of home and hearth. That should be a place where people ought feel 'relaxed and comfortable' (in the campaign slogan of the Australian Prime Minister). But it is one in which Americans can no longer feel safe and secure.

In appointing the first Director of the Office of Homeland Security, President Bush emphasized this theme:

> I know that many Americans at this time have fears. We've learned that America is not immune from attack. We've seen that evil is real. It's hard for us to comprehend the mentality of people that will destroy innocent folks the way they have. Yet, America is equal to this challenge, make no mistake about it. They've roused a mighty giant. A compassionate land will rise united to not only protect ourselves, not only make our homeland as secure as possible – but to bring the evildoers to justice so that our children might live in freedom.[48]

* * * * * * * * * *

In addition to those three principal mechanisms of risk misperception, there are a raft of other familiar psychological forces at work in leading people to overestimate the risks of terrorist attacks.

One, for example, is the 'control bias'. People are far more comfortable running risks that they perceive (rightly or wrongly) as being 'in their control', and they tend to have more exaggerated reactions to risks that they perceive as being 'outside their control'. That is why people are generally much more comfortable running objectively larger risks driving a car than flying commercially: in the one case they are behind the wheel, in the other they are not.[49] A terrorist attack might strike anywhere, and there is virtually nothing one can do to protect oneself if it does. Because of that, 'isolated acts of terrorism involving a small subset of the population can cause far more serious dislocations than are warranted' by the objective magnitude of the risk.[50]

Another is the familiar psychological tendency for people to 'neglect the base rate'.[51] Recall the calculations with which this chapter began concerning the increase in probability of dying in various ways as a result of 9/11: people naturally tend to focus on the percentage increases (between 16 and 33 per cent), forgetting the low base (less than 1 in 10,000) on which those increases come.

Yet another familiar psychological phenomenon is that people are notoriously bad at internalizing and acting on low probabilities. Consider in this connection evidence from betting on horse races. We can calculate the objective probability of a long shot winning from the frequency with which horses at any given odds actually win, and the subjective probability of any given horse winning any given race as the fraction of total money bet in that race on the horse in question. Studies show that people systematically overestimate low objective probabilities, betting more heavily on long shots than objectively they should. Subjective probabilities come in line with objective ones only when the probability of the horse's winning approaches 16 per cent.[52] Nor is this phenomenon confined to the racetrack: other studies show broadly the same occurring in auctions.[53]

Now, the odds of terrorist attacks are well below that, by anyone's estimate. So the tendency to overreact to low-probability events – putting too much money on unlikely horses at the track – is likely to lead similarly to putting too much emphasis on protection against unlikely terrorist threats, politically.[54]

* * * * * * * * * *

In 1987 a RAND analyst complained that 'for years Washington has allowed the natural emotional abhorrence of terrorism to supplant a rational evaluation of the terrorist danger.'[55] Even then, that RAND analyst felt the need to emphasize that he was speaking in his private capacity, rather than on behalf of the RAND Corporation. Post-9/11, perhaps he would not have felt able to speak even with that qualifier.

The point he was making, however, remains as true today as it was back then. There are powerful, familiar, well-understood psychological mechanisms that stand in the way of a rational response to terrorist risks. Political leaders who are genuinely dedicated to serving the public interest, rather than merely seeking re-election, ought take account of those well-known facts and adjust their policy responses accordingly.

Mass-mediated terror

A good way to prevent kidnapping, it has been suggested, is simply to freeze the assets of all relatives of anyone who has been kidnapped. If would-be kidnappers were convinced the ransom could not be paid, and ransom were their only motive, then kidnapping would be pointless.

An analogous strategy is sometimes recommended *vis-à-vis* terrorists more generally. Terrorists, as defined in chapter 3, inflict harm on one person with the intention of influencing various others. If we could somehow block communication of their message to those others whom they are trying to influence, then that too would make terrorism pointless.

Politicians seized by that thought sometimes try to deprive terrorists of the 'oxygen of publicity' by prohibiting the mass media from carrying stories concerning terrorism. That was the phrase employed by British home secretary, Douglas Hurd, in 1988 when invoking his powers under the Broadcasting Act to outlaw the radio or television broadcasting of speeches by representatives or supporters of various named organizations involved in The Troubles, including the IRA, UDA and Sinn Fein. The ban was lifted six years later.[56]

* * * * * * * *

Whether or not the mass media serves terrorists' ends, by communicating points of view (or even just conveying their demands), certainly it helps further their purposes by spreading word of events intended to instil fear.

The trouble is, it is standardly said, the mass media cannot do the job it is supposed to do in an open, democratic society without that as an unavoidable by-product.[57] The public have a 'need to know', and a 'right to know', about important events occurring in their community. Acts of violence causing major destruction and loss of life are just such important events that ought be communicated.

The question is *how* they are communicated. One of the key justifications offered by *Washington Post* publisher Katherine Graham for reporting on such events is that:

> Terrorist acts are impossible to ignore. They are simply too big a story to pass unobserved. If the media did not report them, rumor would abound. And rumors can do much to enflame and worsen a crisis.

But if that is a central justification for reporting news of terrorism, then the reports thus justified must themselves not be inflammatory or alarmist. In part that is a matter of not giving terrorist spokespersons an open microphone or broadcasting their own inflammatory messages. But in part it is a matter of news organizations being reasonably restrained in their own coverage of the events.

One of the pitfalls Katherine Graham particularly points to is 'the amount of coverage devoted to a terrorist incident'. Understandably,

> During a crisis, we all want to know what is happening. But constant coverage can blow a terrorist incident far out of proportion to its real importance. Overexposure can preoccupy the public and government to the exclusion of other issues.

Graham recalls the example of the then recent hijacking of TWA Flight 847 by Lebanese Shiites, when television networks constantly interrupted regularly scheduled programming with news flashes of dubious importance. And one network devoted its entire 22-minute evening newscast to the crisis. More important topics were ignored.[58]

As news organizations themselves acknowledge, saturation coverage of terrorist events can be as inflammatory in its own way as giving the terrorist spokesperson an open microphone for inciting violence. Here the point is being made by a print journalist against her broadcast journalist rivals, and perhaps they are indeed more prone to the error.[59] But clearly it is a point that pertains to both kinds of media.

* * * * * * * *

People's perceptions of risks are systematically distorted by many factors. Among them are the psychological dynamics already discussed. Also among them, however, is the frequency with which people encounter reports about those risks in the media.

In one classic study, people were asked to estimate the number of deaths per year from various causes. The researchers then counted the number of stories in that town's newspaper reporting deaths from those causes. They found that the frequency of newspaper reports was biased towards dramatic events.[60] 'Violent, often catastrophic, events such as tornados, fires, drownings, homicides, motor vehicle accidents and all accidents were reported much more frequently than less dramatic causes of death having similar (or even greater) statistical frequencies.' The researchers further found that people's estimates of the frequency of those events were biased in the same direction, to a very high degree (the correlation was over 85 per cent in the two towns studied, astonishingly high by the standards of social science).[61]

The question of the direction of causation of course remains. Newspaper reporting both shapes people's perceptions of the risks and is shaped by them. People's opinions about what is important (or perhaps just what they are psychologically disposed to find interesting or worrying) influence the media's choice of what to report, just as what is reported shapes people's views on those matters. No doubt both elements are at work.[62] But a substantial body of case-controlled social scientific evidence suggests that much the larger influence is of news (particularly television news) on people's attitudes, rather than vice versa.[63] There can be little doubt, therefore, that biases in media reporting of events shape, to some significant degree, people's perceptions of how common those events are.

It would be easy to complain at this point that it is just a matter of bad journalistic practices misleading the public. Certainly it is true in this case that press coverage of certain events has been disproportionate to the frequency of their actual occurrence; and certainly it is true that public perceptions have been distorted by that distorted press coverage. But is it really 'bad practice' on the part of the media?

Here is the rationale for the media's reporting more heavily the events that they do:

> Stories about floods, forest fires and epidemics become important news, because even if the number of victims is small, the thought that a similar disaster could strike almost anywhere will affect a much larger number of people.[64]

(Ditto 'terrorism', of course.) That fact not only makes news about those events of interest to a much wider group of people than those actually affected. It also makes that news genuinely relevant to that much wider group of people. It would be a disservice to the public not to report news of those events prominently, therefore. Yet the inevitable consequence of reporting those events prominently is that people will inevitably be led to believe that they are more common than they actually are.

* * * * * * * *

'Terrorism' is one subject that is particularly prone to being overreported in the media.

This had been true well before 11 September 2001. Twenty years earlier, the leading RAND researcher on terrorism had observed that:

> It makes no difference that ordinary homicides vastly exceed murders caused by terrorists. The news media do not allocate space or air time proportionally according to the leading causes of death in the world. News in general is about the unusual, the alarming, the dramatic. It is not a summing up of information. It is anecdotal. Because of their frequency, ordinary homicides are, regrettably, just that – ordinary.[65]

Terrorist violence, in contrast, is something special – and newsworthy.

A 1987 study of coverage of international terrorist incidents by television news, for example, found that there was no systematic relation between the frequency of news reports and the frequency of actual terrorist incidents, worldwide. What there *was*, however, was a systematic overreporting of terrorist acts against US targets – particularly against private US citizens.[66] Someone watching any of the three major US television channels could well be forgiven for supposing that international terrorism posed a much greater threat to him or her than truly it did, year in and year out.

With September 11, of course, US television coverage of terrorism soared. 'The number of news stories about terrorism on the three major networks jumped from around 178 in the 12-months prior to September 2001 to 1345 stories in the twelve months afterwards.' Furthermore, 'public concern mirrored the network news coverage.' When asked to name the 'most important problem facing the country', almost half nominated 'terrorism' immediately after 9/11, up from literally zero the year before. Over the following eighteen months, between 15 and 30 per cent of people continued naming 'terrorism' as the 'most important problem', with those fluctuations closely tracking the frequency of television news stories concerning terrorism.[67]

In a study of 1500 people over the six months following the 9/11 attacks, researchers found that people's perceptions of the risks of another major terrorist attack were strongly and positively related to the amount of television news coverage they had seen.[68] Those findings

> confirm the role of television in shaping psychological reactions to a terrorist event. Americans who watched television news more frequently reported higher levels of fear and anxiety after 9/11. These findings raise questions, for example, about the wisdom of replaying coverage of the demise of the World Trade Center towers. Such images are impossible to forget and replaying them may serve to maintain or further amplify fear and anxiety, long after a terrorist incident. The visual imagery of TV seems to be the key to the heightened levels of fear and anxiety among avid media consumers.[69]

* * * * * * * * *

There are, then, these sociological mechanisms governing news operations that work hand in glove with the psychological mechanisms just described, further exacerbating people's propensity to overestimate the risks of terrorist attacks.

These are not 'flaws' or 'perversions' of news reporting (although there are, no doubt, some of those at work as well).[70] The more fundamental problem is this: the very features that make terrorist events genuinely 'newsworthy' (i.e., that make people want and need to know about those events) are ones which, even when reported accurately, interact with the psychological mechanisms just discussed to make people perceive terrorist events as being more common and more harmful than they are.

Risks of really mass destruction

This chapter opened with an attempt to put the events of 9/11 statistically into perspective. The events of that day, awful though they were for those caught up in them, simply were not of such a magnitude as to make a major difference to people's risk of violent death across the US as a whole – at least so long as such events do not recur frequently. The rest of this chapter has been devoted to trying to decide just how likely recurrence of such sorts of events might actually be – discussing along the way some well-known socio-psychological mechanisms that reliably lead people to suppose them to be much more likely than they really are.

In the US Office of Technology Assessment table categorizing terrorist risks, however, 'likelihood' is only one of the elements to be considered. The 'magnitude' of the harms done by different sorts of acts of terrorism must also be considered. I have focused on the harms inflicted on 9/11 because, in the rhetoric of the day, that is treated as the 'worst terrorist attack ever'. Still, it is not the worst one imaginable.

The 9/11 attacks killed 2973 people. But the OTA table contemplates the possibility that an efficient biological attack might kill a million, or that an atomic bomb detonated in a major US city might kill 100,000, or that a successful attack on a nuclear or toxic chemical plant might kill 10,000. A decade ago, OTA regarded the likelihood of those events as 'extremely low' to 'very low'; and perhaps they remain so, contemporary political rhetoric notwithstanding. Still, even a very low probability of such a very grave harm might make those sorts of terrorist risks ones to be taken very seriously.[71]

* * * * * * * *

That is the sort of point that was being made, in the run-up to the invasion of Iraq, about risk of 'weapons of mass destruction' falling into terrorist hands. As it happens, there were no such weapons to be found in Iraq: that was a false reason for that war.

Still, the more general point remains. Even if deaths on the magnitude of 9/11's ought objectively be regarded as posing only modest increases in the risk to people's lives overall, the magnitude of deaths that might occur through the terrorist use of weapons of mass destruction perhaps ought be seen in a different light. As the US attorney general said, 'We cannot wait for terrorists to strike to begin investigations and take action. The death tolls are too high, the consequences too great. We must prevent first – we must prosecute second.'[72]

In that spirit, the US National Security Presidential Directive 17, outlining a National Strategy to Combat Weapons of Mass Destruction, declared

> Weapons of mass destruction (WMD) – nuclear, biological and chemical – in the possession of hostile states and terrorists represent one of the greatest security challenges facing the United States. . . . Some states, including several that have supported and continue to support terrorism, already possess WMD and are seeking even greater capabilities, as tools of coercion and intimidation. . . . We will not permit the world's most dangerous regimes and terrorists to threaten us with the world's most destructive weapons.[73]

* * * * * * *

It was once thought that larger strategic considerations would inhibit terrorists from using weapons of mass destruction. It would simply not be prudent for terrorists who are in pursuit of specific objectives that required broad public sympathy to engage in the radically indiscriminate destruction, such as that entailed by the use of nuclear weapons or the uncontrolled spreading of an epidemic.[74]

Recent decades, however, have seen the emergence of 'new terrorism' of a sort that is more Messianically motivated or millenarian-oriented. Being less concerned with external support among non-believers, such groups might be less reluctant to employ indiscriminately weapons of mass destruction.[75] On the contrary, 'inflicting a scourge on the heretics or infidels may be seen as performing a sacramental act, manifesting divine retribution that morally justifies mass murder.'[76]

Once upon a time it was further thought 'that a biological attack is unlikely precisely because the devastation from such an attack cannot be limited', and would spread to the attackers' own people as well as among those they meant to attack. But again, that may no longer be such a compelling argument, insofar as contemporary terrorists are infused with a spirit of martyrdom that extends that exalted status even to unknowing or unwilling victims of the epidemics that they initiate.[77]

* * * * * * *

Still, terrorists wanting to deploy weapons of mass destruction face serious problems as regards both acquisition and delivery of those weapons.[78]

The danger of nuclear materials being used for terrorist purposes has been discussed virtually since the dawn of the nuclear age.[79] The major barriers to terrorist groups using nuclear weapons have traditionally surrounded acquisition of fissile materials and their assembly into a thermonuclear device. With the end of the Cold War and the loss of controls over Soviet nuclear stockpiles, acquisition of both fissile materials and finished bombs has become far easier.[80] Dirty nukes that work principally through radiation poisoning are more easily assembled, although far less lethal. So while nuclear devices are still regarded as the least likely weapons of mass destruction to be deployed by terrorists, the danger is greater than it used to be.

Chemical weapons seem particularly hard to deliver. It is worth bearing in mind that, however much fear was aroused by mustard gas in World War I, the 'actual mortality rate was low. Of the casualties inflicted by gas, [only] some 2 percent resulted in death.' Similarly, although the absolute numbers of people killed in Iraqi chemical attacks on Halabja were high (estimates are 3000 to 5000), the actual mortality *rate* was modest.[81]

Delivering biological weapons is also tricky. 'Microbial pathogens and toxins are susceptible to environmental stresses such as heat, oxidation and desiccation', and the great challenge in 'weaponizing' them is to 'maintain their potency during weapon storage, delivery and dissemination'.[82] Ebola, for example, is enormously lethal, killing 90 per cent of those infected by it within a week; but its transmissibility is 'limited by its instability in air', and, while it can remain active in blood for up to a month, using that fact to craft a delivery system poses a major challenge.[83] Delivering biological attacks via human carriers is even harder: they will be detected early, and only a limited number of people will come into unprotected contact with conspicuously infected carriers.

* * * * * * * *

Tempting though such weapons would be as instruments of terror, the simple fact remains:

> terrorists have seldom used them. Terrorists have never detonated a nuclear device. They have used chemical agents rarely – most often to poison foods – and biological and radiological agents more rarely still. Except for the chemical attacks carried out by the Aum Shinrikyo cult in Japan in 1994 and 1995, there have been no cases of large-scale, open-air dissemination.[84]

And terrorists have not used such weapons for good reasons.

It would be wrong, however, to take too much comfort from the thought that weapons of mass destruction have not been much used by terrorists to date. Given the enormous number of lives that might potentially be lost in such an attack, 'we cannot wait for terrorists to strike', as the US Attorney General puts it. So precautions of some sort are clearly in order.

* * * * * * * *

The best suggestion anyone seems to have for preventing weapons of mass destruction from falling into terrorist hands is to cut them off at the source.

Developing chemical, biological or nuclear weapons in most cases requires vastly sophisticated laboratories staffed by large teams of research scientists working continuously for several years. That is powerfully true of nuclear weapons production, obviously.[85] It is also strongly true of the production of chemical weapons such as nerve gas.[86] And even the more straightforward production of biological weapons would require 'a modestly sophisticated pharmaceutical industry'.[87]

'Rogue states' (as well as, of course, the United States) have been able to mount sustained research efforts of these sorts. But no known terrorist group has itself been able to sustain the sort of research and development programme that would lead to their independent development of weapons of mass destruction.

The real risk lies in weapons developed in some state-sponsored laboratory falling into terrorist hands. Preventing the transmission of weapons of mass destruction from state-sponsored laboratories to terrorists constitutes the best strategy for controlling that.[88]

If the problem is state-made weapons of mass destruction falling into terrorist hands, however, there are various obvious solutions.

- The most obvious, if also the most utopian, is for *all* states to renounce the use of those weapons themselves and destroy their stockpiles and research laboratories for developing those weapons.
- A more modest but more realistic step in the same direction would be to strengthen international controls over such weapons and research programmes.
- Yet another proposal, moderately utopian but not wildly so, might be for an international programme of buying up weapons of mass destruction and destroying them (and the laboratories that made them), as was begun through the Nunn–Lugar initiative *vis-à-vis* the former Soviet republics.[89]

Those, notice, are all essentially diplomatic strategies – 'diplomacy, arms control, multilateral agreements, threat reduction assistance and export controls – that seek to dissuade or impede proliferant states and terrorist networks.'[90] The US National Strategy to Combat Weapons of Mass Destruction proposes to pursue them as one of its three pillars. Other pillars however take more belligerent forms, ranging from interdiction through 'preemptive measures' all the way to this strong threat:

The United States will continue to make clear that it reserves the right to respond with overwhelming force – including through resort to all of our options – to the use of WMD against the United States, our forces abroad, and friends and allies.[91]

Now, threatening massive retaliation against terrorist attacks is problematic, insofar as terrorist bombs typically come with 'no return address'. You do not know who launched them, sometimes. You do not know where exactly they are, often. Threats of massive retaliation and 'mutually assured destruction' worked well during the Cold War to deter nuclear attacks from states associated with some identifiable territory that could be targeted by counter-measures. Such threats cannot work nearly so well when those who launched the attack are unlikely themselves to be directly targeted in the counter-attack.

Launching wars against countries that are known to have chemical-biological weapons programmes (much less nuclear ones) is not particularly promising as a general strategy, either. There are simply too many of them.[92] Besides, attacking many of them would simply be too risky (not least because they possess weapons of mass destruction, in part perhaps precisely to deter such attacks).

Diplomatically addressing the 'weapons of mass destruction' problem at source – the limited number of state-sponsored research laboratories and stockpiles – rather than trying to track all the shadowy groups of terrorists who might want to use those weapons is surely the smarter strategy. If 'weapons of mass destruction' are the problem, then a concerted diplomatic offensive on the handful of state makers of those weapons is the right response. A 'war' on the myriad possible end users of those weapons, among all the terrorist groups in the world, is not.

Imprudent precautions

We should certainly take the sorts of measures catalogued above to try to prevent 'weapons of mass destruction' from falling into terrorist hands. But how much more than that would it be reasonable to do?

I shall address this question at two levels. First, how much more ought the government itself do? Faced with other catastrophic risks such as global warming, we sometimes think that governments ought adopt a 'precautionary principle', doing everything they possibly can to protect against the worst possible outcome. Would that be a sensible principle to apply to risks of terrorist attacks employing weapons of mass destruction? Second, I shall consider how much more governments ought sensibly ask the populace itself to do. Would it be sensible to mount a Neighbourhood Watch against terrorists, akin to that which many communities already mount against common or garden criminals?

* * * * * *

Of course when risks increase the response ought increase. If some bad outcome is suddenly seen to be twice as costly or twice as likely as it used to be, then we ought spend twice as much as we used to do to protect against it (or perhaps even a little more, if we are 'risk-averse'). No one disputes that. When our perceived risks of terrorist attack rose in the wake of the 9/11 attacks, it therefore was only right that governments began doing more than they used to do to protect against those risks. The question is just 'how much more' they ought to do.

Here what I want to consider, and critique, is the 'pay any price, bear any burden' response. According to this view, we should 'do whatever it takes' to protect ourselves against the risk of attack by terrorists, particularly ones armed with weapons of mass destruction. We ought, on this view, accord 'absolute priority' to protecting ourselves against terrorism of that sort; we ought focus on worst-case scenarios, and make sure that the worst they do to us is as tolerable as we can make it.

Now, in general, protecting against the very worst thing that might happen and totally ignoring all other possible payoffs and their probabilities is not a particularly sensible way of approaching risks.

> If you took [that] . . . principle seriously then you could never cross a street (after all, you might be hit by a car); you could never drive over a bridge (after all, it might collapse); you could never get married (after all, it might end in a disaster), etc. If anybody really acted this way he would soon end up in a mental institution.

In general, Nobel laureate John Harsanyi continues, 'It is extremely irrational to make your behavior wholly dependent on some highly unlikely unfavorable contingencies regardless of how little probability you are willing to assign to them.'[93]

That said, there are sometimes particular sorts of circumstances in which that might constitute a sensible reaction to certain sorts of risks. Here I shall canvass three arguments that might be given for thinking that that might be the case with national security in general and with protection against terrorists (especially terrorists with weapons of mass destruction) in particular. Although upon reflection none of them turn out to be good arguments, unreflectively all of them seem tempting.

One set of reasons has to do with the way in which national security is connected to the nation's very existence.[94] The thought goes something like this. A nation that fails to protect its 'national security' fails, literally, to secure its very nationhood; in the limiting case upon which this thought focuses, it ceases to exist as a nation. Now, existence is a precondition of agency, and hence a precondition of anything else you want to do. That makes protecting national security something akin to what John Rawls calls a 'primary good', a necessary means to any other end you want to pursue.[95] And that makes pursuing national security a priority goal: without that being secured, without our nation's very existence being guaranteed, our nation cannot achieve any of the other goals we harbour for it.

Now, there are lots of things to say about that argument. One is that continuing existence is not, strictly speaking, a necessary condition of achieving absolutely any goal you might have. Sometimes the best way for a flesh-and-blood person to achieve some of her goals is to sacrifice herself so that someone else (her children, her battalion) will better be able to carry her project forward. Ditto with the nation. Furthermore, protecting something too completely sometimes destroys it, or anyway destroys our reason for wanting it in the first place. Long ago, Aquinas observed that the only way to guarantee absolutely the security of a ship is to keep it in harbour for ever – which would, of course, make it pointless to have a ship at all.[96] Ditto, the critics quoted at the end of chapter 2 would say, with a never-ending state of emergency to secure our democracy against terrorism: the emergency measures, implemented in perpetuity, would destroy the very democratic liberties whose existence they were supposed to be securing.

But, beyond all that, is the 'primary good' analogy really apposite here? For that analogy to apply, it must be the case that the nation's very existence is threatened. In total war against a foreign state, it may well be. And Tony Blair sometimes seems to assert that the same is true of terrorism, referring to it as an 'existential' threat.[97] But rhetoric has simply lost any connection to reality in such cases. It is simply not true that terrorist networks are sovereign states with plenipotentiary powers seeking to acquire suzerainty over our country. There is not the remotest prospect of any of the Western states ever coming under the rule of al-Qaeda, in the way Britain came under Norman rule after the Conquest. The War on Terrorism is just not that sort of war.

'Everything changed on 9/11', we are endlessly told. One of the things that changed is, presumably, the scale of the damage that terrorists might be willing and able to inflict; and similarly motivated terrorists armed with weapons of mass destruction might inflict far more damage, yet again.[98] Their aim is to destroy, not to conquer, but if the destruction in view would be sufficiently complete the 'primary good' analogy might nonetheless apply. Destruction of the capacity of the state to exercise its sovereign powers at all (or at all effectively) might still constitute a telling argument for prioritizing national defence, at least against terrorists with weapons of mass destruction.

But pause for a moment to ponder that now familiar phrase: weapons of *mass* destruction, not weapons of *total* destruction. In the worst-case scenario (which, as I have said earlier, is highly unlikely), terrorists might manage to explode a few medium-sized nuclear devices in major cities, or spread a lethal disease through several international airports simultaneously. Millions of people would die; it would be an awful thing. But the destruction caused would be 'mass', not 'total'. Life on earth would not cease to exist, as it might have done had there been an all-out nuclear exchange at the height of the Cold War. Nor even would the United Kingdom cease to exist, as it might have done had it lost World War II. And, remember, something akin to a literal 'threat to the very existence of the country' is what is required to activate the 'primary good' argument for giving absolute priority to national defence against terrorists with weapons of mass destruction.

A second set of reasons for prioritizing defence against terrorists with weapons of mass destruction might have to do with vaguely game-theoretic considerations. In the founding text of modern game theory, von Neumann and Morgenstern focused on zero-sum games, games in which one player's gains always exactly match the other player's losses.[99] The uniquely rational way to play those sorts of games is to follow the 'maximin' rule. That is to say, choose that course of action that has the best worst-possible outcome for you. In a zero-sum game you should make your own choice as if your worst enemy will be assigning you your place, because in a zero-sum game she will.[100] Or, anyway, you will be assigned your place by someone whose interests are diametrically opposed to your own: what is best for her is worst for you, and vice versa; so, among the options your own choice leaves open to her, she is bound to choose the option which is worst for you because (by definition of a zero-sum game) that option is best for her.

How good an argument that is for prioritizing security concerns depends simply on how well the zero-sum game analogy captures the essentials of the situation at hand. That is not a very good way of analysing ordinary international politics. International relations are rarely zero-sum games. Sometimes they are better than that: there are win–win opportunities, gains to be had from cooperating. Sometimes they are worse than that: there are lose–lose situations, where gains and losses sum to something less than zero. But rarely are international relations literally zero-sum affairs.[101]

Again, relations between terrorists and their targets *might* be different. But for that to be the case, terrorists would have to have no goals of their own, beyond inflicting damage on their targets. The gain to the terrorists must be literally exactly what their targets have lost; and any losses to terrorists must constitute corresponding gains to their targets. There must be no way that both of them could lose, or both of them could gain. That is what is required for the situation to be literally zero-sum. Maybe some terrorists somewhere stand in that relation to their target, but it is unlikely that the US and al-Qaeda, for example, stand in that relation. If the US withdrew its infidel troops from Afghanistan, Iraq and Saudi Arabia, for example, and forced Israel to withdraw to its 1967 borders, it looks as if bin Laden's demands would be satisfied. Maybe he is lying, and if the US were to concede that much the US might suddenly find him demanding yet more. But demanding and bargaining are hallmarks of what game theorists call a 'cooperative game' rather than a 'non-cooperative', zero-sum game. In a zero-sum game, there is nothing to bargain over, no gains of trade to be realized.

A third set of arguments for prioritizing national security against WMD-armed terrorists might invoke the 'precautionary principle' often advocated (and occasionally implemented, e.g., in the European Union) in environmental protection policy.[102] The precautionary principle takes many forms, many of them pretty indefensible.[103] There is, however, a 'core' version of the precautionary principle that even its strongest critics have to concede is perfectly defensible.

According to that version of the principle, we should choose the course of action with the best worst-possible outcomes if and only if the following three conditions are all satisfied:

1   there is a plausible risk of some catastrophic outcome;
2   probabilities cannot be credibly assigned to alternative possible outcomes; and
3   the loss from pursuing a cautious policy as compared to some other policy is not great.[104]

Then, even critics of the precautionary principle have to agree, it makes sense to pursue the more cautious course of action.[105]

Of course, if uncertainties run all that deeply, we might not even be able to tell which is the more cautious course: for the same reason we cannot assign probabilities, we might not be able to tell which course of action has the best worst-possible outcomes. Of course, caution is rarely completely cost-free. Of course there are often disagreements over whether the catastrophe in view achieves the threshold of minimum plausibility and over just how unreliable probability estimates might be. But in cases where all those conditions are met, precaution would surely be warranted.

Many would justify prioritizing precautions against terrorists with weapons of mass destruction on some such grounds. If terrorists got and used such weapons, the results would clearly be catastrophic: 'Here were terrorists prepared to bring about Armageddon', Tony Blair said of the 9/11 attackers.[106] Just how probable it is that such terrorists might acquire and employ weapons of mass destruction is hard to calculate with any precision. At one point, Blair describes it as being 'only a matter of time'; at another point, however, he acknowledges that 'it is possible that . . . nothing would have happened.'

At that point, Blair makes the crucial point from the perspective of the precautionary principle. Let me therefore quote that portion of his text at length:

> We cannot be certain . . . But do we want to take the risk? . . . [M]y judgement then and now is that the risk of this new global terrorism and its interaction with states or organisations or individuals proliferating WMD is one I simply am not prepared to run.

. . .

> Let me give you an example. A short while ago, during the war, we received specific intelligence warning of a major attack on Heathrow. To this day, we don't know if it was correct and we foiled it or if it was wrong. But we received the intelligence. We immediately heightened the police presence. At the time it was much criticised as political hype or an attempt to frighten the public. . . . But sit in my seat. Here is the intelligence. Here is the advice. Do you ignore it? . . . [O]f course, intelligence is precisely that: intelligence. It is not hard fact. It has its limitations. . . . But . . . would you prefer us to act, even if it turns out to be wrong? Or not to act and hope it's OK? And suppose we don't act and the intelligence turns out to be right, how forgiving will people be?[107]

Whether or not Blair meant literally to invoke the precautionary principle, that is the most interesting way to read the speech.[108] Certainly that is so, anyway, if that argument is to be seen as constituting a case for according anything like absolute (as opposed to just 'more', maybe 'much more') priority to protecting ourselves against WMD-armed terrorists.[109]

Before turning to assess Blair's arguments in those terms, however, let us pause to note how centrally an argument of that form would bear on various other of the issues raised in this chapter. If this were the right way to look at the risks imposed by terrorists with weapons of mass destruction, then it would be wrong even to try to calibrate the magnitudes of those risks, as I began this chapter trying to do. A precautionary-principle approach accepts that we can never calibrate probabilities in these realms, employing instead a decision rule ('choose the course of action with the best worst-possible outcome') that operates without any knowledge of probabilities. Furthermore, if probabilities did not matter, then neither would it matter that people misjudge the probabilities in all the familiar ways detailed earlier in this chapter. In both those ways, it would be highly convenient if it were appropriate to apply the precautionary principle to terrorists with weapons of mass destruction.

But is the precautionary principle really appropriate there? Are the preconditions set out above for the sensible application of that principle met, even in the case of terrorists armed with weapons of mass destruction?

The first precondition was that there must be 'a plausible risk of catastrophic outcomes'. At first brush, that condition seems easily satisfied: we are talking about terrorists with weapons of mass destruction, after all. But just how catastrophic does the catastrophe in view have to be, in order for the precautionary principle to apply? Think of its core environmental applications: global warming or genetically modified organisms. In explaining why they think the precautionary principle ought apply there, proponents point to possible catastrophes that would involve literally the end of (human) life on earth. Maybe those scenarios fail to meet the threshold of minimum plausibility required for the precautionary principle to apply; that is something we can argue about, but it is not something we need to settle for present purposes. We need only note the size of the possible catastrophes involved in those main applications of the precautionary principle.

Now compare that with the size of the worst minimally plausible catastrophe that would ensue from terrorist attacks, even if they are perpetrated using weapons of mass destruction. Tony Blair talks as if such terrorists might 'bring about Armageddon'.[110] But that is pure hyperbole. Recall the OTA's top estimates: perhaps a million deaths from a bio-terrorist attack using ebola, or 100,000 from the detonation of a nuclear device in a large city. Either would be a major catastrophe, to be sure. But neither is anywhere near the end of human life on earth.

Would catastrophes of those magnitudes nonetheless be 'big enough' for the precautionary principle properly to apply? Well, again, I suppose that that is something we will simply have to discuss. Just note two things at the outset of that discussion, though. First (as I have just said), applying the precautionary principle to terrorists with weapons of mass destruction really would extend that principle *well beyond* its traditional range, to catastrophes of several orders of magnitude smaller than those to which it has traditionally been thought to apply. Note also that applying the precautionary principle to weapons of mass destruction would presumably require that each country destroy, unilaterally if necessary, its own stockpiles of weapons of mass destruction. That, surely, is the course of action with the best worst-possible outcome. (The worst possible outcome from countries retaining weapons of mass destruction is that they might be stolen and used in terrorist attacks, whereas the worst possible outcome of unilaterally destroying them would be that enemies who retained such weapons might blackmail us into doing something we prefer not to do – that would be bad, but presumably not nearly as bad as terrorists using the weapons of mass destruction against us.)[111]

Turning to the second precondition, the precautionary principle applies only if probabilities cannot credibly be assigned to (all) alternative possible outcomes. When it comes to terrorist attacks, that seems likely to be true. Certainly we cannot assign probabilities with any precision. While many things have to 'go right' for terrorists to launch a successful attack, and the probabilities of some of those steps are more reliably estimated than others, one crucial element will always be 'surprise'; and there is simply no reliable way for us to estimate the probability of someone thinking of something we have not yet thought of (flying fully fuelled aeroplanes into skyscrapers, for example).[112] Thus, it looks as if the second precondition for applying the precautionary principle to terrorism is likely to be satisfied.

The third precondition for applying the precautionary principle is that 'the loss from pursuing a cautious policy as compared to some other policy is not great'. Proponents of the precautionary principle might say that this puts it too strongly. Certainly we ought not require that the precautionary course of action be literally costless before the principle is allowed to apply. Just how large a cost of precaution is acceptable is something, once again, we will need to discuss further. Still, this much is surely clear: it must not be the case that the cost of the precautions is of anything like the same order of magnitude as the uncertain catastrophe they are supposed to be protecting us against.

In the case of the War on Terror, the costs are far from negligible. Think just financially, for the moment: while the costs of the 9/11 attacks and their knock-on consequences for the US economy were very great, so too are the ongoing costs of the War on Terror. Ignore the vast expense of literal wars in Afghanistan and Iraq. The US Department of Homeland Security itself has a projected budget of $34.2 billion for 2006, the bulk of which is in direct pursuit of the War on Terror.[113] Quite apart from the financial costs, the War on Terror also imposes other less tangible costs – to people's peace of mind, to civil liberties and so on, in ways already discussed.

Thus, the War on Terror is hardly a 'costless', or even a 'low cost', course of action. As I have said, how costly is 'too costly' for the precautionary principle to justify any course of action is open to further discussion. Nevertheless, with a price tag of this magnitude it seems implausible that the War on Terror can be justified in the precautionary-principle way.

* * * * * * *

What is the proper role of the public more generally in the War on Terror? Given the risk of catastrophic consequences from a terrorist attack using weapons of truly mass destruction, might it be a prudent precaution to mobilize the public to serve as the 'eyes and ears of the police'? Would it be prudent to enlist everyone into a Neighbourhood Watch against terrorism, after the fashion of more familiar Neighbourhood Watch schemes against ordinary crime?

Governments have certainly been tempted by that thought. Something like that was clearly suggested by Tom Ridge, upon assuming command of the US Department of Homeland Security: 'everyone in the homeland must play a part', by offering 'their . . . awareness and their resolve'; 'this job calls for a national effort'.[114] Mass mobilization against terrorism is even more explicit in the Australian government's 'Be alert but not alarmed' campaign. An official brochure delivered to every

Australian household enlisting them in that campaign said, in words straight out of standard Neighbourhood Watch leaflets:

> Some of the best people to spot things that are out of the ordinary in a neighbourhood or workplace are those who are there every day.
>   As we all go about our daily lives, we should keep an eye out for things that may be unusual or suspicious. Be alert, but not alarmed.
>   . . . Look at the situation as a whole. If it doesn't add up, ring up the **24-hour National Security Hotline** on **1800 123 400**. Callers may remain anonymous if they wish.
>   You can cut out the card on the right and carry it in your purse or wallet. If you have a mobile phone, consider putting the number in the memory. You can also report suspicious activity online at **www.nationalsecurity.gov.au**.[115]

And in the UK, local Neighbourhood Watch manuals themselves now typically contain sections on terrorism which end with exhortations such as:

> The police cannot defeat terrorism alone, communities defeat terrorism!
>
> **If you see any suspicious activity:**
>
> **CALL THE FREE CONFIDENTIAL HOTLINE ON 0800 789 321** or contact your local police station.[116]

Just how many useful tips on impending terrorist attacks might come from the public in that way is unclear. (Neighbourhood Watch, it turns out, is not all that useful in catching common or garden criminals: its greater success lies in reassuring the public and improving police–community relations.)[117] What is much more clear is the sense of generalized fear and unease caused by these sorts of campaigns, at least when applied to terrorist activities.

Neighbourhood Watch was of course set up as a response to fear of crime of a more common or garden sort. The thought – internalized more by the watchers than the watched, evidence alluded to above seems to suggest – is that people who know they are being watched will be less likely to commit crimes. But no one who has given the matter a moment's thought can imagine that terrorists who are undeterred by the eyes and ears of MI5 and MI6 will be greatly deterred by the eyes and ears of watchful neighbours. Furthermore, because the objective chances of encountering an actual terrorist in their neighbourhood is vanishingly small, citizens will not get the subjective sense of increased security that Neighbourhood Watchers ordinarily do from informing the police about activities of common or garden miscreants in their communities. In short, a Neighbourhood Watch against terrorism would increase anxiety without increasing security, worrying people rather than reassuring them.

* * * * * * * *

Stirring up the citizenry to be 'on watch' for terrorists deploying weapons of mass destruction is particularly perverse. For a start, just how likely is it that ordinary citizens are going to stumble across a facility for storing enriched uranium or anthrax that the intelligence services have missed? So the 'benefit' side of the equation is unlikely to be very great when it comes to a Neighbourhood Watch for weapons of mass destruction. And, on the 'cost' side, damage to the populace's peace of mind is bound to be unusually high.

It should come as no surprise that the populace overreacts wildly to the risks imposed by terrorists with weapons of mass destruction. Everything said earlier in this chapter about the public's tendency towards misperception of risks of terrorism in general is all the more true of risks of terrorist deployment of 'weapons of mass destruction'. There are certain attributes of 'weapons of mass destruction', most especially, that evoke psychological responses out of all proportion to the actual risks that they pose.

For a start, they are weapons of *mass* destruction, thus posing 'collective risks' of many people being killed at once. Hence the risks associated with such weapons are psychologically overemphasized for that familiar reason. Furthermore, the deaths they would bring are dramatic, vividly described and all too easily imagined. Psychologically, they are easily 'available' and overstated for that reason as well.

The upshot is, as Jessica Stern correctly concludes:

> The technologies and activities we fear most are not necessarily the ones that are the most dangerous. Certain characteristics of risks tend to inspire fear that is out of proportion to the risks themselves. Nuclear, chemical and biological agents possess all the characteristics that are conducive to disproportionate dread.[118]

Everything that has been said about how familiar psycho-social mechanisms lead us to overestimate the dangers of terrorism in general applies in trumps to the dangers of terrorists using weapons of mass destruction.

* * * * * * *

It is tempting to think that it is 'only prudent' to 'pull out all the stops' to protect against terrorists armed with weapons of mass destruction. But that thought turns out to be in error. Mass destruction is not total destruction: it matters just how big the possible losses might be. It also matters just what the odds of those catastrophes might be. Precision is impossible in these realms, but order-of-magnitude thinking can help us frame reasonable, graduated responses to the new terrorist risks that we now run. Stirring up the citizenry with warnings that – given what we know of the familiar psychological mechanisms at work – are bound to be misheard will be counterproductive of that goal of effective risk-management, as well as being destructive of people's peace of mind and even of democratic self-government, as I go on to show in the next chapter.

7

Terrorizing Democracy

Terrorism as a political wrong

Standard acts of terrorism are wrong in many ways. Insofar as terrorism is pursued by means that are themselves morally wrong – killing, maiming and so on – then the act is wrong for all those other reasons, too. In the classic cases of terrorism, those other wrongs doubtless dominate, by a very wide margin, the distinctive wrong that is terrorism itself ('acting with the intention of frightening people for political advantage'). Still, there is something distinctively wrong with terrorism, understood just in that specific sense. That is best understood as a political wrong, as I shall now argue.

* * * * * * * *

One way of analysing the political wrong of terrorism – and surely the most trivial – would be in terms of a wrong done by terrorists to their political adversaries, over whom they thereby acquire some advantage through unfair means.

If terrorism were nothing more than an 'illegitimate means of pursuing political advantage', however, there would be much less wrong with it than there is. Surely the wrong of terrorism is not only, or even principally, to be found in the wrong done to one's political *competitors*. The wrong of terrorism (even when no other moral wrong is done in pursuit of it) is not just akin to the wrong of playing dirty campaign tricks on opponents.

* * * * * * * *

A second and slightly better way of analysing the distinctive wrong of terrorism is in terms of the wrong done to those who have been frightened by it. After all, fear represents an unpleasant mental state; anyone who attaches moral importance to people's mental states would regard that as bad. Other things being equal, it might be thought, it is wrong to act in ways intended to produce bads for people.[1]

That proceeds too quickly, however. Sometimes it is right and proper to be afraid. In some larger sense (not now dealing purely in terms of mental states, obviously), it would be right – correct, even good – for people to be afraid of what they should be afraid of, and wrong for them not to be. So anyone making people frightfully aware of the threat of a large bomb that they should truly fear would be doing them a service, not a disservice – whatever the cost may be to their peace of mind.

Thus, the wrong of terrorism on this second account would have to be couched in terms of something other than just subjectively undesired mental states. Indeed, it would have to be couched in terms of something other than just objectively undesirable mental states, even. After all, it is objectively desirable for people to be duly frightened of and take precautions against an impending epidemic, even if the warner's main motive in issuing the warning were to further her own political cause.

On this second account, then, the wrongness of terrorism would have to be couched in terms of the wrongness of the intentions of the person creating these mental states in us. The wrong would, on this account, lie more in something like 'using people' (by 'taking political advantage of people's fears' or perhaps 'manipulating people's fears in ways that rebound to her political advantage').[2]

* * * * * * * * * *

The third and deepest political wrong of terrorism, I would suggest, is that done to a political community when instilling terror circumvents people's reasoning capacity. Instilling terror undermines people's capacity for autonomous self-government. That is the peculiar and particular wrong done by acts of terrorism in and to a democracy.

People who are terrified do not reason clearly. They are panicked, or cowed. Terrorism, insofar as it succeeds in producing terror, would thus have the effect of undermining people's capacity for autonomous self-government, both individually and collectively. Therein, I suggest, lies the distinctively *political* wrong of terrorism, understood as 'acts intended to frighten people for political advantage'.

'Terror', remember the *OED* telling us, is 'the state of being terrified or greatly frightened; intense fear, fright, or dread'. Those are not states of mind conducive to calm thought. They evoke more visceral than reasoned responses. What they provoke are more 'reactions' than 'reflections'.[3] Terror induces panic and 'short-circuits deliberation'.[4] People who are in the grip of terror are not thinking clearly. They may not be thinking at all.

In a mundane way, we see this in the phenomenology of horror movies. We must 'suspend disbelief' to enjoy them properly. But once we have entered into the spirit of the thing, and given ourselves over to the terror that the director was trying to conjure up, we cease being quite so inclined to query the illogicality of contrived plot lines. Succumbing to terror is the antithesis of succumbing to reason.

What is true of individuals, whether in a fantasy of horrors or a genuinely terrifying situation, is all the more true of collectivities. Terror drives out reason, collectively as well. Phenomena such as 'groupthink' and the 'law of group polarization' ensure that terror feeds on terror, in interpersonal interactions.[5] Collective decision procedures designed to be responsive to the thinking of members of the group unavoidably reflect, too, the terror that its members share. Competitive bidding for people's votes exacerbates it, insofar as people who are terrified tend to back the politicians who seem to be taking what terrifies them most seriously. Any attempt at reasoned and balanced assessments of relative risks will fall on deaf ears among people too frightened to reason clearly and calmly.

* * * * * * * *

The larger political sin of terrorism, then, lies not in the wrong of one political actor's thereby securing some 'unfair advantage' over her political opponents or in the wrong of frightening people. Instead it lies in the way in which terrorism undermines rational discourse across the political community as a whole. In that way, terrorism deprives us collectively of the capacity to be genuinely self-governing, reasoning together.

Terrorists who plant bombs or fly aeroplanes into buildings are greatly to blame for that. So too, however, are democratic politicians who deliberately stoke people's fears for their own political advantages. They, too, are 'acting with the intention of instilling fear in people for one's own political advantage'. They too are thereby intentionally subverting the democratic process. In that sense, they are committing terrorist offences against the polity, every bit as much as the bombers themselves.

Fearlessness as a response

Jean Elshtain writes that, 'when a wound as grievous as that of September 11 has been inflicted on a body politic, it would be the height of irresponsibility and a dereliction of duty for public officials to fail to respond.'[6] Others agree: 'the option of ignoring terrorism is not available. It might be rational, but it is psychologically and politically impossible.'[7]

But overreacting plays into terrorist hands, too. 'Lacking conventional power, extremists use terrorist tactics to create an atmosphere of fear and alarm. It often works. How much security is enough? Extraordinary security measures fulfill the wildest fantasies of the terrorists. They want the mighty to tremble.'[8] Why give terrorists what they want, in that way?

Sometimes 'doing nothing' is the optimal response. Indeed, sometimes it is the only responsible course of action. 'Benign neglect' might not have been a reasonable response to the race problem in the US, as Daniel Patrick Moynihan advised President Nixon. But there are other sorts of problems to which 'neglect' might be precisely the right response.

Terrorism might well be just such a case. If it is attention that evil people are seeking through desperate deeds, then ignoring them might indeed be the best way of making them go away.

* * * * * * * * *

An extreme form of that policy would be to ban journalists from reporting terrorist events. That has been discussed and dismissed in the previous chapter as democratically damaging and pragmatically pointless. It would substitute rumour for fact and, if anything, exacerbate public panic.

A more modest form of that policy would involve a self-denying ordinance on the part of politicians themselves. They can and should eschew any partisan political advantage that might come from the terrorist threat. They can and should make the Wars on Terror, like all wars, non-partisan affairs. They can and should refrain from 'playing the terror card', just as politicians in racially charged situations can and should refrain from playing the 'race card'.[9]

All of those 'can's and 'should's sound like moral exhortations, which might leave realpolitik-inclined readers wondering how they are going to be given any real force. But in a democracy there is a way. Voters might well resent being manipulated, and politicians seen to be doing so might well end up being electorally punished in consequence.

This presupposes that voters are sufficiently self-aware to realize that they have 'hot buttons' that politicians might try to push. But with such self-awareness, it might well be an open question whether voters who see politicians trying to 'push their hot buttons' will get 'hot' or just get mad.

* * * * * * * *

Within the broad tradition of liberal political philosophy dominating Western thinking about politics since the time of Hobbes
and Locke, the primary task of governments and leaders is to
free people from fear, allowing them to go about their affairs
in ways of their own choosing.

The fears that might intrude on people's living their lives as
they please, and against which governments are to protect
people, include fears both of other citizens and of government
itself. And of course there is a tradeoff between those two:
people have to be in fear of the power of the state to sanction
them, if they are to be free of fear of others harming them. So
there is a balance to be struck – more of which below. But
within the liberal tradition the prime directive in striking that
balance is to do so in such a way that minimizes fear overall.[10]

On this classic understanding, what governments and their
leaders are supposed to do is to quell their people's fears. They
are supposed to do so through their actions, taking measures
to protect people against threatened harms and thus reducing
the grounds for fear. But they are supposed to do so through
words as well as deeds. It is the job of political leaders in liberal
democracies to reassure people, as appropriate, that matters are
in hand and to tell them, where true, that there is nothing
(much) to fear.

Recall the catch-phrase of Franklin Roosevelt's First Inaugural, 'We have nothing to fear but fear itself.' In the midst of the
Great Depression, the task of democratic leadership was to
reassure people that government had put in place effective
strategies for getting the country out of the depression, which
would work just so long as people responded to them soberly
and steadfastly rather than in a panicked frenzy.[11]

* * * * * * *

Terrorism could in principle be tackled in the same way.

British administrators confronted with Jewish terrorism in
Palestine – Fighters for the Freedom of Israel (Lechi: the 'Stern

Gang'), the National Military Association (Etzel), and the like – always insistently labelled those groups 'terrorists'. But the British Army always hesitated in so designating them, precisely on the grounds that it resisted 'the implication that its troops were frightened by them'.[12]

That, I suggest, might be a model response, well worth emulating. The terminological ploy is the lesser part of the story: it is of little (but perhaps not literally 'no') consequence whether we call these people 'terrorists' or not. The issue rather is how we respond to their acts. The deeper strategy underlying the British Army's response suggests that it might be best to deprive terrorists of their power simply by refusing to let them frighten us.

Just as the British Army in Palestine was (at least officially) nonplussed by the bombing of its headquarters in the King David Hotel by Jewish terrorists, so too (whatever their private thoughts) were Londoners in public response to German terror bombing during World War II. The principal effect of the Blitz was to strengthen rather than weaken their resolve. This pattern is common enough that it ought give terrorist tacticians pause.[13]

* * * * * * *

Downplaying terrorist violence has been politically attempted from time to time. In 1971 the Home Secretary, Reginald Maudling, announced that it was the British government's aim to confine The Troubles in Northern Ireland to an 'acceptable level of violence'.[14] The government thereby acknowledged that eliminating terrorism altogether in the province was, for the foreseeable future, not a realistic ambition. But what the government could hope to do was contain the violence, so that it interfered minimally with people in the course of their daily lives.

The further objective to be achieved, by describing the situation in those terms, was to emphasize to citizens that the risks of terrorist violence really could be kept down to 'acceptable' limits, and people really could reasonably get on with their lives. 'If terrorism cannot be eliminated, it must perforce at some level be tolerated – and it can be.' That was Maudling's message.[15]

Ideally, of course, no one ought ever have to face the risk of violent death. But the real world is non-ideal, in that as in so many other respects. We run risks of violent death every time we cross the road or board a train. Within certain limits, we deem those to be 'acceptable risks'.[16] The Home Secretary's message, in framing his government's Northern Ireland policy in these terms, was to invite people to see the risk of terrorist violence as within those parameters.

That notion of an 'acceptable level of violence' was 'half-accepted, half-repudiated' as official government policy for Northern Ireland throughout the 1970s.[17] But whatever its status as official policy, that way of thinking about terrorism seems to have had considerable impact on everyday life in the province. Psychologists report that, 'while the "Troubles" ... play[ed] ... some sort of role in adding to the stresses of everyday life in Northern Ireland, their contribution is probably only a relatively small one.' They go on to explain that 'it is not actual levels of violence that are the primary source of stress . . . , but rather it is the way in which people perceive that violence.'[18] People in the 'acceptable risk' frame of mind can 'distance' themselves psychologically from the violence. In that way, what would commonly be regarded as 'high' levels of terrorist violence can be prevented from producing very high levels of social stress, at least as long as the violence does not actually touch them directly (and it did not actually touch most people in Northern Ireland directly).

This social psychological evidence is borne out by survey data of a more general sort. Asked 'how serious do you feel terrorism is here in [your own country]?', fully 60 per cent in the US (where there were no terrorist events of consequence in 1978, the year in question) responded 'very serious', whereas only 30 per cent in the UK (where there were eighty-eight deaths from terrorist violence in Northern Ireland in 1978) thought it was 'very serious'.[19]

Clearly, the way political elites approach terrorist issues can have a significant impact on public perceptions. Adopting a low-key approach, such as Reginald Maudling's 'acceptable level of violence' doctrine and its policy heirs, helps calm public fears of terrorist violence. It avoids exaggerated assessments of the risks, and extreme psychological responses. That is both healthier for the citizenry and healthier for democracy.

* * * * * * * *

There is a salutary contrast between the UK and the US regarding the way post-9/11 warnings of the risk of terrorism have been handled. The contrast is nicely summed up by the Tory Shadow Minister responsible for homeland security (whose own predilections in the matter are diametrically opposed to my own):

> How alert to terrorism is this country? The fact is that we have been at a higher alert state than America since the attacks on British targets in Turkey last November. But who is aware of this? The only way that this was put in the public arena at first was via a leak from BBC Radio 4. Now, it is true, there are Home Office and MI5 websites where the alert state is available, but neither serves to tell the man on the street exactly how much danger he is in. When the Home Office is challenged on this point their reply is that . . . too much information is thought likely to induce panic.

Whereas, in the US approach, President Bush boasts:

> In the face of this threat what has the USA done? It has raised its alert state and told everybody that it has done so. Then, its security forces have been placed in highly visible positions so that they can deter terrorists. Next, it has told American institutions overseas that they might be targets as well; but most of all, it has been honest with its people on the scale of the threat. Some call this alarmism; but many recognise it for what it is – sensible precautions taken to avoid another scar being inflicted on America.[20]

The Tory Shadow Minister thinks that the UK suffers in that comparison. But the UK approach to risks of international terrorism is clearly continuous with its traditional approach to terrorism in Northern Ireland. And that approach, as we have just seen, has had considerable benefits both for the psychological health of the community and for realistic assessments of risk in the political process.

* * * * * *

Ironically, an ostensibly 'calming' message formed a large part of the immediate post-September 11 response, even of US and Australian political leaders who subsequently traded shamelessly upon people's fear of terrorism to win re-election.

When President Bush addressed the US Congress in the immediate aftermath of the attacks of September 11, he said,

> I know many citizens have fears tonight, and I ask you to be calm and resolute, even in the face of a continuing threat ... It is my hope that in the months and years ahead, life will return almost to normal. We'll go back to our lives and routines, and that is good.[21]

Similarly, in Australia, 'Be alert but not alarmed' was the official slogan in an official brochure delivered to every Australian household, under a cover letter from the Prime Minister himself.[22]

Even those initial messages were double-edged, of course. In the self-same sentence in which Bush asked people to be calm, he ended by coyly reminding them of the 'continuing danger'. He expressed the hope that life would 'return *almost* to normal': 'almost', but not quite; a reminder that 'everything changed' on September 11. Or, again, the same slogan that told Australians not to be 'alarmed' also reminded them of the need to be wary. As Jürgen Habermas astutely observed of his time in Manhattan in October 2001, 'the repeated and utterly nonspecific announcements of possible new terror attacks and the senseless calls to "be alert" further stirred a vague feeling of angst ... – precisely the intention of the terrorists.'[23]

As election campaigns got underway, the message became more univocal. Reassurances fell away, and the dangers were re-emphasized. The White House's fact sheet on 'Three Years of Progress in the War on Terror', released on the third anniversary of the September 11 attacks (and two months before the 2004 presidential election), begins with this quotation from a speech by President Bush:

> [W]e're still not safe. ... We are a Nation in danger. We're doing everything we can in our power to confront the danger. We're making good progress in protecting our people and bringing our enemies to account. But one thing is for certain: We'll keep our focus and we'll keep our resolve and we will do our duty to best secure our country.[24]

* * * * * *

Matters came to a head towards the end of the 2004 US presidential election. In an interview published in the *New York Times Magazine*, Democratic candidate John Kerry was quoted as endorsing essentially the UK approach to terrorist warnings.

Addressing the question of 'what it would take for America to feel safe again', Kerry replied:

> We have to get back to the place we were, where terrorists are not the focus of our lives, but they're a nuisance. As a former law enforcement person, I know we're never going to end prostitution. We're never going to end illegal gambling. But we're going to reduce it, organized crime, to a level where it isn't on the rise. It isn't threatening people's lives every day, and fundamentally, it's something you continue to fight, but it's not threatening the fabric of your life.[25]

Kerry's remarks were immediately ridiculed by the Bush campaign saying, 'He equated [terrorism] to prostitution and gambling, a nuisance activity. You know, quite frankly, I just don't think he has the right view of the world. It's a pre-9/11 view of the world.'[26]

These themes were picked up by President Bush on the campaign trail, in a call-and-response speech posted without shame on the White House website. To my reading, this is on a par with the 'I have a scream' speech that was deemed to disqualify Governor Howard Dean from the presidency earlier that year.[27] But allow me to quote the encounter at some length, and invite readers to judge for themselves.

THE PRESIDENT: During the decade of the 1990s, our times often seemed peaceful on the surface. Yet, beneath that surface were currents of danger. Terrorists were training and planning in distant camps. In 1993, terrorists made their first attack on the World Trade Center. In 1998, terrorists bombed American embassies in Kenya and Tanzania. And then came the attack on the USS Cole in 2000, which cost the lives of 17 American sailors. In this period, America's response to terrorism was generally piecemeal and symbolic. The terrorists concluded this was a sign of weakness, and their plans became more ambitions [*sic*], and their attacks became more deadly.

Most Americans still felt that terrorism was something distant, and something that would not strike on a large scale in America. That is the time that my opponent wants to go back to.

AUDIENCE: Booo!

THE PRESIDENT: A time when danger was real and growing, but we didn't know it. A time when some thought terrorism was only a "nuisance."

AUDIENCE: Booo!

THE PRESIDENT: But that very attitude is what blinded America to the war being waged against us. And by not seeing the war, our government had no comprehensive strategy to fight it. September the 11th, 2001 changed all that. We realized that the apparent security of the 1990s was an illusion.

The people of New Jersey were among the first to understand how the world changed. On September the 11th, from places like Hoboken and Jersey City, you could look across the Hudson River and see the Twin Towers burning. We will never forget that day, and we will never forget our duty to defend America. (Applause.)

. . .

September the 11th also changed the way we should look at national security. But not everyone realizes it. The choice we face in this election, the first presidential election since September the 11th, is how our nation will defeat this threat. Will we stay on the offensive against those who want to attack us –

AUDIENCE: Yes!

THE PRESIDENT: – or will we take action only after we are attacked?

AUDIENCE: No!

THE PRESIDENT: Will we make decisions in the light of September the 11th, or continue to live in the mirage of safety that was actually a time of gathering threats? And in this time of choosing, I want all Americans to know you can count on me to fight our enemies and defend our freedom. (Applause.)

. . .

My opponent has a fundamental misunderstanding on the war on terror. A reporter recently asked Senator Kerry how September the 11th changed him. He replied, 'It didn't change me much at all'.

AUDIENCE: Booo!

THE PRESIDENT: His unchanged world view is obvious from the policies he still advocates. He has said this war is 'primarily an intelligence and law enforcement operation.' He has declared, we should not respond to threats until they are – quote – 'imminent'. He has complained that my administration – quote – 'relies unwisely on the threat of military preemption against terrorist organizations'. Let me repeat that. He says that preemptive action is 'unwise', not only against regimes, but even against terrorist organizations.

AUDIENCE: Booo!

THE PRESIDENT: Senator Kerry's approach would permit a response only after America is hit.

AUDIENCE: Booo!

THE PRESIDENT: This kind of September the 10th attitude is no way to protect our country. (Applause.) The war on terror is a real war, with deadly enemies, not simply a police operation. In an era of weapons of mass destruction, waiting for threats to arrive at our doorsteps is to invite disaster. Tyrants and terrorists will not give us polite notice before they attack our country. As long as I'm the Commander-in-Chief, I will confront dangers abroad so we do not have to face them here at home. (Applause.)

In fairness, it *was* a campaign rally. (In fairness, so too was Howard Dean's.) But whatever you say about it, that clearly indicated an aversion to any attempt at putting the risks of terrorism in their proper place. Still less did it represent any genuine attempt by the President positively to correct for the familiar ways (discussed in the previous chapter) in which even the most neutral warnings of terrorism will inevitably be exaggerated in their transmission and their reception.

When you know that the medium of transmission and reception will inevitably amplify the message in ways described in the previous chapter, the responsible thing to do is to moderate the inputs so that the outputs will come out about right. That is what the British strategy, so lamented by the Tory Shadow Minister, did. That is the very opposite of what the US President, on the hustings, chose to do.

In that speech and many like it, President Bush was clearly himself acting with the intention of instilling fear of terrorism to advance his own political agenda. And on the definition I have offered and defended in chapter 3, that would count as an act of terrorism in itself.

Hobbesian solutions to non-Hobbesian problems

Political theorists, like everyone, have a limited range of tools in their intellectual toolkits. Presented with real-world events, they rummage around to see what among their standard equipment best fits this occasion, rather than necessarily doing any first-order philosophy on the situation at hand.

When confronted with large-scale terrorism, such as the events of 9/11, what comes most immediately to the political theorist's mind is the Hobbesian 'war of all against all'.[28]

The echoes are there. Both in the Hobbesian state of nature and in the newly uncertain world of random terror, we do not know where the threat might come from. Both are characterized by an overwhelming sense of diffuse fear and danger.

Hear what some distinguished political theorists said about 9/11, then. From Benjamin Barber:

> In binding us to our own fear through what the anarchist Bakunin called the 'propaganda of the deed', the terrorists have in a certain sense undone the social contract, bringing us full circle back to a kind of 'state of nature'. For the last four hundred years, we travelled a road from anarchy, insecurity and fear (the state of nature postulated by social contract theorists like Hobbes and Locke) to law and order (lawful order), political safety and the enjoyment of civil liberty. Operating outside the law, making insecurity ubiquitous and turning liberty into risk, terrorism pushes us backwards into a quasi-anarchy.[29]

Similarly, Jean Bethke Elshtain says:

> None of the goods that human beings cherish ... can flourish without a measure of civil peace and security. What ... goods do I have in mind? Mothers and fathers raising their children; men and women going to work; citizens of a great city making their way on

streets and subways; ordinary people flying to California to visit grandchildren or to transact business with colleagues – all of these actions are simple but profound goods made possible by civil peace. . . . Human beings are fragile creatures. We cannot reveal the fullness of our being, including our deep sociality, if airplanes are flying into buildings or snipers are shooting at us randomly or deadly spores are being sent through the mail. . . . We know what happens to people who live in pervasive fear. The condition of fearfulness leads to severe isolation as the desire to protect oneself and one's family becomes overwhelming. It encourages harsh measures because, as the political theorist Thomas Hobbes wrote in his 1651 work *Leviathan*, if we live in constant fear of violent death we are likely to seek guarantees to prevent such.[30]

These sorts of overly dramatic analogies might be forgiven in the immediate aftermath of 9/11. But even before that, writers on terrorism had been saying the same in rather more moderate tones:

every political community has understood that random and indiscriminate violence is the ultimate threat to social cohesion, and thus every political community has some form of prohibition against it. Terrorism allowed full sway would reduce civil society to the state of nature where there is in Hobbes' fine description, 'continual fear of violent death, and the life of man solitary, poor, nasty, brutish and short'. No political society can sanction terrorism, for that would be a self-contradiction, as the very reasons for entering civil society were to escape precisely those conditions imposed by the terrorists.[31]

* * * * * * * *

Are the analogies apt?

While the fear that 9/11 provoked may be analogous to the fear that Hobbes invoked, the *source* of the fear is importantly different. There was no breakdown of law and order on 9/11, no breakdown of civil society or public services overall. There was no 'war of all against all'. And that is true of virtually all cases of terrorist violence. The terrorists' goal may be to 'destroy the existing order'. But it is simply not the case that terrorist acts, taken individually or usually even taken altogether, succeed in that larger aspiration. They might succeed in killing a lot of people, and in frightening a lot more. They might succeed in instilling widespread fear. But they do not usually come close to succeeding in causing social breakdown.[32]

In Hobbesian terms, notice, absolutist government is a solution *not* to the problem of 'fear' but *rather* to the problem of 'war of all against all'. Fear may be what prompts one to accede to absolutist government. But it is not what rationalizes that accession.

Furthermore, acceding to an absolutist government does not solve the problem of fear. On the contrary, fear is what makes people obey the absolutist state. And it is not just fear of the state and its agents: it is fear of one's fellows and their willingness to serve as agents of the state in enforcing its will.[33] So generalized fear – 'fear by all of all' – remains in the absolutist state.

Terrorism might replicate the fear found in a Hobbesian state of nature. But it does not replicate what Hobbes describes as the grounds of that fear. Even in a world of rampant terrorism, we do not face a war of 'all against all', the solution to which is installing one 'common power' over them all. Instead we face a war of 'some against all'.

In Hobbes's famous phrase, a war of all against all makes 'the life of man solitary, poor, nasty, brutish and short'.[34] In a 'war of all against all' people inevitably lead 'solitary' lives because each is at war with each other. Each knows the other is her enemy. Fear *thus* motivated would indeed constitute a barrier to the emergence of cooperative social relations in the first place. And fear of sliding back into that sort of situation would indeed tend to 'erode the quality or stability of an existing social order'.[35]

But it is what we are afraid *of* – not fear as such – that has that tendency to destabilize or degrade social order. It is fear that our fellows might be systematically untrustworthy, that they might all be our enemies, that we might be in a 'war of all against all'.

Terrorists too harm some people in hopes of instilling fear in far more people, and they often do so in hopes of destabilizing or degrading the existing social order. There are many ways they might envisage that occurring: by undermining confidence in the government to protect people, by undermining consumer confidence and depressing the economy, by forcing people to stay home at night rather than keeping up social contacts. All of those represent significant alterations to 'the character of society and the quality of daily life', owing to the fear of terrorism.[36]

But none of that amounts to a 'war of all against all'. True, under the influence of terrorism social trust is eroded by the thought that 'anyone might be a terrorist'. But even that mildly paranoid thought is importantly different from the genuinely Hobbesian thought that 'everyone *is* my enemy'. Even if I am uncertain which, or how many, of my fellows can be trusted, that is importantly different from being certain that literally none of them can be.

* * * * * *

A 'war of *some* against all' is simply not a 'war of *all* against all'. Substantial central power might be needed to circumvent the power that the 'some' have to harm 'all'. But the same power might be used to harm as well as to protect 'all', and the way that that might balance out cannot be presumed in advance of careful questioning.

It is a balancing act not required in a literally Hobbesian world. There, we are in a Prisoner's Dilemma situation in which we are certain that each will take advantage of the other unless there is some external power to prevent them from doing so. There, the external power must be strong enough to compel all at once. Where only some pose threats, such absolute power is not strictly required.

The Hobbesian analogy seriously misleads. It suggests that the case in favour of absolutist government, in the face of fear, is open and shut. In truth, it is anything but.

* * * * * * * *

Turning immediately to Hobbes in this context is slightly unimaginative, even for those looking for off-the-shelf theories to apply to the post-9/11 terror. Even off-the-shelf political theory offers other resources. Judith Shklar wrote famously of the 'liberalism of fear', C. B. Macpherson of the initial liberal model of 'protective democracy'.[37]

The reason for resisting any immediate turn to Hobbes, and for recalling those other political philosophical resources instead, lies of course in the alternative solutions they suggest to the problem of 'fear'. Hobbes famously used our fear of, and in, the state of nature as justification for an all-powerful sovereign. And this is precisely the path being followed in the push for 'homeland security'.

Recall the words of Tom Ridge upon assuming his position as director of the new US Office of Homeland Security:

> We will work to ensure that the essential liberty of the American people is protected, that terrorists will not take away our way of life. It's called Homeland Security. While the effort will begin here, it will require the involvement of America at every level. Everyone in the homeland must play a part. I ask the American people for their patience, their awareness and their resolve. This job calls for a national effort. We've seen it before, whether it was building the Trans-Continental Railroad, fighting World War II, or putting a man on the moon.[38]

Now, perhaps we ought forgive a man a bit of hyperbole on the day of his acceptance speech in the White House. And, in many respects, what he says is both obvious and innocuous. Still, there is an uncomfortably totalitarian edge to Ridge's call for the total commitment of the total community to the project of homeland security.

Shades of an absolute Hobbesian ruler are seen, too, in the 'restriking of the balance between liberty and security' that is proceeding apace in the wake of 9/11. Some of the new laws enacted to deal with terrorism amount to nothing more than updating existing statutes to reflect new technologies: in an age of mobile phones, the law that required authority to wiretap be tied to a specific landline obviously needed updating, independently of the events of 9/11.[39] But many of the provisions of the USA PATRIOT Act, and especially the use of military tribunals, do indeed amount to 'restriking the balance' decidedly towards security at the cost of liberty and due process.[40]

In short, 'superterrorism' – as terrorist spectaculars such as 9/11 are sometimes called[41] – has been presented as a Hobbesian problem, calling forth the standard Hobbesian solution, an increasingly absolutist state.

* * * * * * * * *

Terrorists induce fear, or anyway they do their best to do so. So do governments, when threatening people with criminal sanctions. An absolutist state governs through a 'rule of fear'. But even in decent liberal states of the ordinary sort, people comply with the law in part out of 'fear of punishment'.

What keeps 'fear of punishment' from shading into the sort of fear induced by terrorists – both state terrorists (such as absolutist governments) and non-state terrorists – is that the punishments are not arbitrary. Where a society is governed according to the 'rule of law', punishments attach in known and avoidable ways to actions. People who avoid performing such actions have nothing to fear, honest mistakes apart.[42]

Contrast that with the case of a state not bound by the 'rule of law'. People are held by the police without charge, for protracted periods. Law-enforcement officials have vast discretionary power in interpreting the laws, so that there is no way for people to know in advance what is or is not a violation of them. The possibility of retrospective legislation means that you might come to be guilty of a crime for doing something that was not criminal at the time you did it. In a society like that, we would be tempted to say that the state is indeed terrorizing its citizens, exercising through a 'rule of fear' of arbitrary punishment rather than a 'rule of law'.[43] We must be careful, in the War on Terrorism, not to create a terrorist state.

Of tyrants and terrorists

A moment's reflection upon the politics of fear reminds us that government, too, is something to fear. We need protection against it, as much as we need it to protect us against one another or terrorist outsiders. And we need all the more protection against government, the stronger that government is. That is the original liberalism of limited government, checks and balances, democratic restraints on arbitrary rule.

In giving government greater powers to do what we want it to do, we ought pause to consider the possibility that it will use those powers to do things we do not want it to do. We might guard against that eventuality in either of two ways: by tightly defining the circumstances in which the powers may legally be used, thus ensuring that they will be used only in ways we want; or by throwing governors out of office if they use powers in ways we do not want.

Each of those protections is strictly limited, however. Terrorists are nothing if not creative; and if we circumscribe the new powers narrowly they can easily be circumvented by that creativity, terrorists using mobile telephones to avoid wiretaps on landlines for example. If we want to write the rules in such a way as to increase substantially (one can never 'ensure') the prevention of terrorism, those rules must be relatively open-textured. That in turn opens the very real possibility they might be used in ways we do not want.

* * * * * * *

Ideally, in a democracy we ought always be able to employ the next election as at least a *post hoc* check (which ought in turn serve as an *ex ante* deterrent) on these new powers being used in ways we do not want. But, by its nature, much of the work of the secret services is and must remain secret: the electorate never really knows to what (all) uses they are putting their new powers, or anyway not until very much later. Furthermore, the very enactment of these new security measures sets in train a cycle of fear that precludes clear thinking on these matters.

I refer here neither to deep psychological drives nor to cynical political manipulation. No doubt both are at work, as I have said earlier. But nothing so fancy is required to explain the cycle of fear I here have in view. All we need assume is that people are 'intuitive Bayesians' in their everyday affairs. The more they are delayed at airports waiting to go through metal detectors, the more reason they naively assume there must be for those security precautions. Even people who firmly believe otherwise – who firmly believe the security threat is vastly exaggerated – naturally find themselves in unreflective moments being insidiously sucked into this 'intuitive Bayesian' reasoning that 'there must be something to the threat if we're being made to wait like this.'

* * * * * * * * * *

If we cannot rely on either of those two ways of checking abuse of powers granted to the new anti-terrorist Leviathan, then we are faced with the grim choice of either not granting those extended powers to combat terrorism or else granting them and accepting the Hobbesian consequences. The risk on the one side is terrorism. The risk on the other side is tyranny.

Where we should strike the balance obviously depends on how big each risk is, both in the sense of how likely each outcome is to occur and in the sense of how harmful each outcome would be if it did occur.

Of the risk of tyranny, human history offers abundant evidence. We have a pretty clear idea how much harm strong states can do, if unchecked. And we have a pretty clear idea of how likely that is to occur, eventually if not immediately.

Emergency powers work well in time-limited emergencies. Once the emergency is past, the extra powers vanish.[44] Most – but certainly not all – Roman dictators handed back power at that point. A few – but too few – of their successors have done likewise.

The situation is far more problematic when what we face is (as discussed in chapter 2) a permanent state of emergency. If the War on Terror can never be won – as President Bush himself proclaims[45] – then the anti-terrorist Leviathan will be in permanent possession of emergency powers. The emergency becomes a way of life. The corrosive effects on limited government can only be imagined. But it does not take much imagination to surmise that they might be very deleterious indeed. Harold Lasswell warned that something similar might result from the permanent mobilization of armed forces in 'The Garrison State' that he foresaw the US becoming after World War II.[46] However injurious communist witch-hunts were to American civil liberties during the Cold War, one can only imagine much greater injury still when confronted with a more diffuse foe.

8

Conclusions

Like the warnings of terrorist attack discussed in chapter 6, this book's own warnings – in its case, warnings of the danger of warnings of terrorism – constitute a message that is at risk of being misread (perhaps wilfully so) in all too many quarters. Let me therefore say as conspicuously and as clearly as possible what I am *not* saying.

I am *not* saying that Western political leaders who do nothing more than warn of terrorist attacks for partisan purposes are 'as bad as bin Laden'. There are many other moral offences listed on his charge sheet that are absent from theirs, starting with 2973 murders on 11 September 2001. So too in my fictitious IRA bomber examples in chapter 5: Kevin, the terrorist who actually planted the bomb which he then rang the police to warn about, is guilty of two offences (first, planting the bomb; second, issuing a terrorist warning); whereas Pat, the IRA sympathizer who merely discovered the bomb in the rubbish and rang in the warning for political purposes, is guilty merely of one offence (issuing a terrorist warning). So let us be clear: bin Laden is undoubtedly 'worse' than Bush and Blair and Howard and their ilk.

What I *am* saying is merely that there is one important respect in which they all might be broadly the same. Insofar as all of them act with the intention of frightening people for their own political purposes (and I am prepared to leave that as an open question), they would be committing what ought be regarded as a capital crime against democratic politics. They would all be intentionally undermining people's capacity for democratic self-government, by evoking visceral responses rather than reasoned reflections. That, I have argued, is the distinctive feature of terrorism. That is what distinguishes it from murder and destruction perpetrated for other purposes. And that is a feature that 'democratic' politicians' Wars *on* Terror can sometimes share with terrorists' Wars *of* Terror.

* * * * * * *

I hesitate to describe my conclusions in terms of real people – bin Laden, Bush, Blair, Howard and so on. I do so for various reasons.

I hesitate in part because that would require conducting an all-in assessment of the moral character and actions of real people, in a way I have avoided here. A full assessment of bin Laden would have to take account of all sorts of things that he did on days other than 11 September 2001; a full assessment of the others would have to take into account all sorts of other things that they have done, beyond their responses to the events of that day. Some philosophers have attempted to do that.[1] I have not. Here I have focused instead on a narrower subset of that larger project: the moral assessment of the phenomenon of terrorism and reactions to it. I have limited myself accordingly to the moral assessment of only a small part of people's overall character and behaviour.

I further hesitate to describe my conclusions in terms of real people because I do not have the full facts about what they did and why, what they knew and when. I think I know some things, and I suspect lots of others: it is plenty for forming my own private judgement, but not nearly enough for me to tell anyone else (in print, as opposed to the pub) how they ought form theirs. On this account as well, I am content to leave the overall assessment of the moral character of named individuals to St Peter, whose big book contains all the relevant facts and in any case whose job it is.

My aim in writing the present book is not to tell readers *what* to think about terrorism and wars on it but, rather, to help them see *how* to think about those things. What are the crucial facts that we would need to know, and what are the crucial considerations that we ought bear in mind, in forming moral assessments of terrorists and of those who declare war upon them?

* * * * * * *

Much though I would like to avoid talking in terms of the names of real people, I find when discussing the arguments of the book that audiences simply will not allow me to do so. The names of real people seem to have some irresistible attraction.

So let me compromise. Let me talk in terms of some people *somewhat like* their real-world counterparts: B'ush, B'lair, H'oward, b'in Laden. Using that semi-fictionalized cast of characters, I can express the broad conclusions of this book without embroiling myself in messy factual disputes of a sort that are better left to the historians.

Who knows what the real bin Laden thinks and does? But imagine his semi-fictionalized counterpart, b'in Laden. B'in Laden, let us suppose, organizes for aeroplanes to be hijacked and crashed into occupied buildings. Suppose, furthermore, he does so with the intention of both (a) causing death and destruction and (b) causing general fear in the target population in order to further his socio-political purposes. And, again, who knows what (if anything) goes through the mind of the real Bush? But imagine his semi-fictionalized counterpart, B'ush. B'ush, let us suppose, issues warnings of imminent terrorist attacks; and let us suppose he does so purely with the intention of causing general fear in his electorate in order to further his own socio-political purposes (re-election, say).

Now, think of St Peter's task as akin to an exercise in double-entry bookkeeping. He keeps the moral equivalent of a 'charge sheet', on which everyone's good and bad deeds are all separately itemized. Then, come the Final Judgement, he adds them all up to come to his overall assessment.

On that charge sheet, b'in Laden gets ticks under two headings:

(a) intentionally causing death and destruction; and
(b) intentionally causing general fear in a target population
     in order to further his socio-political purposes.

On his charge sheet, B'ush gets a tick under heading (b) alone
– which is of course the 'bad deed' that distinctively characterizes terrorism, on the analysis I have been giving of it in this
book.

So, to the crucial questions:

1) Is b'in Laden 'worse' than B'ush?
    Of course. B'in Laden is guilty of two bad deeds – (a) and
    (b) – whereas B'ush is guilty of (b) alone. Furthermore,
    the bad deed that is peculiar to b'in Laden alone is far
    worse than the bad deed that B'ush and b'in Laden share
    in common.
2) Are b'in Laden and B'ush both guilty of terrorism?
    Yes: they both have a tick in column (b).
3) Is b'in Laden any 'more guilty' of terrorism than B'ush,
    merely because he gets a tick in column (a) as well as
    (b)?
    No reason to think so: they are separate offences. B'in
    Laden is guilty of two crimes (murder and terrorism)
    whereas B'ush is guilty of one alone (terrorism). But b'in
    Laden is not 'more of a terrorist' for being a murderer as
    well.

If that last conclusion still seems strange, consider this
analogy. Suppose Sam and Sue jointly kidnapped Zeke, whom
Sam then proceeded to murder without Sue's knowledge or
assistance. Sam would be guilty of two crimes ('kidnapping'
and 'murder'), whereas Sue would be guilty of one alone
(just 'kidnapping'). They would both be kidnappers. But Sam
is not 'more of a kidnapper' for being a murderer as well. Nor
is Sue any 'less of a kidnapper' for not being a murderer as
well.

* * * * * * *

Here is another way of interrogating recent political history for traces of the distinctive sort of moral offence that I see as peculiarly associated with terrorism.

In the final days of the 2004 US presidential election campaign, the real Osama bin Laden broadcast a message through Aljazeera, addressed directly to US voters.[2] It was a puzzling message in many respects. But on one crucial point it was crystal clear: the US ought expect further death and destruction if it persists in the policies of George W. Bush.[3]

The real George W. Bush responded to bin Laden's broadcast in a brief, disjointed statement from the tarmac of a windswept Dayton airfield. He did not say in so many words, 'The US will suffer further death and destruction if the US does not persist in the policies of George W. Bush.' But that was the unmistakable message.[4]

Now, each of them – the real Osama bin Laden and the real George W. Bush – has also said and done a great many other things. What they said on that day must no doubt be seen against the background of all that. But for the purposes of this more philosophical enquiry, I want to abstract away from all the complications that that involves.

So let us imagine their semi-fictionalized counterparts, b'in Laden and B'ush, making similar statements. Let us imagine that each of them does so purely with the intention of frightening people and, by so doing, of thereby influencing the outcome of the 2004 US presidential election. Furthermore, let us imagine, what each delivered was a warning pure and simple. Specifically, let us suppose that b'in Laden was completely incapable of initiating an attack himself and completely powerless to influence anyone else to do so or to refrain from doing so. His message, let us suppose, was purely a prediction of and warning about what would be done by others with no connection with himself, were B'ush re-elected. That may or may not be an accurate characterization of either the real Bush or the real bin Laden. But let us imagine a semi-fictionalized B'ush and b'in Laden of whom it is true, and ask how we ought in that case assess their actions.

In the case as described, it seems to me that we would have no choice but to assess the messages of b'in Laden and B'ush strictly on a par. Both warn of some frightening prospect. Both do so purely in order to manipulate the same political outcome (albeit in opposing directions). In the construction of our semi-fictionalized characters, we have assumed away any other wrongs that either of the speakers might do or have done; so, in the semi-fictionalized story, B'ush and b'in Laden do not differ in any other respect. Thus, there are simply no grounds for drawing any distinction between what they have done. Any wrong done by b'in Laden's warning of terrorism on the eve of the US election is perfectly matched by a strictly analogous wrong done by B'ush's warning of terrorism on the eve of the US election, and vice versa.

*   *   *   *   *   *   *   *

Campaigns of fear undermine the democratic process by undermining people's capacity for self-government. That is a non-trivial wrong.

It is wrong to take by force what you cannot win by persuasion. That is why theft is worse than trade, war is worse than diplomacy, a coup is worse than an election. It is similarly wrong to take by *fear* of force what you cannot win by persuasion.

Terrorists do that by bombings and threats and warnings of bombings. We are all too familiar with that. We are less familiar – less familiar than we should be – with the fact that political leaders can do something similar, frightening people (with warnings of terrorist bombs, among other things) instead of reasoning with them.

Terrorism and warnings of terrorism are not unique in undermining the democratic process in this way. The same is true of 'playing the race card' in racially divided societies. That evokes visceral responses and circumvents reasoned political argument in just the same way as 'playing the terrorism card' does in a world traumatized by 9/11. And in a great many less dramatic ways, marketing experts who advise politicians how to push people's 'hot buttons' are doing the same sorts of things. So the damage that 'playing the terrorism card' does to democratic self-government is nowise unique. Instead, it is broadly similar to the damage done by lots of other actors and acts that seem simply sleazy rather than deeply sinister.

That conclusion seems to be correct on both scores. Political manipulators are morally worse than we might initially have imagined, and their moral badness is in direct proportion to their political successfulness. But terrorism as such – what is distinctive about terrorism, as opposed to the (and typically far worse) means through which it is carried out (kidnapping, murder, etc.) – is morally no worse than that. The defining feature of terrorism is, I have argued, its attempt to manipulate socio-political outcomes by playing on people's fears. That is continuous with many forms of political manipulation practised by marketing experts. And it is continuous, too, with politicians' attempts to manipulate political outcomes by playing on people's fears of what terrorists might do.

Saying that does nothing to mitigate the badness of the many other things that terrorists also do in the process of engendering that fear. Mass murder is wrong, whether conducted for political purposes or any other; and among the suite of wrongs mass-murdering terrorists commit, that is much the worst wrong.

The distinctive wrong of terrorism, however, is that it is committed for distinctively political purposes. And it is a wrong that can be committed by those reacting against mass murderers, as well as by those acting in league with them.

* * * * * * *

Perhaps we ought welcome warnings of terrorist attacks before they occur, from whatever source those warnings might come and for whatever purpose they might be issued. Assuming such warnings would allow us to mitigate the effects of the attacks (or perhaps even to foil them altogether), it is surely better to be warned of the attacks. And at a pinch, it is better to receive such warnings of terrorist attacks from terrorists, for terrorist purposes (even if they succeed in instilling fear), rather than not to receive any warnings at all. Likewise, it is better to have warnings of terrorist attacks from self-serving politicians, issued for strictly analogous and equally morally offensive purposes of instilling fear for their own political purposes, than it would be not to have warnings at all.

That is simply to say that the second-best is always better than the worst outcome, in this case, the bombs actually exploding and doing their awful damage. But it would be *better still* were those warnings to come from people with purer intentions, wanting just to save lives and property. And it would be far better if those warnings were issued in a low-key British way rather than in the American way, so as not to instil undue fear or subvert democratic self-government in the process.

Of course, it would be better still if there were no terrorist threats to warn anyone about. Nice though that world would be, I concur with Bush, Blair and myriad others in judging that world to be beyond our reach. Terrorists will be with us for the foreseeable future, doing, threatening and warning of frightening things in furtherance of their nefarious socio-political aims. We simply have to take that as given.

What might be within our power to change is the conduct of our own elected representatives. Must we continue to tolerate them, *too*, perverting our political process, through the same sorts of frightening warnings, purely for their own political purposes? Is it not bad enough that we have to suffer terrorist bombers doing that, without suffering the same from our elected representatives as well?

Notes

Preface

1 Freedland (2005); Lawson (2005); Meek (2005).

Introduction

1 Just as there are many wrongs which those who practise terrorism protest; although unlike Honderich (2003a, 2003b) I am not prepared to allow that fact to excuse terrorists their own wrongs. For a much more careful discussion of circumstances under which terrorism might be morally justified, see Corlett (2003, chs 5–6).
2 For a partial survey and potted history, see Robin (2004).
3 Frightened people often end up killing lots of other people, however; and for that, politicians who intentionally instilled that fear might be largely to blame.
4 As I have been insisting for some time, now (Goodin 1982, ch. 1).
5 Not to mention the public, more generally. Martha Nussbaum (2003, 233) recounts the tale of 'a baseball game I went to at Comiskey Park, the first game played in Chicago after September 11 ... [A]s the game went on and the beer began flowing, one heard, increasingly, the chant, "U-S-A, U-S-A", a chant left over from the Olympic hockey match in which the United States defeated Russia, expressing the wish for America to defeat, abase, humiliate, its enemies. Indeed, the chant USA soon became a general way of expressing the desire to crush one's enemies, whoever they were. When the umpire made a bad call against the Sox, the same group in the bleachers turned to him, chanting "U-S-A".

Anyone who crosses us is an evil terrorist, deserving of extinction.'
Or anyway such was the mindset of the White Sox fans on that
day.

6 Aglionby (2004). Arroyo's own phrasing was ambiguous but at least
admits of this reading.

7 Pear (2004). The reporter has Paige saying the NEA 'was *like* "a
terrorist organization"'; but Paige's own spokesperson reports, 'He
said he considered the NEA to be a terrorist organization.'

8 India (2002), sec. 3 (1)(a).

Chapter 2 Terrorism as Unjust War

1 For reasons I shall discuss below, contemporary just-war theorists
typically prefer to talk in terms of 'non-combatants' rather than
'innocents' when they are being precise; but the language of 'innocence' dominates the public discourse, and is a clear reference to
notions of just and unjust war even if technical versions of that
discourse have moved on.

2 UN (1949).

3 His focus in that earlier book was, as its title suggested, principally
on war. He remarks only in passing on terrorism more generally, in
the following terms: 'The systematic terrorizing of whole populations is a strategy of both conventional and guerilla war and of
established governments as well as radical movements. Its purpose
is to destroy the morale of a nation or class, undercut its solidarity;
its method is the random murder of innocent people' (Walzer 1977,
197). It is unclear to what extent that is intended as a definition
of terrorism, and to what extent it is intended as a set of empiri-
cal generalizations about how terrorists ordinarily conduct
themselves.

4 Walzer (2004, 136, 51).

5 Primary among them: Coady (1985, 53; 2001); Teichman (1989,
511); and Primoratz (1990, 134: 'terrorism is so very wrong primarily . . . because it is violence inflicted on the innocent'). Those with
a focus on violence more broadly include: Wellman (1979, 250);
Baier (1991); Held (1984, 606; 1991, 62–72); Quinton (1990);
indeed, 'violence' is part of what on some accounts represents the
'consensus' definition of 'terrorism' (Wilkinson 1990, 45–6; Schmid
and Jongman 1988).

6 US CIA (2003); US Department of State (2003). The FBI (1998)
employs the more general definition written into *Code of Federal*

Regulations, title 28, sec. 0.85: 'unlawful use of force and violence against persons or property to intimidate or coerce a government, the civilian population, or any segment thereof, in furtherance of political or social objectives.'

7   US Army (ca. 1993, 2).
8   Bush 2001a.
9   Kean and Hamilton (2004, xvi).
10 Elshtain (2003, 59, 20; see also e.g. pp. 10–11).
11 Chomsky (2002, 119–20).
12 UN (1997b, 2).
13 UN (1999, art. 2(1)(b)). A variation on this (substituting 'non-combatant' for the 'any other person' clause) is proposed as a matter of urgency by the UN Secretary-General's High-Level Panel (2005, para. 164).
14 UN Office on Drugs and Crime (2004), quoting a 1992 proposal by A. P. Schmid to the United Nations Crime Branch.
15 Elshtain (2003, 19).
16 I thus share the sentiment expressed by Primoratz (1990/2004, 22): 'Most of us feel that terrorism is so very wrong primarily, but not solely, because it is violence inflicted on the innocent; intimidation and coercion through intimidation are *additional* grounds for moral condemnation, an insult added to injury.'
17 *Hansard Parliamentary Debates (Lords)*, 14 Sept 2001, col. 22; quoted in Keohane (2003, 111).
18 Held (2004, 64) points out, and Coady (2001/2004, 10) accepts, this possibility, at least with respect to workers in the Pentagon.
19 Blunkett (2004, i); see similarly Card (2003, 178). For what it is worth, however, Osama bin Laden (2004) claims to have issued several since 1996, and US 9/11 Commission (2004, 47) explicitly describes his 1998 *fatwah* as 'a declaration of war'.
20 Again, bin Laden (1996; 2004) would beg to differ. In any case, if the US government succeeds in expanding just-war doctrine to permit 'pre-emptive' wars (Byers 2003), a clear intention on the part of the US to make war on bin Laden would justify his pre-emptively making war on them.
21 As Held (2004, 64) notes, defining terrorism in those just-war terms would have the counter-intuitive consequence of making terrorist murder of soldiers never count as 'terrorism'. However 'innocent', soldiers are never 'civilians'. But 'blowing up the US Marine barracks in Lebanon in 1983 and killing hundreds of marines, and blowing a hole in the US destroyer USS Cole . . . are routinely

described as examples of terrorism. Although we might say that such descriptions are simply wrong, I am inclined to think they are not.' Freedman (2005, 162) comments similarly that 'The IRA were not called terrorists only when they murdered 11 civilians at Enniskillen on Armistice Day 1987 but something else when they killed 18 soldiers at an ambush in Warren Point in 1979.'

22 Note that the Geneva Protocol II (UN 1977) extends the rules of war to 'non-international armed conflicts': i.e., to combatants regardless of whether they represent a state; and to 'armed conflict' rather than just war alone.

23 Franck and Lockwood (1974, 88–9) actually advocate that, 'if an organized terrorist movement directs and confines its use of force to officials of the government against which they are fighting . . . , members of that movement are entitled, if captured, to treatment analogous to that accorded to belligerents in a civil war, even by the opponent government (i.e., they may not be brought to trial or subjected to punishment other than humane detention).' Franck and Lockwood acknowledge that this clause 'is unlikely to appeal to states', but go on to observe that, 'if the officials of governments genuinely want terrorism confined to attacks on the terrorists' enemies, they must create differential treatment for those who do.' Cf. Gilbert (1990, 19–20); Coady (1985, 62); Teichman (1986, 67, 95).

24 I am grateful to David Rodin for discussion of these issues. He, like McMahon (2004, 708–18), thinks that the whole just-war tradition can and should be revised on this point.

25 Walzer (1977, 21).

26 French (2003, 42–3).

27 Nowadays, anyway, if not according to the earlier Church fathers; legally, anyway, if not necessarily morally. Cf. Walzer (1977, 299); Mapel (1998).

28 The League of Arab States' 1998 Convention for the Suppression of Terrorism, for example, stipulates that 'All cases of struggle by whatever means, including armed struggle against foreign occupation and aggression for liberation and self-determination, in accordance with the principles of international law, shall not be regarded as an offense' (Arab League 1998).

29 It has other costs, however, as I shall discuss below.

30 There is evidence in the fact that Protocol II to the Geneva Conventions (UN 1977) extends them, and the just-war thinking

embodied in them, to internal ('non-international') armed conflicts. It is unclear, however, whether this extends those rules to 'terrorism' rather than simply to 'internal war'. Article 1.2 says that 'This Protocol shall not apply to situations of internal disturbances and tensions, such as riots, isolated and sporadic acts of violence and other acts of a similar nature, as not being armed conflicts.' Article 2.1 goes on to say, 'Nothing in this Protocol shall be invoked for the purposes of affecting the sovereignty of a State or the responsibility of the government, by all legitimate means, to maintain or re-establish law and order in the State or to defend the national unity and territorial integrity of the State.'

31　Morally that might excuse but of course does not justify his fighting (Fullinwider 1975; cf. Mapel 1998, 177–80).

32　She is 'materially innocent' if not 'morally innocent' (Walzer 1977, 299–301). See similarly Townshend (2002, 7–8).

33　Nagel (1972); Fullinwider (1975; 2003); McMahon (1994); Elshtain (2003, 19). Cf. Zohar (2004).

34　Heymann (2003, 28), referring to the period circa 1981.

35　Habermas (2003, 34–5) is offended on precisely this point: 'I consider Bush's decision to call for a "war against terrorism" a serious mistake, both normatively and pragmatically. Normatively, he is elevating those criminals to the status of war enemies; and pragmatically, one cannot lead a war against a "network" if the term "war" is to retain any definite meaning.'

36　UN (1949).

37　Jenkins (1986, 779).

38　UN (1997a, art. 11); identical language appears in another UN Convention (1999, art. 14) and similar language in the EU Convention on the Suppression of Terrorism (1977, art. 1–2). This practice dates back to 1856 when, 'after an attempted assassination of Napoleon III, Belgium excluded the assassination of a head of state or member of his family from the category of a political offence and thereafter this exclusionary clause – known as the *attentat* or Belgian clause – was included in many extradition treaties' (Dugard 1974, 68; see also Anon. 1935; Franck and Lockwood 1974, 83–4). Similarly, extradition of anarchists was permitted on grounds that they were not the political opponents of any particular government but rather 'the enemy of all Governments' (*In re Meurnier* [1894] 2 Q.B. 415 at 419, quoted in Dugard 1974, 68). So too are war criminals extraditable, on grounds that 'a crime against humanity or the rules of war is of international concern and should not be protected because it happens to have a national political objective' (Fawcett 1958, 391; Dugard 1974, 78).

39 The equivalent language in the Arab League's Convention for the Suppression of Terrorism is clearer on this score: 'None of the terrorist offences indicated in the preceding article shall be regarded as a political offence. In the application of this Convention, none of the following offences shall be regarded as a political offence, even if committed for political motives' (1998, art. 2(b)).

40 Jenkins (1999, v). See similarly Gilbert (1994, chs 4, 11).

41 Jenkins (1986, 780).

42 Luban (2003, 51).

43 Tribe (2004, 235).

44 This discussion draws on Luban (2003); see similarly Jenkins (1999, xii). On the military orders establishing special military tribunals to try foreigners accused of terrorism, see Murphy (2002, 253–5); Fitzpatrick (2002); Anon. (2003).

45 That aspect of the UK Prevention of Terrorism Act attracted much negative comment in the heated House of Lords debate on its renewal (1–8 March 2005), available at: http://www.publications. parliament.uk/pa/ld199900/ldhansrd/pdvn/allddays.htm (accessed 30 March 2005).

46 In Luban's (2003) gloss on standard/traditional/unrevised versions of just-war theory – although, as I said at the outset, just-war casuistry is endlessly inventive and many refinements would doubtless be urged by revisionists (to do, perhaps most especially, with 'military necessity').

47 Note especially the prefatory note attached to the British 'Bill of Particulars' justifying joining the war on Afghanistan: 'This document does not purport to provide a prosecutable case against Usama Bin Laden in a court of law. Intelligence often cannot be used evidentially, due both to the strict rules of admissibility and to the need to protect the safety of sources. But on the basis of all the information available HMG is confident of its conclusions as expressed in this document' (UK 2002). See similarly Walzer (2004, 137–8). As long ago as 1985, a US Secretary of State had announced that the US might be compelled to resort to force 'before each and every fact is known or on evidence that would not stand up in an American court' (George Schultz, quoted in Jenkins 1986, 774).

48 Note that none of this is true of the 'humane treatment' required for prisoners of 'non-international armed conflicts' by Protocol II extending the Geneva Conventions to the sorts of cases that might involve domestic terrorism (UN 1977, art. 4–6).

49 Luban (2003). See further: Heymann (2003, ch. 2); Tribe (2004).

50 And, on some views, conditions of 'supreme emergency' might permit violation of the laws of war (Walzer 1977, ch. 16).

51 US Constitution, art. 1, sec. 9, cl. 2.

52 Ferejohn and Pasquino (2006). Ackerman (2004).

53 Dershowitz (2002, 6).

54 Tribe (2004, 233, 235; see further pp. 260–82). On the civil liberties costs, see Heymann (2003, ch. 5).

55 In an interview aired on NBC's 'Today Show' on 30 Aug 2004, subsequently subject to endless 'clarification' (Allen 2004).

56 Bush 2005b.

57 Heymann (2003, xii). He goes on to add, 'And we cannot allow such small and hostile groups to impose on us for decades the costs we would be prepared to bear for a few years to protect ourselves against the vast powers of an advanced foreign state' (p. xii and, more generally, ch. 2).

58 US 9/11 Commission (2004, 365; see similarly p. 383).

59 Borger (2005).

60 Blunkett (2004, i).

61 Elster (1990); Axelrod (1984).

62 Tribe (2004, 236). See further Karstedt (2003).

63 Dershowitz (2002, 11).

64 So the Law Lords held; see Clare Dyer, Michael White and Alan Travis, 'Judges condemn anti-terror laws', *Guardian Weekly*, 172 (24 Dec 2004–6 Jan 2005), p. 8. US lower courts held similarly, requiring arraignment of detainees in Camp X at Guantánamo Bay; see *Hamdi v. Rumsfeld*, 124 S. Ct. 2633 (2004).

65 A memo from the US Assistant Attorney-General to the White House Counsel acknowledges the violation of international law, incorporated into US domestic law by accession to the relevant Convention, but asserts that 'necessity', 'self-defence' or the president's powers as commander-in-chief particularly in time of war might render the violation nonetheless constitutional (Bybee 2002).

66 Luban (2003). This is clear in the US 'Military Order of November 13, 2001 on Detention, treatment and trial of certain non-citizens in the war against terrorism' (Anon. 2003).

Chapter 3   Terrorism as a Political Tactic

1   Quoted in Keohane (2003, 113).
2   Barber (2003, 76).
3   Netanyahu (1986, 204, 29–30).
4   US Army (ca. 1993). One might however compare this description of the terrorist mentality with that in evidence in President George W. Bush's 2002 State of the Union address describing a grab-bag of disparate countries as an 'axis of evil' and insisting that other countries are 'either with us or against us' in the war on terror (Bush 2002a).
5   US Army (ca. 1993); see further Townshend (2002, 54–60).
6   Walzer (2004, ch. 3). Likewise legally: constitutional lawyers appeal to 'necessity' to justify abrogating international treaties, relaxing constitutional restraints on executive power, and so on (Bybee 2002).
7   Gilbert (1994, 5).
8   In the gloss offered by Townshend (2002, 13). Note that one of the few organizations that explicitly accepted the term 'terrorist' – the Fighters for the Freedom of Israel (Lehi) – explicitly embraced the key elements of that philosophy (Shamir 1943; see further Townshend 2002, 89).
9   Under the influence of the Bakuninist wing of the Berne Congress in 1876; for a brief historical gloss, see McCormick (2003, 475–81).
10   The strategic thinking at the core of terrorism, and ways we might use that to manipulate terrorist behaviour, is nicely set out in McCormick (2003, 480–90) and Frey (2004).
11   Waldron (2004, 6). See similarly Freedman (2005).
12   US 9/11 Commission (2002, 362).
13   p. 775.
14   Title 22, US Code, sec. 2656f(d); quoted in US CIA (2003) and US Department of State (2003).
15   28 Code of Federal Regulations, sec. 0.85; quoted in US FBI (1998, 3).
16   UN (1994, I.3).
17   UN (1999, art. 2(1)(b)).
18   US Army (ca. 1993, 1).
19   Jenkins (1986, 779–80). As he explains, the RAND Corporation insistently defines 'terrorism . . . objectively . . . , by the quality of the act, . . . not by the identity of the perpetrators or the nature of

their cause'. Listing the many features characteristically associated with terrorist acts, Jenkins says: they 'involve violence or the threat of violence, sometimes coupled with explicit demands. The violence is usually directed against noncombatants. The purposes are political. The actions are often carried out in a way that will achieve maximum publicity. The perpetrators are usually members of an organized group. Their organizations are by necessity clandestine, but . . . often claim credit for their acts.' See further Jenkins (1981b).

20 Dumas (2003, 67); this, Dumas goes on to emphasize, is a 'conceptual definition of terrorism as a tactic', which 'has nothing to do with the ultimate goals of those who choose this tactic' (see similarly Thornton 1964; Gilbert 1994, ch. 4). For a more long-winded version, here is what Schmid and Jongman (1988, 28) offer as the 'academic consensus definition': 'Terrorism is an anxiety-inspiring method of repeated violent action, employed by (semi-) clandestine individual, group or state actors, for idiosyncratic, criminal or political reasons, whereby – in contrast to assassination – the direct targets of violence are not the main targets. The immediate human victims of violence are generally chosen randomly (targets of opportunity) or selectively (representative or symbolic targets) from a target population, and serve as message generators. Threat- and violence-based communication processes between terrorist (organization), (imperiled) victims, and main targets are used to manipulate the main target (audience(s)), turning it into a target of terror, a target of demands, or a target of attention, depending on whether intimidation, coercion, or propaganda is primarily sought.' The latter definition is quoted approvingly by the UN Office on Drugs and Crime (2004).

21 Coady (1985, 53). See similarly: Schmid and Jongman (1988, 19); Wellmer (1984, 285–93); Freedman (2005, 168).

22 As Held (1991, 62) rightly replies to Coady (1985, 53).

23 Elliott (2002).

24 Olson (1993).

25 Bakunin (1873/1975, 333).

26 See for example his 'Revolutionary catechism' (Bakunin 1866); see further Ignatieff (2004, ch. 5).

27 Camus (1953, 137).

28 Gilbert (2003).

29 Lesser (1999, 111, 109).

30 Habermas (2003).

31 Lesser (1999, 101).
32 Jenkins (2003, 2).
33 Townshend (2002, 113), who continues: 'With such violence we reach what may be seen either as the purest, or the most absurd, reduction of terrorism to symbolic gesture.'
34 Metraux (1995, 1553–4) reports that Aum is widely seen as such a blatantly political movement that it 'has forced many Japanese to question the effectiveness of the 1951 Religious Corporation Law, which provides designated religions with various privileges.'
35 Ibid.
36 Rapoport (1984, 660, 663; emphasis added).
37 Bin Laden 1996; his declaration of jihad issued on 12 October 1996 was reiterated in his *fatwah* of February 1998. See further: US 9/11 Commission (2004, 47 ff.); UK (2002, para. 22); Murphy (2002, 239–40).
38 Townshend (2002, 111). For the text of the *fatwah*, see Bin Laden (1996); but better insight into his thinking perhaps comes from Parekh's (2004) fictionalized exchange between bin Laden and Gandhi.
39 US Army (ca. 1993).
40 Townshend (2002, 107).
41 Habermas (2003).
42 See more generally Rapoport (1988). As Coady (2004, 41) says, in advocating inclusion of 'for political purposes' in his own definition of 'terrorism', 'When religion or ideology employs violent means to undermine, reconstitute or maintain political structures for the further transcendent ends of the religion or ideology, then that counts as "political purposes". War is a paradigm political activity . . . and it would be strange to say that the medieval Crusaders, for example, were not involved in politics when they invaded the Holy Lands.'
43 Anthony (2004, 15).
44 Teichman (1989, 511). That was her first thought; her second thought, wrong in my view, was that the association between terror and terrorism should be seen as merely a very strong contingent one.
45 In post-9/11 demonizing of al-Qaeda, it was sometimes said that that group has no further aims or goals beyond simply killing as many Americans as it can. That is untrue, in ways I have already discussed in chapter 2. But it is particularly untrue to say that

al-Qaeda did not intend its attacks to induce fear. Just hear bin Laden's (2004) words addressed to Americans on the eve of the US presidential election: 'No one except a dumb thief plays with the security of others and then makes himself believe he will be secure. Whereas thinking people, when disaster strikes, make it their priority to look for its causes, in order to prevent it happening again. . . . Your security is in your own hands. And every state that doesn't play with our security has automatically guaranteed its own security.'

46 In these discussions, I persist in the colloquial practice of equating 'terror' with 'chronic fear', although I take the point that this colloquial usage varies from psychologists' technical one. 'In psychiatry terror is an extreme form of anxiety, often accompanied by aggression, denial, constricted affect, and followed by frightening imagery and intrusive, repetitive recollection' (Schmid and Jongman 1988, 19, quoting F. Ochberg). That is not the psychological state that terrorists typically strive to produce: they want the citizenry and the government to respond in a rational way, giving them what they desire after sober reflection on the increasing costs that the terrorists will impose if they do not; and it would be counter-productive of a terrorist's socio-political ends 'to produce such generalized gibbering terror in the hearts of . . . her target population that their normal activities ground to a halt' (Baier 1991, 36; cf. Wellman 1979, 255).

47 Quoted in Weinberger (2003, 66). See also: www.terrorismfiles. org/encyclopedia/terrorism.htlm (accessed 18 Jan 2005).

48 League of Nations (1937).

49 UK (1974, pt. III, sec. 9(1)). A more expansive version appears in the Terrorism Act 2000:

(1) In this Act 'terrorism' means the use or threat of action where –
  (a) the action falls within subsection (2),
  (b) the use or threat is designed to influence the government or to intimidate the public or a section of the public, and
  (c) the use or threat is made for the purpose of advancing a political, religious or ideological cause.
(2) Action falls within this subsection if it –
  (a) involves serious violence against a person,
  (b) involves serious damage to property,

(c)   endangers a person's life, other than that of the person committing the action,

(d)   creates a serious risk to the health or safety of the public or a section of the public, or

(e)   is designed seriously to interfere with or seriously to disrupt an electronic system. (UK 2000, 1)

50   Jenkins (1986, 779–80). See further Jenkins (1981b).

51   Among philosophers, note, e.g., Wellman's (1979, 252) remark that 'terrorism and coercion are inextricably linked as means and end. . . . Just as coercion is the essential end of terrorism, so terror is its essential means.' See similarly: Held (1984, 606; 1991, 62–5); Quinton (1990, 35–43); Baier (1991); cf. Coady (1985, 53; 2001); Teichman (1989, 511); Primoratz (1990, 134). The emphasis is standard among those specializing in the study of terrorism. Wardlaw (1982, 16), for example, offers the following definition: 'political terrorism is the use, or threat of use, of violence by an individual or a group, whether acting for or in opposition to established authority, when such action is designed to create extreme anxiety and/or far-inducing effects in a target group larger than the immediate vicitims with the purpose of coercing that group into acceding to the political demands of the perpetrators.' See similarly Wilkinson (1990, 45–6); Schmid and Jongman (1988).

52   Cf. Teichman, quoted in Primoratz (1990/2004, 21).

53   Although, even in that Convention, this clause is second behind the primary terrorist offences, defined in terms of 'the intent to cause death or serious bodily injury'; UN (1997a, art. 2, clauses 1(b) and 1(a) respectively).

54   UN (1999, art. 2, clause 1); EU (1977, art. 2, clause 2).

55   Franck and Lockwood (1974, 76).

56   Walzer (1988, 238; 2004, 51).

Chapter 4   States Can Be Terrorists, Too

1   And before: writing in 1990, Primoratz (1990/2004, 22) observed, 'Terrorism is often presented as a method employed solely by rebels and revolutionaries, and state terrorism is thus defined out of existence. This may be good propaganda, but it is poor analysis.'

2   Bush (2001a, 2).

3   Maybe non-state actors cannot even logically engage in war: recall Habermas (2003) saying that 'one cannot lead a war against a

"network" if the term "war" is to retain any definite meaning.' Or again, Thornton (1964) distinguishes 'terrorism' from even 'internal "guerilla" war': for him, the defining feature of 'war' is that it is 'instrumental'; 'guerilla war' meets that condition; and Thornton thinks terrorism is 'symbolic' in its orientation, instead.

4 One commentator observes: 'In the state's view, only the state has the right to use force – it has, as academics tend to say, a monopoly on the legitimate use of violence' (Townshend 2002, 5). Another observes that, from a just-war perspective, 'the gravest charge against terrorists is that they wage war without *proper authority*. . . . [That] is necessary . . . for something properly to count as war, for a distinction needs to be drawn between private killing . . . which ordinarily counts as murder, and public killing such as takes place in war, which ordinarily does not so count. Authority [in just-war theory] . . . derives from a sovereign who administers the law. Resort to private killing in a settlement of disputes is disallowed since such matters are to be judged by the sovereign' (Gilbert 1994, 28).

5 Might there be, for example, some problem – maybe moral, maybe logical – in a state 'declaring war' on non-state actors such as terrorists? A 'state of war' is fundamentally a relational notion, implying 'between X and Y'. If such non-state actors are not the sorts of actors that are entitled to conduct war, is it fair/reasonable/just (is it even logically coherent) to name them as respondents in a cause they are not entitled to defend? Apropos the 9/11 attackers, one response might be that they declared war on the US through their actions; they are capable of waging *de facto* war, even if they are not *de jure* (morally or legally) entitled to do so. So, in declaring war on them, the US was merely acknowledging that a 'state of war' already existed between the US and al-Qaeda. But that does not solve the problem sketched above as to how the US might morally (or perhaps even logically) initiate a state of war against terrorist groups that have not yet initiated war against it.

6 p. 775; quoted in Weinberger (2003, 66).

7 Hare (1979); Young (2004); French (2003); Freedman (2005, 170).

8 Doubtless another reason is the desire of states to promulgate 'persuasive definitions' of terrorism, tarring their opponents but not themselves with that odious label – more of which below.

9 Gurr (1986, 53).

10 Aristotle, *Politics*, 1313–1314a; quoted in Walzer (2004, 64). Montesquieu, *Spirit of the Laws*, III.ix; quoted in Kelly (1980, 19).

11 *US Code*, title 22, sec. 2656f(d); quoted in US CIA (2003) and US Department of State (2001; 2003). This definition invariably appears in the preliminaries of the annual report that the State Department is required to deliver to Congress on *Patterns of Global Terrorism*.

12 Per Article 15 of the 1958 Geneva Convention on the High Seas, codifying customary international law on this point (emphasis added).

13 Henkin et al. (1987, § 522, Comment b and Reporter's Note 2).

14 See, e.g., Arendt (1970, 45–8) and Lomasky (1991).

15 Townshend (2002, 45).

16 Walzer (1977, 197).

17 Here is another deeply cynical example of the sort that abounds in international conventions. The Arab League's Convention for the Suppression of Terrorism specifies that 'All cases of struggle by whatever means, including armed struggle, against foreign occupation and aggression for liberation and self-determination, in accordance with the principles of international law, shall not be regarded as an offence' of terrorism. But the Convention then goes on to add, 'This provision shall not apply to any act prejudicing the territorial integrity of any Arab State' (1998, art. 2(a)).

18 US FBI (1998, 3), quoting *Code of Federal Regulations*, title 28, sec. 0.85.

19 This leaves open the possibility that public officials who exceed their legitimate authority when performing such acts could count as terrorists, which is more than the CIA/State Department definition admits: note, however, that a still-classified National Security Decision Directive signed by President Reagan on 13 November 1984, 'reportedly [grants] a *carte blanche* exemption from US legal proceedings for operatives engaged in anti-terrorist activities outside the US that otherwise would be punishable under US law' so long as the actions were 'taken "in good faith"' (CDI 2002).

20 The Prevention of Terrorism Act of 1974, updated periodically since but not essentially changed on this score, defined 'terrorism' as 'the use of violence for political ends including the use of violence for the purpose of putting the public or any section of the public in fear' (UK 1974). Public officials would presumably claim exemption on grounds that any violence used pursuant to their official duties was not 'for political ends'.

21 Henkin et al. (1987, § 522, Reporter's Note 2); Freedman (2005, 161).

22 UN (1997a).

23 In resisting the suggestion that 'any definition [of terrorism] should include States' use of armed forces against civilians', the UN Secretary-General's High-Level Panel (2005, para. 160) makes precisely this point: 'We believe that the legal and normative framework against State violations is far stronger than in the case of non-State actors.'

24 Townshend (2002, 47).

25 Insofar as they were all aimed at discrete targets rather than inculcating a diffuse sense of fear, they would be non-paradigmatic cases from my own point of view.

26 Franck and Lockwood (1974, 73–4, n. 27).

27 Ibid.

28 Ibid.

29 UN Secretary-General (1987).

30 Townshend (2002, 6).

31 Jones (2005).

32 Alperovitz (2002, 13).

33 'Modern terrorists', Jenkins (1986, 776) goes on to say, merely 'extended this concept'.

34 Townshend (2002, 6). See further Walzer (1977); Lackey (2004).

35 Walzer (2004, 130). See similarly: Primoratz (1997, 222); Townshend (2002, 6).

36 William D. Leahy, quoted in Alperovitz (1995, 627).

37 This objection is put by Teichman (1989, 511), who insists that 'terrorism is not only terror-producing behaviour. If it were, almost all warfare would be terrorism, and so would a lot of other human activities. . . . Our definitions must include the idea that causing terror is the usual feature even if not an invariable feature of central, or core cases.' Coady (1985, 53) similarly objects to that sort of definition, on the grounds that 'the fear effect [is] . . . associated with all uses of political violence, including open warfare where civilian populations are involved though not attacked directly'; 'it would surely be counterintuitive to see all or most military engagements as terrorist' (Coady 2001/2004, 9); 'whatever verdict we give on war, it is surely just confusing to equate all forms of it, including resistance to Adolf Hitler, with terrorism' (Coady 2004, 38).

38 This is an option that Coady (2001/2004, 9) passes over curiously briskly.

39 For one famous example, Ivan Kaliayev refused to throw his bomb at Grand Duke Sergei when he realized that the latter's family was in the carriage with him; he succeeded in killing him in a subsequent attempt (Townshend 2002, 58).

40 *Pace* realists following Clausewitz (1989, 87), for whom 'war is . . . a political instrument, a continuation of political intercourse, carried on with other means' and which always 'involves the employment of lethal force for a political end'.

41 Glover (1991). So too, perhaps, were the US air strikes on Iraq before the 2003 invasion, depending on whether 'Shock and Awe' was principally intended to be instilled in the Iraqi military or in the Iraqi populace at large.

42 Keeny and Panofsky (1981–2); Lackey (2004).

43 Quinton (1990, 41–3); Gilbert (1994, chs 9–10).

44 The Revolution itself was, in part, against the 'terrorism' involved in the arbitrary rule of the *ancien régime*: what was 'originally understood as the Terror' was 'the *lettre de cachet*, not the *glaive de la loi*' (Kelly 1980, 29).

45 'France: the reign of terror', in *Encylopedia Britannica* (1999).

46 Walzer (2004, 130). See similarly Townshend (2002, 46–8).

47 See further: Solzhenitsyn (1974–5); Conquest (1968).

48 Shawcross (1987).

49 President Videla defined a 'subversive' as 'anyone who opposes the Argentine way of life' and promised to 'combat, without respite, subversive delinquency in all of its forms until its total annihilation' (quoted in Pion-Berlin and Lopez 1991, 71). Perhaps as many as 20,000 were killed (Townshend 2002, 47). See also Timerman (1981); Feldman (1997).

50 NKVD (1983), quoted in Schmid and Jongman (1988, 11, 24). They add, 'The authenticity of this document, which reached the West in the early 1950s, has not been fully established; however, even if the NKVD was not the originator, it provides profound insights into Communist practices' (p. 209). See, e.g., Trotsky (1931/2004).

51 As the Soviet NKVD (1983), quoted in Schmid and Jongman (1988, 24), observes, 'This goal [of "enlightened terror"] can be attained if one repeats the same action constantly and systematically. But naturally such a method – the repetition of the action – is uneconomical.'

52 Ryan (1991).

53 Mason and Krane (1989, 175). If repressive violence is thus bound to backfire, eventually, then why do governments engage in it?

Mason and Krane's answer is simply that these regimes have no choice: they lack 'the institutional machinery, economic resources or political will to address opposition challenges through more accommodative programs of reform' (ibid.).

54 Laws, Hobbes (1651, ch. 16) says, are ineffectual 'without the terror of some power, to cause them to be observed . . .'

55 As Sinnott-Armstrong (1999) objects to a similar definition (Primoratz 1990).

56 See, e.g., Pontara (1978, 22).

57 Perhaps that is merely to say that we need to incorporate a few additional just-war style considerations into our domestic analogue, at this point, in ways that will be suggested below.

58 *US Code*, title 22, sec. 2656f(a). This report is published annually as *Patterns of Global Terrorism* (e.g., US Department of State 2001).

59 US Department of State (2003, 85).

60 Townshend (2002, 130–1); US Department of State (1986).

61 Bush (2002a).

62 US Department of State (2003, 85).

63 Ibid., p. 86.

64 Bush (2001a, 2).

65 Bush, quoted in Murphy (2002, 246).

66 Bush (2001b, 2).

67 UN (1970, 1).

68 UN (1994, art. II.4).

69 Feldman (1997).

70 UN (1997a, art. 2, clause 3). See similarly EU (1977, art. 1 (f) and 2 (3)).

Chapter 5 Warnings Can Be Terroristic, Too

1 For at least many, if not absolutely all, of the politicians participating in them. See Allen (1957); Hofstadter (1965); Ignatieff (2004, ch. 3).

2 Nozick (1972, 120–7). On terrorist 'offers' see O'Neill (1990).

3 Or what Nozick (1972) calls a 'non-threatening warning'.

4 A 'culpable omission' (failing to do something one could and should have done) counts as a 'doing' for these purposes.

5 Ball (1981).

6 That is how a 'threat' is distinguished from an 'offer', for example: a threat expresses a conditional intention to do something that

would make the person threatened worse off, whereas an offer
expresses a conditional intention to do something that would make
the person being made the offer better off (Nozick 1972).

7 Either for deontological reasons (because it is wrong to form a
conditional intention to do something it would be wrong to do) or
for consequentialist ones (because so intending increases the risk
that the wrong will actually be done). The wrongness of 'conditional
intentions to do something that would be wrong' was much discussed in connection with nuclear deterrence: the issue there was
whether, if it is wrong to use nuclear weapons, it is also wrong to
threaten to use them (McMahan 1985).

8 Notice that this is phrased in terms of 'intentions' rather than
'effects': the warning might have other effects (perhaps even securing the person issuing it a £100,000 reward); this condition is met,
however, so long as 'averting the harm' is the 'sole reason for which
the person acted' (or 'the sole description under which he chose
that action'), even if the person also clearly foresaw those other
effects. This is the 'double effect' doctrine that figures so largely in
just-war doctrine, for example.

9 I am not in general particularly enamoured of moral theories that
turn fundamentally on people's intentions and motives, but even in
a fundamentally consequentialist moral theory motives and intentions will have at least a derivative role to play. Disentangling mixed
motives can sometimes pose insurmountable problems, however
(Goodin 1995, ch. 3).

10 Being members of IRA and UVF cells, respectively, they may well
have done just that on other occasions and be properly described
as 'terrorists' by virtue of those other acts. Or, insofar as joining
terrorist groups and swelling their membership is an act intended
to instil fear in people for political advantage, their sheer membership in those groups might make them 'terrorists'. My present discussion brackets all that, however, and focuses narrowly upon the
act of their warning of this particular bomb that they have discovered in the rubbish.

11 Of course, membership of a terrorist association – the sheer act of
joining, or the support one's membership gives to those actually
detonating bombs – might itself count as a terrorist act. If so,
that is just *another* moral offence to add to the catalogue. Note that
it can plausibly be analysed in the terms I propose: the more
members a frightening organization has, the more frightening it
is; so the sheer act of joining the IRA can be seen as an act

intentionally instilling fear in people for one's own political advantage.

12   This is not the complete parody it may seem: something like it is the view underlying the dominant Schumpeterian view of party competition in contemporary political science (Schumpeter 1950; cf. Wittman 1983).

13   The primary *OED* definition of 'alarmist' is 'one ... who raises alarm on very slight grounds, or needlessly'. But after that comes a semicolon, followed by the words, 'a panic-monger', which the *OED* defines as 'one who endeavours to bring about or foster a panic, esp. on a political, social or financial question' (with no mention of the panic in question being 'needless' or 'on slight grounds'). Similarly, note that the *OED* ends the definition of 'terrorist' quoted in the text above by equating that with 'an alarmist, a scaremonger'; and, while the primary definition of 'alarmist' carries that implication of the alarm being groundless, the definition of 'scaremonger' does not. It refers merely to 'one who occupies himself in spreading alarming reports' (again, with no mention of those reports being groundless or the alarm needless).

14   That is to say, some serious moral offence other than, and in addition to, the moral offence associated with the sheer fact of 'acting with the intention of instilling fear in people for one's own political advantage'.

15   As per Walzer (1988, 238; 2004, 52).

16   I am indebted to Adrian Walsh for a version of this suggestion.

17   Waldron (2004, 11) remarks that 'the coercer demonstrat[ing] the threat by actually imposing harms of the kind that he is threatening' is a feature that 'is present in most terrorist situations'. But 'most' is not 'all', thus denying any analytic necessity. Waldron is thus prepared to contemplate, as an atypical instance, a case in which no harm is imposed (beyond the issuing of a threat).

18   UK (1974).

19   Title 22, *US Code*, sec. 2656f(d); quoted in US CIA (2003) and US Department of State (2001).

20   *Code of Federal Regulations*, title 28, sec. 0.85; as quoted in US FBI (1998, 3).

21   Indeed, 'violence' is part of what on some accounts represents the 'consensus' definition of 'terrorism' (Schmid and Jongman 1988, 28). See similarly: Wellman (1979, 250); Baier (1991); Held (1984, 606; 1991, 62–72); Quinton (1990, 35–43); Pontara (1985, 20). Cf.

Wardlaw (1982, 16); Alperovitz (2003, 12–13); Primoratz (1990, 134).

22 The closest the OED gets is when it defines a 'terrorist' as 'any one who attempts to further his views by a system of *coercive* intimidation'.

23 Coady (1985, 53) is firm on this point; Teichman (1989, 511) ends up conceding this, as well.

24 One example that has been offered is of a terrorist blackmailer who pursues his political objectives through a threat to reveal facts about a political leader that the leader is genuinely frightened of having made public. However morally odious that threat may be, Wellman (1979, 251) thinks that it can hardly count as a threat of 'violence'. I am not so sure: one can surely 'do violence to someone's reputation', and perhaps more than merely metaphorically.

25 Galtung (1969); Pontara (1978); Honderich (1989, 2003a, 2003b); Keane (2004).

26 Cf. Wellman (1979, 251), discussed in a previous note.

27 For which I am grateful to Chuck Beitz.

Chapter 6   Warnings Bound to Be Misheard

1 Ignatieff (2004, 54).

2 US 9/11 Commission (2004, 311).

3 'Innocent' in the sense of not members of paramilitary organizations, killed between 1969 and 1986; see Curran and Miller (2001, 74).

4 Townshend (2002, 75).

5 Fischhoff (2002, 58). Of course, it is not as if each American were literally equally likely as each other to be a terrorist victim, so we have to forgive Fischhoff some slight hyperbole here.

6 US Census (2005, 80, Table 103) reports there were 20,308 homicides in the US in 2001, of which 2973 were attributable to those attacks.

7 In the last years for which this statistic was reported in the *US Statistical Abstract*, it hovered around 700 per year (US Census 2001, 86, Table 114). US 9/11 Commission (2004, ch. 1) reports 246 people (not counting the hijackers themselves) aboard the four flights that crashed that day.

8 US Census (2005, 80, Table 114) reports that 8,303 people died in workplace accidents (not including the 9/11 attacks, which are

coded as homicides). Of course some of the homicides and suicides also occurred 'at work'; adding all of those into the denominator would reduce the percentage reported in the text.

9 These calculations are based on the sources as above, together with the 2001 US population estimate of 285,321,000 (US Census 2005, 7, Table 2).

10 US Census (2005, 80, Table 103).

11 Blair (2005a).

12 US Census (2005, 79, Table 102).

13 Ibid., 83, Table 106.

14 US OTA (1993a); reprinted in O'Hanlon et al. (2002, 6).

15 The magnitude of 'possible fatalities' in US OTA's 1993 table, at least, seems stable, judging from the similar estimates offered by the UN Secretary-General's High-Level Panel (2005, paras 107–16).

16 Although there is a well-known psychological mechanism, the 'representativeness bias', that leads people to draw unwarranted inferences from small samples – a phenomenon Kahneman and Tversky aptly describe as 'belief in the law of small numbers' (in Kahneman et al. 1982, ch. 2; see chs 1–6 more generally).

17 US Department of Homeland Security (2005; emphasis added). Implicitly, those attacks are supposed to be 'imminent'. Of course the risk of a terrorist attack *sometime* in the future (tomorrow, next month, next year, next decade, next century) has to be high, indeed, virtually certain; if that is all the warning conveyed, it would be meaningless.

18 As Habermas (2003, 29) observes, 'In Israel people at least know what can happen to them if they take a bus, go into a department store, discotheque, or any open area – and how frequently it happens. In the USA or Europe [post-9/11] one cannot circumscribe the risk; there is no realistic way to estimate the type, magnitude or probability of the risk, nor any way to narrow down the potentially affected regions.'

19 As Frey (2004, 127) reports, they were in an earlier period, ca. 1989 – when he notes that people's perceptions of the risk were all the more exaggerated ('fully 14 percent of Americans believed that, when flying, they were likely to be skyjacked or blown up by a bomb smuggled onto a plane by terrorists').

20 US Census (2005, 678, Table 1054); the exact number was 10,840,000 in 2003, which is the latest year for which those statistics are reported.

21 Brennan (2003). As Gambetta (2004) says, 'almost all the scary cases "uncovered" since 9/11 – and widely discussed by politicians and the press – have turned out to be false alarms', leading him to conclude that '9/11 is a wild outlier among terrorist acts' and its 'perpetrators themselves seem to be far out on the spectrum of dangerous individuals. While there is no dearth of suicide-mission volunteers, very few people share Mohamed Atta's traits: highly skilled, methodically inclined, and ready to die . . . The lucidity and composure required by an organizer stand in contrast with the trance-like state needed to go on a suicide mission.'

22 Huddy et al. (2003, 265).

23 Jenkins (2003, 1).

24 Tribe (2004, 260).

25 Giddens (2005b, col. 150), glossing arguments he had elaborated in an article published a couple of months earlier (Giddens 2005a).

26 On the eve of the Queen's Speech announcing the Blair Government's new anti-terrorism measures, unidentified sources told the *Daily Mail* that British security services had thwarted plots for September 11-style terror attacks on Canary Wharf (Anon. 2004a). But the Leader of the House of Commons denied the report, saying, 'If there was a specific threat to Canary Wharf or anywhere else, we would have said so. . . . That leak, if it was a leak, did not come from a government minister or as far as I know a government source' (Grice 2004). Whom to believe here is anyone's guess.

27 Furthermore, 'only three of those cases relate to allegations of Islamic extremism. The other convictions involved Irish paramilitaries – both republican and loyalist – a Sikh extremist group and the Tamil Tigers' (Dodd et al. 2005).

28 Bush (2005a).

29 Eggen and Tate (2005) add, 'Most of the others were convicted of relatively minor crimes such as making false statements and violating immigration law – and had nothing to do with terrorism.'

30 For summaries of recent work, see Kahneman's Nobel Lecture (2003) and Pidgeon et al. (2003).

31 Breyer (1993, 35).

32 Goodin (1995, ch. 8).

33 Slovic et al. (1980/1982, 468–70).

34 Starr (1969).

35 That would be a subspecies of 'ambiguity aversion' (Ellsberg 1961), which experimental evidence suggests is quite common (Luce 2000).

36 Tversky and Kahneman (1974); Gilovich et al. (2002); Slovic et al. (2002); Kuran and Sunstein (1999); Sunstein (2005b, chs 3–4).

37 Slovic et al. (1980/1982, 265–7); Fischhoff et al. (1981, 29); Pidgeon et al. (2003).

38 Monbiot (2004).

39 Being struck by lightning or savaged by your pet are pretty dramatic too, in their own ways. But the 'availability' mechanism works, psychologists suggest, by there being an instance that is readily called to mind. How many movies have you seen involving the heroine being killed by a lightning strike or a domestic pet?

40 Sunstein (2003, 121).

41 They were willing to pay, on average, $14.12 versus $12.03 (Johnson et al. 1993). Clearly, one or the other of those would rationally have to be revised. But the design of the experiment does not allow us to determine whether, having had the discrepancy pointed out to them, subjects would increase the amount they are willing to pay for the more inclusive ('any reason') policy or decrease the amount they would be willing to pay for the less inclusive ('terrorism') one.

42 Rowntree and Land (1996).

43 Howard (2005).

44 Tribe's (2004, 227) description is most evocative: 'In the weeks following the tragic events of September 11, 2001, more than a few otherwise sober, thoughtful people became accustomed to saying in one form or another: "This changes everything. Nothing will ever be the same again".... September 11 was this generation's Pearl Harbor. But it was worse, because it was magnified, amplified, repackaged and reproduced through the most potent channels of our modern media. The bone-chilling images of jets crashing into the two great towers have been burned into our memory – seared into our senses along with the feeling of abject terror and utter helplessness that overtook nearly all who watched that day's horror unfold. And the conspicuous ease with which the terrorists used crude, low-technology box-cutters to bring down an unmistakable symbol of Western influence and prosperity revealed a haunting, asymmetrical inversion of power that no one can soon forget.'

45 Gaddis (2001); Kaplan (2003).

46 Heymann (2003, 38).

47 Gaddis (2001, 10). Benjamin Barber (2004, 75) remarks similarly, 'The diabolical intelligence behind the World Trade Center and Pentagon attacks was evident not so much in the crude but demonically imaginative use of passenger planes as firebombs but in the ensuing manipulation of fear that closed down the air transportation system and the stock markets.'

48 Bush (2001c). Before Bush's adoption of it as a theme, of course, 'homeland security' was a term already politically in the air. The US National Commission on National Security, chaired by former Senators Gary Hart and Warren Rudman, had warned in its January 2001 report that 'the combination of unconventional weapons proliferation with the persistence of international terrorism will end the relative invulnerability of the US homeland to catastrophic attack. A direct attack against American citizens on American soil is likely over the next quarter century'; and it recommended that 'security of the American homeland [from terrorism] should be the primary national security mission of the US government' (quoted in Jamieson and Waldman 2003, 163; see further Kaplan 2003).

49 Kahneman et al. (1982, pt 5); Sunstein (2003, 121–2).

50 Sunstein (2003, 122).

51 Tversky and Kahneman (1974); Kahneman et al. (1982, pt 2).

52 Griffith (1949); Rosenkrantz (1981, 2.3–5).

53 Preston and Baratta (1948). Although psychologists studying these data interpret them as evidence of subjective misperception of low probabilities, economists prefer to try to rationalize them in terms of risk-preferences (particularly the preference of people with low capital to take low-probability, high-payoff gambles) (Ali 1977).

54 Of course, racetrack betting involves prospects of gains whereas terrorist attacks involve prospects of losing; but if 'prospect theory' is true, people will be even more oversensitive to prospects of losses than of gains (Kahneman and Tversky 1979; see more generally Kahneman and Tversky 2000).

55 Jeffrey Simon, quoted in Townshend (2002, 117).

56 Because it had generally been seen to be ineffective, and also because of 'the need to bring the banned leaders back into the political "peace process"' (Townshend 2002, 138).

57 'Publicity may be the oxygen of terrorists', *Washington Post* publisher Katherine Graham (1986, 25) says, 'But . . . news is the life-blood of liberty.'

58 Ibid., pp. 24–5.

59　A BBC journalist reported as far back as 1985 a widespread feeling (from which he disassociated himself) that 'keeping a sense of proportion in the face of terrorist atrocity may seem a counsel of appeasement. What moral constraint, after all, binds the terrorist?' (David Jessel, quoted in Townshend 2002, 116–17).

60　The print media equivalent of the television news rule, 'if it bleeds it leads', has long been observed (Gans 1980, 155–7).

61　Slovic et al. (1980/1982, 468), discussing Coombs and Slovic (1979).

62　Bruchner (1973).

63　Behr and Iyengar (1985); Iyengar and Kinder (1987).

64　Gans (1980, 151).

65　Jenkins (1981a, 2).

66　Delli Carpini and Williams (1987, 57, 59). See similarly: Gans (1980); Jenkins (1980); Weimann and Winn (1994, 131); Kern et al. (2003, 288–90).

67　Ibid., pp. 290–1.

68　And not vice versa: 'in a series of two-stage-least-squares analysis . . . , TV viewing had considerable impact on fear, but fear had no significant impact on TV viewing. Our cautious conclusion based on these analyses is that TV viewing elevates perceptions of risk and fear and anxiety' (Huddy et al. 2003, 264).

69　Ibid., p. 273.

70　Wardlaw (1982, ch. 9); Nacos (2002).

71　Cynically, one might suppose that 'the scenarios of biological or chemical warfare painted in detail by the American media during the months after September 11, the speculations over the various kinds of nuclear terrorism, only betray the inability of the government to at least determine the magnitude of the danger' (Habermas 2003, 29). After all, the destruction threatened by 'weapons of mass destruction' is massive: and if the potential cost is truly massive, then it does not really matter exactly how probable it might be; we ought take all possible precautions against it, just the same. Still, orders of magnitude *should* matter.

72　Ashcroft (2001, 4).

73　Bush (2002b, 1).

74　Thornton (1964, 81); Blair and Brewer (1977, 392); Jenkins (1985); Stern (1999, 78–80).

75　Stern (1999, 71–2).

76　Kellman (2000, 435). See similarly Dershowitz (2002, 181–6). Many commentators point in this regard to the May 2003 treatise by Saudi cleric Shaykh Nasir bin Hamid al-Fahd, 'Treatise on the legal Status of Using Weapons of Mass Destruction Against Infidels' (May 2005, 6).

77 Ibid.
78 US OTA (1993b); Stern (1999, ch. 4).
79 Rosenbaum (1977); Blair and Brewer (1977).
80 Stern (1999, ch. 6); Allison (2004); Etzioni (2004). There was plenty of enriched uranium floating around even before that: Gambetta (2004) tells of a botched 1998 attempt to entrap eleven Italian Mafiosi who were attempting to sell eight cylinders of enriched uranium given by the US to the Congo as nuclear fuel, which disappeared from Kinshasa during the 1997 downfall of the Mobutu regime; one of the cylinders was seized, but the other seven are still in circulation.
81 Stern (1999, 40).
82 US OTA (1993b, 9).
83 Stern (1999, 41); 'the deliberate creation of an infectious aerosol' is one suggestion, although it is unclear how that proposal articulates with ebola's instability in air.
84 Ibid., p. 48.
85 US OTA (1993b, 3–6).
86 Ibid., pp. 6–7, reports: 'Synthesis of nerve agents, however, includes some difficult . . . steps involving highly corrosive or reactive materials. A sophisticated production facility to make militarily significant quantities of one class of nerve agents might cost between $30 and $50 million, although dispensing with modern waste-handling facilities might cut the cost in half.' While pesticide plants could in principle be converted for the production of nerve gas, that would take 'weeks or months'.
87 Ibid., p. 8.
88 Heymann (2003, 24). To adapt a recommendation by US OTA (1993b, 1): 'Those steps [in the production of nuclear, chemical and biological weapons] that are particularly time-consuming or difficult for proliferants to master without outside assistance can be exploited to control proliferation.'
89 Lugar (2005). Etzioni (2004) elaborates how this might be expanded with particular reference to highly enriched uranium, which he reasonably regards as the greatest terrorist threat. See more generally Allison (2004).
90 Bush (2002b, 2).

91 Ibid., p. 3. The *Washington Times* (31 Jan 2003) reported that the classified version of this document read 'including potentially nuclear weapons' (www.fas.org/irp/offdocs/nspd/nspd-17.html).

92 The CIA estimates there are twenty such countries; many are US allies, of course, but many also have 'known links' to terrorists (Stern 1999, 49).

93 Harsanyi (1975, 595).

94 I canvass and critique this and various other similar arguments for the 'priority of national defence' in Goodin (1982, ch. 11).

95 Rawls (1971, sec. 15).

96 Aquinas (1942, pt I–II, q. 2, art. 5).

97 Blair (2005b); cf. Runciman (2005).

98 As Blair (2005b) and Giddens (2005a, 31; 2005b, col. 150), for example, emphasize.

99 von Neumann and Morgenstern (1944).

100 Rawls (1958, 172).

101 Schelling (1967, 106).

102 As enunciated in the 1992 Rio Declaration, the Precautionary Principle holds that, 'Where there are threats of serious or irreversible damage, lack of full scientific certainty shall not be used as a reason for postponing cost-effective measures to prevent environmental degradation' (UN 1992, principle 15).

103 Sunstein (2005a, 2005b).

104 Gardiner (2006).

105 Sunstein (2005b, ch. 1).

106 Blair (2005b).

107 Ibid.

108 Hahn and Sunstein (2005) critically canvass other attempts to apply the precautionary principle to homeland security.

109 Cf. Runciman (2005).

110 Blair (2005b). His agent in the Lords elaborates: 'The consequences of old-style terrorism may be horrific, but can be weathered. The same is not true of a large-scale [new-style] terrorist attack: just one episode could be devastating, and one involving a nuclear device cataclysmic. . . . We have to avoid even a single successful attack' (Giddens (2005a, 31).

111 Just as the precautionary principle would have recommended unilateral nuclear disarmament at the height of the Cold War. After all, the worst-possible outcome of a continuing nuclear standoff would be an all-out nuclear war leading to the annihilation of life

on earth, whereas the worst-possible outcome of unilateral disarmament would be the hegemony of the other side – which would be bad, but not nearly as bad as the end of life on earth (Goodin 1985).

112 Betts (1978). The same is true in war planning, of course: whether that means that the generals should choose strategies based on the precautionary principle there depends, then, just on whether the other two preconditions are also met (which presumably neither ordinarily is).

113 US OMB (2005).

114 Bush (2001c).

115 Australia (2003, 7).

116 Cambridgeshire Constabulary (2005).

117 For a semi-official review of studies of its effectiveness, see Laycock and Tilley (1995).

118 Stern (1999, 47).

Chapter 7   Terrorizing Democracy

1 Wellman (1979, 255) offers a version of this sort of argument: 'The experience of terror is intrinsically undesirable. . . . Terrorism is *prima facie* wrong just because it uses terror, something that is necessarily bad, as its central means.' Acting with the intention of producing this bad is bad, even if the act fails to achieve what it intended.

2 Goodin (1980).

3 In Arendt's terms, 'total terror . . . inexorably paralyzes everything that is not mere reaction' (quoted in Waldron 2004, 15).

4 Waldron (2004, 15).

5 Janis (1982); Sunstein (2002).

6 Elshtain (2003, 59).

7 Townshend (2002, 116).

8 Jenkins (1983).

9 Mendelberg (2001).

10 Shklar (1989).

11 Roosevelt (1933/1995).

12 Townshend (2002, 88–9).

13 Wellmer (1984, 285–93).

14 Townshend (2002, 26). Western governments commonly adopt this attitude towards terrorism, without actually announcing it; see Gal-Or (1991).

15 Townshend (2002, 26).

16 In the very title of the book by Fischhoff et al. (1981).

17 Townshend (2002, 26).

18 Cairns and Wilson (1989, 621), summarizing Cairns and Wilson (1984); see similarly Curran and Miller (2001).

19 De Boer (1979, 412), reporting the results of a December 1977 Harris poll in the US and a June 1978 SOC poll in the UK. UK deaths from terrorist violence from Curran and Miller (2001, 74, table 1).

20 Mercer (2004).

21 Bush (2001b, 4, 5).

22 Australia (2003, 7).

23 Habermas (2003, 26).

24 White House (2004, 1).

25 Quoted in Bai (2004); CNN (2004).

26 Ibid.

27 Quoted and discussed by Jackson (2006).

28 I shall focus on the version of this argument that applies the Hobbesian 'characterization to relations among people, newly frightened by terrorism. There is another version of this argument that applies that characterization to relations among states – although that neglects the very different way Hobbes characterizes states and individuals and the consequences of those differences for states' capacities to "operate under conditions of lawfulness". The perceived lesson of 9/11 was to elide those differences, making the state as mortal and hence as fearful as blood-and-bone individuals, thus creating a "post-Hobbesian international order".' Runciman (2003) elucidates that logic well, but accepts rather too quickly the view that the lesson of 9/11 (or even a version of it conducted with weapons of mass destruction) is that, internationally as well as interpersonally, '"the weakest has strength to kill the strongest", or they would do, if only they could get their hands on the necessary equipment'. Such an attack would kill a lot of people, to be sure; but in what sense would it, literally or even metaphorically, kill the state?

29 Barber (2003, 75–6); see further Barber (2004).

30 Elshtain (2003, 46–7). And many other less famous folk follow in those footsteps. Meisels (2005, 169–70) for example writes that, 'While it is far-fetched to describe the US at present as facing a Hobbesian war of all against all, one needn't be an alarmist in order to recognize that terror threatens the future of a political society

far more substantially than the civil war Hobbes had in mind. . . . Where terrorists attack commuter buses, railways and air travel, freedom of movement is seriously impeded. When places of worship become targets of attack, freedom of religion is diminished. Since terrorists aim to attack large concentrations of people, terrorized citizens will often refrain from exercising their right of assembly.'

31 Phillips (1984, 89), quoted in Gilbert (1994, 37–8), who goes on to dismiss that view in terms similar to mine.

32 'Usually', because occasional cases can be found. J. D. Mabbott (1947, 21–2) describes one case where a near-Hobbesian scenario had occurred: 'I lived for a month in Ireland in 1922. There was no actual loss of life near us during that time, only a few shots audible in the night. Yet there was fear and suspicion everywhere and all peaceful avocations had come to an end. Fear and veiled hostility had destroyed the whole structure of social life.'

33 As Kavka points out, 'rule by fear' in the Hobbesian state cannot work through a pyramid of fear, with citizens fearing the police, and lower-level officers fearing the ones above them all the way up to the king. The physical strength of the absolute ruler is not that impressive; 'typically rulers are older and weaker than their nearest aides and are not armed' (Kavka 1983, 602). Instead, the 'rule of fear' works instead by each person fearing each other person as being someone who might possibly be disposed to obey the king's command to punish him if he breaks the law. It is a network of fear, rather than a hierarchy of fear.

34 Hobbes (1651, ch. 13, para 9).

35 Scheffler (2006, 7).

36 Ibid., pp. 7–8.

37 Shklar (1989); Macpherson (1977, ch. 2).

38 'Gov. Ridge sworn in to lead Homeland Security', 8 October 2001, http://www.whitehouse.gov/news/releases/2001/10/20011008-3.html; quoted in Kaplan (2003, 60).

39 Ashcroft (2001, 6).

40 Waldron (2003); Etzioni and Marsh (2003); Darmer et al. (2004); Tribe (2004).

41 Townshend (2002, 32–5).

42 Scheffler (2006).

43 As the Nazi regime did its population, for example (Waldron 2004, 19–21).

44 Ackerman (2004); Ignatieff (2004, ch. 2).

45 Asked in an NBC television interview whether America would win the 'war on terror', Bush replied: 'I don't think you can win it. But I think you can create conditions so that . . . those who use terror as a tool are less acceptable in parts of the world' (Anon. 2004b).

46 Lasswell (1941). He thought history bore out his fears (Lasswell 1962).

Chapter 8   Conclusions

1 E.g., Singer (2004); Miller (2003).

2 Bin Laden (2004).

3 The crucial passages read, 'People of America this talk of mine is for you and concerns the ideal way to prevent another Manhattan, and deals with the war and its causes and results'; and 'In conclusion, I tell you in truth, that your security is not in the hands of Kerry, nor Bush, nor al-Qaida. No. Your security is in your own hands. And every state that doesn't play with our security has automatically guaranteed its own security' (bin Laden 2004). Thus, while it was not literally a party-political intervention, it was most definitely a policy-oriented one, and political in that sense.

4 In full, Bush's (2004b) text reads: 'Earlier today I was informed of the tape that is now being analyzed by America's intelligence community. Let me make this very clear: Americans will not be intimidated or influenced by an enemy of our country. I'm sure Senator Kerry agrees with this.

I also want to say to the American people that we're at war with these terrorists and I am confident that we will prevail.

Thank you very much. Thank you.'

References

Académie Française. 1796. *Dictionnaire de l'Académie Française, Supplément*. Paris: Académie Française.

Ackerman, Bruce A. 2004. The emergency constitution. *Yale Law Journal*, 113: 1029–91.

Aglionby, John. 2004. Philippines bans logging after fatal floods. *Guardian Weekly*, 171, 10–16 December: 4.

Ali, Mukhtar. 1977. Probability and utility estimates for racetrack bettors. *Journal of Political Economy*, 85: 803–15.

Allen, Frederick Lewis. 1957. *Only Yesterday: An Informal History of the Nineteen-Twenties*. New York: Harper.

Allen, Mike. 2004. Bush tones down talk of winning terror war. *Washington Post*, 30 August. Available at: www.washingtonpost.com/wp-dyn/articles/A47707-2004Aug30.html (accessed 1 Dec 2004).

Allison, Graham T. 2004. *Nuclear Terrorism: The Ultimate Preventable Catastrophe*. New York: Times Books.

Alperovitz, Gar. 1995. *The Decision to Use the Atomic Bomb*. New York: Knopf.

Alperovitz, Gar. 2002. Terrorism: what is it? In *Globalization, Terrorism & Democracy: International Roundtable II Report, Berlin, June 2–4, 2002*. College Park: Democracy Collaborative, University of Maryland: 12–13.

Anon. 1935. Harvard Research Draft Convention on Extradition. *American Journal of International Law*, 29 (supplement).

Anon. 2003. Instructions for military commissions on trying aliens charged with terrorism. *American Journal of International Law*, 97: 706–9.

Anon. 2004a. Al Qaeda attack on Canary Wharf foiled. *Daily Mail*, 23 November. Available at: www.dailymail.co.uk/pages/live/articles/news/news.html?in_article_id=328011&in_page_id=1770&ct=5 (accessed 16 Feb 2005).

Anon. 2004b. War on terror cannot be won, Bush admits. *Guardian Weekly*, 171, 3–9 September: 6.

Anthony, Andrew. 2004. A knife in the Dutch heart. *Guardian Weekly*, 171, 17–23 December: 15–16.

Aquinas, Thomas. 1942. *Summa Theologica*. London: Burns Oates & Washburn.

Arab League. 1998. Convention for the Suppression of Terrorism. Available at: www.al-bab.com/arab/docs/league/terrorism98.htm (accessed 15 Jan 2005).

Arendt, Hannah. 1970. *On Violence*. New York: Harcourt, Brace.

Aristotle. 1946. *The Politics*, trans. and ed. Ernest Barker. Oxford: Clarendon Press.

Ashcroft, John C. 2001. A clear and present danger: testimony before the House Committee on the Judiciary, 24 September. In Amitai Etzioni and Jason H. Marsh, eds, *Rights vs. Public Safety after 9/11: America in the Age of Terrorism*. Lanham, MD: Rowman & Littlefield, 2003: 3–8.

Australia, Commonwealth Government. 2003. *Let's Look Out for Australia: Protecting our Way of Life from a Possible Terrorist Threat*. Written by Eric Abetz, special minister of state; distributed to every Australian household, under a cover letter from the prime minister, John Howard, 3 February. Canberra: Commonwealth Government.

Axelrod, Robert. 1984. *The Evolution of Cooperation*. New York: Basic Books.

Bai, Matt. 2004. Kerry's undeclared war. *New York Times Magazine*, 10 October: 38ff. Available at: www.nytimes.com/2004/10/10/magazine/10KERRY.html?ex=1108875600&en=7d98d2ee23c086b0&ei=5070&oref=login&oref=login&pagewanted=all&position= (accessed 18 Feb 2005).

Baier, Annette C. 1991. Violent demonstrations. In R. G. Frey and Christopher W. Morris, eds, *Violence, Terrorism and Justice*. New York: Cambridge University Press: 33–58.

Bakunin, Mikhail. 1866. Revolutionary catechism. In Sam Dolgoff, trans. and ed., *On Anarchy: Selected Works by the Activist-Founder of World Anarchism*. London: Allen & Unwin, 1975: 76–97.

Bakunin, Mikhail. 1873. *Statism & Anarchy*. Excerpted in *On Anarchy: Selected Works by the Activist-Founder of World Anarchism*, trans. and ed. Sam Dolgoff. London: Allen & Unwin, 1975: 323–50.

Ball, Desmond. 1981. *Can Nuclear War be Controlled?* Adelphi Papers no. 169. London: International Institute for Strategic Studies.

Barber, Benjamin R. 2003. The war of all against all: terror and the politics of fear. In Verna V. Gehring, ed., *War after September 11*. Lanham, MD: Rowman & Littlefield: 75–91.

Barber, Benjamin R. 2004. *Fear's Empire: War, Terrorism & Democracy*. New York: Norton.

Behr, Roy L., and Shanto Iyengar. 1985. Television news, real-world cues and changes in the public agenda. *Public Opinion Quarterly*, 49: 38–57.

Betts, Richard K. 1978. Analysis, war & decision: why intelligence failures are inevitable. *World Politics*, 31: 61–89.

bin Laden, Osama. 1996. Declaration of war against the Americans occupying the Land of the Two Holy Places. Available at: www.mideastweb. org/osamabinladen1.htm (accessed 15 Jan 2005).

bin Laden, Osama. 2004. Full text of bin Laden's speech. Available at: english.aljazeera.net/NR/exeres/79C6AF22-98FB-4A1C-B21F-2BC36E87F61F.htm (accessed 1 Dec 2004).

Blair, Bruce G., and Garry D. Brewer. 1977. The terrorist threat to world nuclear programs. *Journal of Conflict Resolution*, 21: 379–403.

Blair, Tony. 2005a. New government action to help Africa. Available at: www.number-10.gov.uk/output/Page6873.asp (accessed 15 Jan 2005).

Blair, Tony. 2005b. Speech to Sedgefield constituency, 5 March 2005. Available at: news.bbc.co.uk/2/hi/uk_news/politics/3536131.stm (accessed 19 June 2005).

Blunkett, David. 2004. Foreword by the Home Secretary. In *Counter Terrorism Powers: Reconciling Security and Liberty in an Open Society – A Discussion Paper*. Cmd 6147: i–iii. Available at: www.hmso.gov.uk/ information/cmpapers/cm_ghi.htm#ho (accessed 16 Jan 2005).

Borger, Julian. 2005. Permanent jails for US-held suspects: Pentagon tactic avoids terrorism trials. *Guardian Weekly*, 172, 7–13 January: 6.

Brennan, Geoffrey. 2006. Terrorism and its discontents. In Tilman Brück, ed., *The Economic Analysis of Terrorism*. London: Routledge.

Breyer, Stephen. 1993. *Breaking the Vicious Circle*. Cambridge, MA: Harvard University Press.

Bruchner, H. 1973. *Communication in Power*. New York: Oxford University Press.

Bush, George W. 2001a. Address to a Joint Session of Congress and the American people, United States Capitol, Washington, DC, 20 September. Available at: www.whitehouse.gov/news/releases/2001/09/20010920-8.html (accessed 1 Jan 2004).

Bush, George W. 2001b. Address to the United Nations General Assembly, 10 November, UN Headquarters, New York. Available at: www. whitehouse.gov/news/releases/2001/11/20011110-3.html (accessed 16 Jan 2005).

Bush, George W. 2001c. Gov. Ridge sworn in to lead Homeland Security, 8 October, White House. Available at: www.whitehouse.gov/news/releases/2001/10/20011008-3.html (accessed 11 Jan 2005).

Bush, George W. 2002a. Address before a joint session of Congress: State of the Union, 29 January. Available at: www.whitehouse.gov/news/releases/2002/01/20020129-11.html (accessed 28 Jan 2005).

Bush, George W. 2002b. National Strategy to Combat Weapons of Mass Destruction. National Security Presidential Directive 17, 11 December. Available at: www.whitehouse.gov/news/releases/2002/12/WMDStrategy.pdf (accessed 17 Feb 2005).

Bush, George W. 2004a. President's remarks on homeland security in New Jersey. Remarks by the president at Evesham Recreation Center, Marlton, Burlington County, New Jersey, 18 October. Available at: www.whitehouse.gov/news/releases/2004/10/print/20041018-11.html (accessed 15 Feb 2005).

Bush, George W. 2004b. We will not be intimidated: statement by the president, Toledo Express Airport, Toledo, Ohio, 29 October. Available at: www.whitehouse.gov/news/releases/2004/10/20041029-18.html (accessed 1 Dec 2004).

Bush, George W. 2005a. President discusses Patriot Act, Ohio State Highway Patrol Academy, Columbus, Ohio, 9 June. Available at: www.whitehouse.gov/news/releases/2005/06/20050609-2.html (accessed 15 June 2005).

Bush, George W. 2005b. President's radio address, 18 June. Available at: www.whitehouse.gov/news/releases/2005/06/20050618.html (accessed 19 June 2005).

Bybee, Jay S. 2002. Memorandum for Alberto R. Gonzales, Counsel to the President. Reprinted in part in M. Katherine B. Darmer, Robert M. Baird and Stuart E. Rosenbaum, eds, *Civil Liberties vs. National Security in a Post-9/11 World*. Amherst, NY: Prometheus Books, 2004: 303–15.

Byers, Michael. 2003. Preemptive self-defense: hegemony, equality and strategies of legal change. *Journal of Political Philosophy*, 11: 171–91.

Cairns, Ed, and Ronnie Wilson. 1984. The impact of political violence on mild psychiatric morbidity in Northern Ireland. *British Journal of Psychiatry*, 145: 631–5.

Cairns, Ed, and Ronnie Wilson. 1989. Coping with political violence in Northern Ireland. *Social Science & Medicine*, 28: 621–4.

Cambridgeshire Constabulary. 2005. *Neighbourhood Watch Manual*. Available at: www.cambs.police.uk/camcom/nhw/manual/terrorism.asp (accessed 23 July 2005).

Camus, Albert. 1953. Individual terrorism. In *The Rebel*, trans. Anthony Bower. London: Hamish Hamilton: 120–47.

Card, Claudia. 2003. Making war on terrorism in response to 9/11. In James P. Sterba, ed., *Terrorism and International Justice*. New York: Oxford University Press: 171–205.

CDI (Center for Defense Information). 2002. Presidential orders and documents regarding foreign intelligence and terrorism. Available at: www.cdi.org/friendlyversion/printversion.cfm?documentID=1654 (accessed 24 Jan 2005).

Chomsky, Noam. 2002. *9-11*. New York: Seven Stories Press.

Clausewitz, Carl von. 1989. *On War*, ed. and trans. Michael Howard and Peter Paret. Princeton, NJ: Princeton University Press.

CNN. 2004. Bush campaign to base add on Kerry terror quote. 11 October. Available at: www.cnn.com/2004/ALLPOLITICS/10/10/bush.kerry. terror (accessed 18 Feb 2005).

Coady, C. A. J. 1985. The morality of terrorism. *Philosophy*, 60: 47–69.

Coady, C. A. J. 2001. Terrorism. In *Encyclopedia of Ethics*, ed. Lawrence C. Becker and Charlotte B. Becker. 2nd edn, New York: Routledge, Vol. 2: 1696–9. Reprinted, expanded, in Igor Primoratz, ed., *Terrorism: The Philosophical Issues*. London: Palgrave, 2004: 3–14.

Coady, C. A. J. 2004. Terrorism and innocence. *Journal of Ethics*, 8: 37–58.

Conquest, Robert. 1968. *The Great Terror*. London: Macmillan.

Coombs, B., and P. Slovic. 1979. Newspaper coverage of causes of death. *Journalism Quarterly*, 56: 837–43.

Corlett, J. Angelo. 2003. *Terrorism: A Philosophical Analysis*. Dordrecht: Kluwer.

Curran, Peter S., and Paul W. Miller. 2001. Psychiatric implications of chronic civilian strife or war: Northern Ireland. *Advances in Psychiatric Treatment*, 7: 73–80.

Darmer, M. Katherine B., Robert M. Baird and Stuart E. Rosenbaum, eds. 2004. *Civil Liberties vs. National Security in a Post-9/11 World*. Amherst, NY: Prometheus Books.

De Boer, Connie. 1979. The polls: terrorism and hijacking. *Public Opinion Quarterly*, 43: 410–18.

Delli Carpini, Michael X., and Bruce A. Williams. Television and terrorism: patterns of presentation and occurrence, 1969 to 1980. *Western Political Quarterly*, 40: 45–64.

Dershowitz, Alan M. 2002. *Why Terrorism Works: Understanding the Threat, Responding to the Challenge*. New Haven, CT: Yale University Press.

Dodd, Vikram, Duncan Campbell and Richard Norton-Taylor. 2005. Ex-grammar school boy gets 13 years for shoe bomb plot. *Guardian Weekly*, 172, 29 April–5 May: 9.

Dugard, John. 1974. International terrorism: problems of definition. *International Affairs*, 50: 67–81.

Dumas, Lloyd J. 2003. Is development an effective way to fight terrorism? In Verna V. Gehring, ed., *War after September 11*. Lanham, MD: Rowman & Littlefield: 65–74.

Eggen, Don, and Julie Tate. 2005. U.S. campaign produces few convictions on terrorism charges. *Washington Post*, 12 June: A1. Available at: www.washingtonpost.com/wp-dyn/content/article/2005/06/11/AR1005061100381_pf.html (accessed 14 June 2005).

Elliott, Michael. 2002. The shoe bomber's world. *Time*, 16 February. Available at: www.time.com/time/world/article/0,8599,203478,00.html (accessed 14 Feb 2005).

Ellsberg, Daniel. 1961. Risk, ambiguity and the Savage axioms. *Quarterly Journal of Economics*, 75: 643–69.

Elshtain, Jean Bethke. 2003. *Just War Against Terror*. New York: Basic Books.

Elster, Jon. 1990. Norms of revenge. *Ethics*, 100: 862–85.

Etzioni, Amitai. 2004. *Pre-empting Nuclear Terrorism in a New Global Order*. London: Foreign Policy Centre.

Etzioni, Amitai, and Jason H. Marsh, eds. 2003. *Rights vs. Public Safety after 9/11: America in the Age of Terrorism*. Lanham, MD: Rowman & Littlefield.

EU (European Union). 1977. European Convention on the Suppression of Terrorism. Available at: untreaty.un.org/English/Terrorism.asp (accessed 15 Jan 2005).

Fawcett, J. E. S. 1958. Note: some recent applications of international law by the United States. *British Year Book of International Law*, 34: 384–91.

Feldman, Glenn. 1997. Soft opposition: elite acquiescence and Klan-sponsored terrorism in Alabama, 1946–1950. *Historical Journal*, 40: 753–77.

Ferejohn, John, and Pasquale Pasquino. 2006. The constitutional theory of emergency powers. In *Oxford Handbook of Political Theory*, ed. John Dryzek, Bonnie Honig and Anne Phillips. Oxford: Oxford University Press.

Fischhoff, Baruch. 2002. Assessing and communicating the risks of terrorism. In A. H. Teich, S. D. Nelson and S. J. Lita, eds, *Science and Technology in a Vulnerable World: Supplement to AAAS Science and*

Technology Policy Yearbook 2003. Washington, DC: American Association for the Advancement of Science: 51–64. Available at: www.hss.cmu. edu/departments/sds/faculty/fischhoff.html (accessed 14 Feb 2005).

Fischhoff, Baruch, Sarah Lichtenstein, Paul Slovic, Stephen L. Derby and Ralph L. Keeney. 1981. *Acceptable Risk*. Cambridge: Cambridge University Press.

Fitzpatrick, Joan. 2002. Jurisdiction of military commissions and the ambiguous war on terrorism. *American Journal of International Law*, 96: 345–54.

Franck, Thomas M., and Bert B. Lockwood, Jr. 1974. Preliminary thoughts towards an international convention on terrorism. *American Journal of International Law*, 68: 69–90.

Freedland, Jonathan. 2005. 'The world in one city' unites in hope, not hate. *Guardian Weekly*, 173, 22–8 July: 7.

Freedman, Lawrence. 2005. Strategic terror and amateur psychology. *Political Quarterly*, 76: 161–70.

French, Shannon E. 2003. Murderers, not warriors: the moral distinction between terrorists and legitimate fighters in asymmetric conflicts. In James P. Sterba, ed., *Terrorism and International Justice*. New York: Oxford University Press: 31–46.

Frey, Bruno S. 2004. *Dealing with Terrorism: Stick or Carrot?* Cheltenham: Edward Elgar.

Fullinwider, Robert K. 1975. War & innocence. *Philosophy & Public Affairs*, 5: 90–7.

Fullinwider, Robert K. 2003. Terrorism, innocence & war. In Verna V. Gehring, ed., *War after September 11*. Lanham, MD: Rowman & Littlefield: 21–35.

Gaddis, John Lewis. 2001. And now this: lessons from the old era for the new one. In Strobe Talbott and Nayan Chanda, eds, *The Age of Terror: America and the World After September 11*. New York: Basic Books: 1–21.

Gal-Or, Noemi. 1991. Do Western societies tolerate terrorism? In Noemi Gal-Or, ed., *Tolerating Terrorism in the West*. London: Routledge: 143–65.

Galtung, Johan. 1969. Violence, peace and peace research. *Journal of Peace Research* 6: 167–91.

Gambetta, Diego. 2004. Reason & terror: has 9/11 made it hard to think straight? *Boston Review*, 20, April/May: 32–6. Available at: bostonreview.net/BR29.2/gambetta.html (accessed 25 Feb 2005).

Gans, Herbert J. 1980. *Deciding What's News*. New York: Vintage.

Gardiner, Steven. 2006. The core precautionary principle. *Journal of Political Philosophy*, 14.

Giddens, Anthony. 2005a. Scaring people may be the only way to avoid the risks of new-style terrorism. *New Statesman*, 18, 10 January: 29–31. Available at: www.newstatesman.com/200501100020 (accessed 30 March 2005).

Giddens, Anthony. 2005b. Speech on the Prevention of Terrorism Bill. *Hansard's Parliamentary Debates (Lords)*, 670 (pt 45) (1 March): cols 148–51. Available at: www.parliament.the-stationery-office.co.uk/pa/ld/ldvol670.htm (accessed 2 Aug 2005).

Gilbert, Paul. 1990. Community and civil strife. In Martin Warner and Roger Crisp, eds, *Terrorism, Protest & Power*. Aldershot: Edward Elgar: 17–34.

Gilbert, Paul. 1994. *Terrorism, Security & Nationality: An Introductory Study in Applied Political Philosophy*. London: Routledge.

Gilbert, Paul. 2003. *New Terror, New Wars*. Edinburgh: Edinburgh University Press.

Gilovich, Tom, Dale Griffin and Daniel Kahneman, eds. 2002. *Heuristics and Biases: The Psychology of Intuitive Judgement*. Cambridge: Cambridge University Press.

Glover, Jonathan. 1991. State terrorism. In R. G. Frey and Christopher W. Morris, eds, *Violence, Terrorism and Justice*. New York: Cambridge University Press: 256–75.

Goodin, Robert E. 1980. *Manipulatory Politics*. New Haven, CT: Yale University Press.

Goodin, Robert E. 1982. *Political Theory & Public Policy*. Chicago: University of Chicago Press.

Goodin, Robert E. 1985. Nuclear disarmament as a moral certainty. *Ethics*, 95: 641–58.

Goodin, Robert E. 1995. *Utilitarianism as a Public Philosophy*. Cambridge: Cambridge University Press.

Graham, Katherine. 1986. Terrorists need the press, but so does a free society. *Washington Post National Weekly Edition*, 5 May: 24–5.

Grice, Andrew. 2004. Hain denies Canary Wharf terror threat. *The Independent*, 27 November. Available at: www.ladlass.com/intel/archives/007430.html (accessed 16 Feb 2005).

Griffith, R. M. 1949. Odds adjustments by American horse-race bettors. *American Journal of Psychology*, 62: 290–4.

Gurr, Ted Robert. 1986. The political origins of state violence & terror: a theoretical analysis. In Michael Stohl and George A. Lopez, eds, *Government Violence & Repression*. Westport, CT: Greenwood Press: 45–71.

Habermas, Jürgen. 2003. Fundamentalism and terror: a dialogue with Jürgen Habermas. In Giovanna Borradori, ed., *Philosophy in a Time of*

Terror. Chicago: University of Chicago Press: 25–43. Excerpts available at: www.press.uchicago.edu/Misc/Chicago/066649.html (accessed 18 Oct 2004).

Hahn, Robert W., and Cass R. Sunstein. 2005. The precautionary principle as a basis for decision making. *Economists' Voice*, 2 (2): article 8. Available at: www.bepress.com/ev/vol2/iss2/art8 (accessed 29 March 2005).

Hare, R. M. 1979. On terrorism. *Journal of Value Inquiry*, 12: 240–9.

Harsanyi, John C. 1975. Can the maximin principle serve as a basis for morality? *American Political Science Review*, 69: 594–606.

Held, Virginia. 1984. Violence, terrorism and moral inquiry. *Monist*, 67: 605–26.

Held, Virginia. 1991. Terrorism, rights and public goods. In R. G. Frey and Christopher W. Morris, eds, *Violence, Terrorism and Justice*. New York: Cambridge University Press: 59–85. Reprinted in Igor Primoratz, ed., *Terrorism: The Philosophical Issues*. London: Palgrave, 2004: 65–79.

Held, Virginia. 2004. Terrorism & war. *Journal of Ethics*, 8: 59–75.

Henkin, Louis et al. 1987. *Restatement of the Law (Third): The Foreign Relations Law of the United States*. Washington, DC: American Law Institute.

Heyman, Philip B. 2003. *Terrorism, Freedom and Security: Winning Without War*. Cambridge, MA: MIT Press.

Hobbes, Thomas. 1651. *Leviathan*. London: Andrew Crooke.

Hofstadter, Richard. 1965. *The Paranoid Style in American Politics*. New York: Knopf.

Honderich, Ted. 1989. *Violence for Equality*. London: Routledge.

Honderich, Ted. 2003a. *After the Terror*. Rev. edn, Edinburgh: Edinburgh University Press.

Honderich, Ted. 2003b. *Terrorism for Humanity*. London: Pluto. (Revised edition of Honderich 1989.)

Howard, Michael. 2005. People deserve to feel safe in their homes. Available at: www.conservatives.com/tile.do?def=news.story.page&obj_id=119426 (accessed 15 Feb 2005).

Huddy, Leonie, Stanley Feldman, Gallya Lahav and Charles Taber. 2003. Fear & terrorism: psychological reactions to 9/11. In Pippa Norris, Montague Kern and Marion Just, eds, *Framing Terrorism: The News Media, the Government & the Public*. New York: Routledge: 255–80.

Ignatieff, Michael. 2004. *The Lesser Evil: Political Ethics in an Age of Terror*. Edinburgh: Edinburgh University Press.

India. 2002. The Prevention of Terrorism Act, 2002. Available at: www.satp.org/satporgtp/countries/india/document/actandordinances/POTA.htm (accessed 15 Jan 2005).

Iyengar, Shanto, and Donald R. Kinder. 1987. *News that Matters: Television & American Opinion*. Chicago: University of Chicago Press.

Jackson, Patrick Thaddeus. 2006. The present as history. In *Oxford Handbook of Contextual Political Analysis*, ed. Robert E. Goodin and Charles Tilly. Oxford: Oxford University Press.

Jamieson, Kathleen Hall, and Paul Waldman. 2003. *The Press Effect: Politicians, Journalists & Stories that Shape the Political World*. New York: Oxford University Press.

Janis, Irving L. 1982. *Groupthink*. 2nd edn, Boston: Houghton Mifflin.

Jenkins, Brian Michael. 1980. *International Terrorism: Choosing the Right Target*. RAND Paper P-6563. Santa Monica, CA: RAND.

Jenkins, Brian Michael. 1981a. *The Psychological Implications of Media-Covered Terrorism*. RAND Paper P-6627. Santa Monica, CA: RAND.

Jenkins, Brian Michael. 1981b. *The Study of Terrorism: Definitional Problems*. RAND Paper P-6597. Santa Monica, CA: RAND.

Jenkins, Brian Michael. 1983. *Terrorism: Between Prudence & Paranoia*. RAND Paper P-6946. Santa Monica, CA: RAND.

Jenkins, Brian Michael. 1985. *The Likelihood of Nuclear Terrorism*. RAND Paper P-7119. Santa Monica, CA: RAND.

Jenkins, Brian Michael. 1986. Defense against terrorism. *Political Science Quarterly*, 101: 779–81.

Jenkins, Brian Michael. 1999. Foreword. In Ian O. Lesser et al., *Countering the New Terrorism*. Santa Monica, CA: RAND: iii–xiv.

Jenkins, Brian Michael. 2003. *Remarks before the National Commission on Terrorist Attacks upon the United States, March 31, 2003*. RAND Testimony CT-203. Santa Monica, CA: RAND.

Johnson, Eric J., John Hershey, Jacqueline Meszaros and Howard Kunreuther. 1993. Framing, probability distortions & insurance decisions. *Journal of Risk & Uncertainty*, 7: 35–51. Reprinted in Daniel Kahneman and Amos Tversky, eds, *Choices, Values & Frames*. Cambridge: Cambridge University Press & Russell Sage Foundation, 2000: 224–40.

Jones, Jonathan. 2005. Visual bombardment. *Guardian Weekly*, 172, 14–20 January: 21.

Kahneman, Daniel. 2003. Maps of bounded rationality: psychology for behavioral economics. *American Economics Review*, 93: 1449–75.

Kahneman, Daniel, and Amos Tversky. 1979. Prospect theory: an analysis of decision under risk. *Econometrica*, 47: 263–91.

Kahneman, Daniel, and Amos Tversky, eds. 2000. *Choices, Values & Frames*. Cambridge: Cambridge University Press & Russell Sage Foundation.

Kahneman, Daniel, Paul Slovic and Amos Tversky, eds. 1982. *Judgement under Uncertainty: Heuristics & Biases*. Cambridge: Cambridge University Press.

Kaplan, Amy. 2003. Homeland insecurities: transformations of language and space. In Mary L. Dudziak, ed., *September 11 in History: A Watershed Moment?* Durham, NC: Duke University Press: 55–69.

Karstedt, Susanne. 2003. Terrorism and 'new wars'. In Bülent Gökay and R. B. J. Walker, eds, *11 September 2001: War, Terrorism and Judgement*. London: Frank Cass: 139–54.

Kavka, Gregory S. 1983. Rule by fear. *Nous*, 17: 601–20.

Kean, Thomas H., and Lee H. Hamilton. 2004. Preface. In *The 9/11 Commission Report: Final Report of the National Commission on Terrorist Attacks upon the United States*. New York: Norton: xv–xviii.

Keane, John. 2004. *Violence & Democracy*. Cambridge: Cambridge University Press.

Keeny, Spurgeon M. Jr., and Wolfgang K. H. Panofsky. 1981–2. MAD versus NUTS. *Foreign Affairs*, 60: 287–304.

Kellman, Barry. 2000. Clashing perspectives on terrorism. *American Journal of International Law*, 94: 434–8.

Kelly, George Armstrong. 1980. Conceptual sources of the terror. *Eighteenth-Century Studies*, 14: 18–36.

Keohane, Dan. 2003. The response of the British government to the attack on America. In Bülent Gökay and R. B. J. Walker, eds, *11 September 2001: War, Terrorism and Judgement*. London: Frank Cass: 110–28.

Kern, Montague, Marion Just and Pippa Norris. 2003. The lessons of framing terrorism. In Pippa Norris, Montague Kern and Marion Just, eds, *Framing Terrorism: The News Media, the Government & the Public*. New York: Routledge: 281–302.

Kuran, Timur, and Cass R. Sunstein. 1999. Availability cascades and risk regulation. *Stanford Law Review*, 51: 683–768.

Lackey, Douglas. 2004. The evolution of the modern terrorist state: area bombing and nuclear deterrence. In Igor Primoratz, ed., *Terrorism: The Philosophical Issues*. London: Palgrave: 128–38.

Lasswell, Harold. 1941. The garrison state. *American Journal of Sociology*, 46: 455–68.

Lasswell, Harold. 1962. The garrison-state hypothesis today. In Samuel Huntington, ed., *Changing Patterns of Military Politics*. New York: Free Press: 51–70.

Lawson, Mark. 2005. Public enemy number two: some security measures can alarm rather than reassure us. *Guardian Weekly*, 173, 29 July–4 August: 14.

Laycock, Gloria, and Nick Tilley. 1995. Appendix: the effectiveness of Neighbourhood Watch: a review of the published literature. In *Policing and Neighbourhood Watch: Strategic Issues*. Police Research Group, Crime Detection & Prevention Series, Paper 60. London: Home Office Police Department: 21–40. Available at: www.homeoffice.gov.uk/rds/prgpdfs/cdp60bf.pdf (accessed 23 July 2005).

League of Nations. 1937. Convention for the Prevention and Punishment of Terrorism. Doc. C.546 M.383 1937 V (1937); adopted 16 Nov 1937. Reprinted in *Official Journal*, 19 (1938): 23–5.

Lesser, Ian O. 1999. Countering the new terrorism: implications for strategy. In Ian O. Lesser et al., *Countering the New Terrorism*. Santa Monica, CA: RAND: 85–144.

Lomasky, Loren. 1991. The political significance of terrorism. In R. G. Frey and Christopher W. Morris, eds, *Violence, Terrorism and Justice*. New York: Cambridge University Press: 86–115.

Luban, David. 2003. The war on terrorism and the end of human rights. In Verna V. Gehring, ed., *War after September 11*. Lanham, MD: Rowman & Littlefield: 51–65.

Luce, R. D. 2000. *Utility of Gains and Losses: Measurement-Theoretical and Experimental Approaches*. London: Lawrence Erlbaum.

Lugar, Richard G. 2005. Nunn–Lugar cooperative threat reduction program. Available at: lugar.senate.gov/nunnlugar.html (accessed 19 June 2005).

Mabbott, J. D. 1947. *The State & the Citizen*. London: Hutchinson.

McCormick, Gordon H. 2003. Terrorist decision making. *Annual Review of Political Science*, 6: 473–507.

McMahan, Jeff. 1985. Deterrence & deontology. In Russell Hardin, John J. Mearsheimer, Gerald Dworkin and Robert E. Goodin, eds, *Nuclear Deterrence: Ethics & Strategy*. Chicago: University of Chicago Press: 141–60.

McMahan, Jeff. 1994. Innocence, self-defense and killing in war. *Journal of Political Philosophy*, 2: 193–221.

McMahan, Jeff. 2004. The ethics of killing in war. *Ethics*, 114: 693–733.

Macpherson, C. B. 1977. *The Life and Times of Liberal Democracy*. Oxford: Clarendon Press.

Mapel, David R. 1998. Coerced moral agents? Individual responsibility for becoming a soldier. *Journal of Political Philosophy*, 6: 171–90.

Mason, T. David, and Dale A. Krane. 1989. The political economy of death squads: toward a theory of the impact of state-sanctioned terror. *International Studies Quarterly*, 33: 175–98.

May, Thomas. 2005. Funding agendas: has bioterror defense been over-prioritized? *American Journal of Bioethics*, 5 (4): 34–44.

Meek, James. 2005. Altered streets. *Guardian Weekly*, 173, 15–21 July: 15–16.

Meisels, Tamar. 2005. How terrorism upsets liberty. *Political Studies*, 53: 162–81.

Mendelberg, Tali. 2001. *The Race Card: Campaign Strategy, Implicit Messages and the Norm of Equality*. Princeton, NJ: Princeton University Press.

Mercer, Patrick. 2004. Britain needs a minister for homeland security. Conservative Party, 13 September. Available at: www.conservatives. com/tile.do?def=news.show.article.page&obj_id=115529 (accessed 18 Feb 2005).

Metraux, Daniel A. 1995. Religious terrorism in Japan: the fatal appeal of Aum Shinrikyo. *Asian Survey*, 35: 1140–54.

Miller, Richard. 2003. Terrorism, war and empire. In James P. Sterba, ed., *Terrorism and International Justice*. New York: Oxford University Press: 186–205.

Monbiot, George. 2004. Why I'm a wolf man. *Guardian Weekly*, 171, 17–23 December: 13.

Murphy, Sean D., ed. 2002. Terrorist attacks on World Trade Center and Pentagon. *American Journal of International Law*, 96: 237–55.

Nacos, Brigette L. 2002. *Mass-Mediated Terrorism*. Lanham, MD: Rowman & Littlefield.

Nagel, Thomas. 1972. War & massacre. *Philosophy and Public Affairs*, 1: 123–44.

Netanyahu, Benjamin. 1986. *Terrorism: How the West Can Win*. New York: Farrar, Straus, Giroux.

NKVD. 1983. Document on terrorism. Reprinted in *The Morality of Terrorism*, ed. David C. Rapoport and Yonah Alexander. New York: Pergamon Press.

Nozick, Robert. 1972. Coercion. In Peter Laslett, W. G. Runciman and Quentin Skinner, eds, *Philosophy, Politics and Society*, 4th series. Oxford: Blackwell: 110–35.

Nussbaum, Martha C. 2003. Compassion and terror. In James P. Sterba, ed., *Terrorism and International Justice*. New York: Oxford University Press: 229–52.

O'Hanlon, Michael E. et al. 2002. *Protecting the American Homeland: A Preliminary Analysis*. Washington, DC: Brookings Institution.

Olson, Mancur, Jr. 1993. Dictatorship, democracy and development. *American Political Science Review*, 87: 567–76.

O'Neill, Onora. 1991. Which are the offers *you* can't refuse? In R. G. Frey and Christopher W. Morris, eds, *Violence, Terrorism and Justice*. New York: Cambridge University Press: 170–95.

Parekh, Bhikhu. 2004. Why terror? *Prospect*, no. 97 (April). Available at: 9-11.haikolietz.de/backup/040400_Why_terror-_(Prospect).html (accessed 30 March 2005).

Pear, Robert. 2004. Teachers union called 'terrorist': education secretary accuses the NEA. *New York Times*, 24 February. Available at: www.house.gov/lantos/sfgate_040224.NEA.pdf or sfgate.com/cgi-bin/article.cgi?file=chronicle/archive/2004/2/24/MNGO056V7M1.DTL (accessed 16 Jan 2005).

Phillips, Robert. 1984. *War & Justice*. Norman: University of Oklahoma Press.

Pidgeon, Nick, Roger E. Kasperson and Paul Slovic, eds. 2003. *The Social Amplification of Risk*. Cambridge: Cambridge University Press.

Pion-Berlin, David, and George A. Lopez. 1991. Of victims & executioners: Argentine state terror, 1975–1979. *International Studies Quarterly*, 35: 3–86.

Pontara, Giuliano. 1978. The concept of violence. *Journal of Peace Research*, 15: 19–32.

Preston, M. G., and P. Baratta. 1948. An experimental study of the auction-value of an uncertain outcome. *American Journal of Psychology*, 61: 183–93.

Primoratz, Igor. 1990. What is terrorism? *Journal of Applied Philosophy*, 7: 129–83. Reprinted in Igor Primoratz, ed., *Terrorism: The Philosophical Issues*. London: Palgrave, 2004: 15–27.

Primoratz, Igor. 1997. The morality of terrorism? *Journal of Applied Philosophy*, 14: 221–33.

Primoratz, Igor, ed. 2004. *Terrorism: The Philosophical Issues*. London: Palgrave.

Quinton, Anthony. 1990. Reflections on terrorism & violence. In Martin Warner and Roger Crisp, eds, *Terrorism, Protest & Power*. Aldershot: Edward Elgar: 35–43.

Rapoport, David C. 1984. Fear & trembling: terrorism in three religious traditions. *American Political Science Review*, 78: 658–77.

Rapoport, David C. 1988. Messianic sanctions for terror. *Comparative Politics*, 20: 195–213.

Rawls, John. 1958. Justice as fairness. *Philosophical Review*, 67: 164–94.

Rawls, John. 1971. *A Theory of Justice*. Cambridge, MA: Harvard University Press.

Robin, Corey. 2004. *Fear: The History of a Political Idea*. New York: Oxford University Press.

Roosevelt, Franklin D. 1933. First inaugural address. Reprinted in Brian MacArthur, ed., *Historic Speeches*. Harmondsworth: Penguin, 1995: 473–7.

Rosenbaum, David M. 1977. Nuclear terror. *International Security*, 1: 140–61.

Rosenkrantz, R. D. 1981. *Foundations & Applications of Inductive Probability*. Altascadero, CA: Ridgeview.

Rowntree, Pamela Wilcox, and Kenneth Land. 1996. Perceived risk versus fear of crime. *Social Forces*, 74: 1353–76.

Runciman, David. 2003. A bear armed with a gun. *London Review of Books*, 25, 3 April: 3–6. Available at: www.lrb.co.uk/v25/n07/print/runc01_.html (accessed 19 June 2005).

Runciman, David. 2005. The precautionary principle. *London Review of Books*, 26, 1 April. Available at: www.lrb.co.uk/v26/n07/print/runc01_.html (accessed 19 June 2005).

Ryan, Alan. 1991. State and private: red and white. In R. G. Frey and Christopher W. Morris, eds, *Violence, Terrorism and Justice*. New York: Cambridge University Press: 230–55.

Scheffler, Samuel. 2006. Is terrorism morally distinctive? *Journal of Political Philosophy*, 14: 1–18.

Schelling, Thomas C. 1967. The strategy of inflicting costs. In Roland M. McKean, ed., *Issues in Defense Economics*. New York: National Bureau of Economic Research: 105–27.

Schmid, Alex P., and Albert J. Jongman et al. 1988. *Political Terrorism*. 2nd edn, Amsterdam: North-Holland.

Schumpeter, Joseph A. 1950. *Capitalism, Socialism & Democracy*. 3rd edn, New York: Harper & Row.

Shamir, Yitzhak. 1943. *Hehbazit*, Summer 1943; reprinted in part in *Middle East Report*, no. 152, May–June 1988: 55.

Shawcross, William. 1987. *Sideshow*. Rev. edn, New York: Simon & Schuster.

Shklar, Judith N. 1989. The liberalism of fear. In Nancy Rosenblum, ed., *Liberalism and the Moral Life*. Cambridge, MA: Harvard University Press: 21–38.

Singer, Peter. 2004. *The President of Good and Evil: The Ethics of George W. Bush*. New York: Dutton.

Sinnott-Armstrong, Walter. 1999. On Primoratz's definition of terrorism. *Journal of Applied Philosophy*, 8: 115–20.

Slovic, Paul, Baruch Fischhoff and Sarah Lichtenstein. 1980. Facts versus fears: understanding perceived risk. In R. Schwing and W. A. Albers, Jr., eds, *Societal Risk Assessment*. New York: Plenum Press. Reprinted in Daniel Kahneman, Paul Slovic and Amos Tversky, eds, *Judgement under Uncertainty: Heuristics & Biases*. Cambridge: Cambridge University Press, 1982: 463–89.

Slovic, Paul et al. 2002. The affect heuristic. In Tom Gilovich, Dale Griffin and Daniel Kahneman, eds, *Heuristics and Biases: The Psychology of Intuitive Judgement*. Cambridge: Cambridge University Press.

Solzhenitsyn, Alexander. 1974–5. *The Gulag Archipelago*, trans T. P. Whitney. New York: Harper & Row.

Starr, Chauncey. 1969. Social benefit versus technological risk. *Science*, 165: 1232–8.

Stern, Jessica. 1999. *The Ultimate Terrorists*. Cambridge, MA: Harvard University Press.

Sunstein, Cass R. 2002. The law of group polarization. *Journal of Political Philosophy*, 10: 175–95.

Sunstein, Cass R. 2003. Terrorism and probability neglect. *Journal of Risk & Uncertainty*, 26: 121–36.

Sunstein, Cass R. 2005a. Cost–benefit analysis and the environment. *Ethics*, 115: 351–85.

Sunstein, Cass R. 2005b. *Laws of Fear: Beyond the Precautionary Principle*. Cambridge: Cambridge University Press.

Teichman, Jenny. 1986. *Pacifism and the Just War*. Oxford: Blackwell.

Teichman, Jenny. 1989. How to define terrorism. *Philosophy*, 64: 505–17.

Thornton, Thomas Perry. 1964. Terrorism as a weapon of political agitation. In Harry Eckstein, ed., *Internal War*. New York: Free Press: 71–99.

Timerman, Jacobo. 1981. *Prisoner Without a Name, Cell Without a Number*, trans. Toby Talbot. New York: Knopf.

Townshend, Charles. 2002. *Terrorism: A Very Short Introduction*. Oxford: Oxford University Press.

Tribe, Laurence H. 2004. The Constitution in crisis: from *Bush v. Gore* to the War on Terrorism. *Tanner Lectures on Human Values*, 24: 173–284.

Trotsky, Leon. 1931/2004. A defense of the 'Red Terror'. In Igor Primoratz, ed., *Terrorism: The Philosophical Issues*. London: Palgrave, 2004: 31–43.

Tversky, Amos, and Daniel Kahneman. 1974. Judgment under uncertainty: heuristics & biases. *Science*, 185: 1124–31. Reprinted in Daniel Kahneman, Paul Slovic and Amos Tversky, eds, *Judgement under Uncertainty: Heuristics & Biases*. Cambridge: Cambridge University Press, 1982: 3–20.

UK. 1974. Prevention of Terrorism (Temporary Provisions) Act. Available at: cain.ulst.ac.uk/hmso/pta1974.htm (accessed 16 Jan 2005).

UK. 2000. Terrorism Act. Available at: www.hmso.gov.uk/acts/acts2000/20000011.htm (accessed 16 Jan 2005).

UK. 2002. *Responsibility for the Terrorist Atrocities in the United States, 11 September 2001: An Updated Account*. London: 10 Downing Street. Available at: www.number-10.gov.uk/output/page3682.asp (accessed 1 Jan 2005).

UN (United Nations). 1949. Geneva Conventions of 1949 and 1977. Available at: www.genevaconventions.org (accessed 16 Jan 2005).

UN (United Nations). 1958. Convention on the High Seas. Available at: www.un.org/law/ilc/texts/hseafra.htm (accessed 28 Jan 2005).

UN (United Nations). 1970. Declaration on Principles of International Law concerning Friendly Relations and Co-operation among States in Accordance with the Charter of the United Nations. Available at: www.un.org/documents/ga/res/25/ares25.htm (accessed 28 Jan 2005).

UN (United Nations). 1977. Protocol II: Additional to the Geneva Conventions of 12 August 1949, and relating to the Protection of Victims of Non-International Armed Conflicts, 8 June 1977. Available at: www.genevaconventions.org (accessed 16 Jan 2005).

UN (United Nations). 1992. Rio Declaration on Environment and Development. Annex I to Report of the United Nations Conference on Environment and Development, Rio de Janeiro, 3–14 June. Available at: www.un.org/documents/ga/conf151/aconf15126-1annex1.htm (accessed 23 June 2005).

UN (United Nations). 1994. General Assembly Resolution 49/60: Measures to Eliminate International Terrorism. A/RES/49/60. Available at: www.un.org/documents/resga.htm (accessed 28 Dec 2004).

UN (United Nations). 1997a. International Convention for the Suppression of Terrorist Bombing. A/RES/52/164. Available at: www.un.org/documents/resga.htm or untreaty.un.org/English/Terrorism.asp (accessed 28 Dec 2004).

UN (United Nations). 1997b. General Assembly Resolution 52/133: Human Rights and Terrorism. A/RES/52/133. Available at www.un.org/documents/resga.htm (accessed 28 Dec 2004).

UN (United Nations). 1999. International Convention for the Suppression of the Financing of Terrorism. Available at: untreaty.un.org/English/Terrorism.asp (accessed 15 Jan 2005).

United Nations. Office on Drugs and Crime. 2004. Definitions of Terrorism. Available at: www.unodc.org/unodc/terrorism_definitions.html (accessed 30 Dec 2004).

United Nations. Secretary-General. 1987. Ruling pertaining to the differences between France and New Zealand arising from the Rainbow Warrior affair. *American Journal of International Law*, 81: 325–8.

United Nations. Secretary-General's High-Level Panel on Threats, Challenges & Change. 2005. *A More Secure World: Our Shared Responsibility*. Report. Available at: www.un.org/secureworld/ (accessed 26 March 2005).

US Army. ca 1993. Combatting terrorism. Ch. 8 of *Field Manual 100–20, Stability and Support Operations* (Final Draft). Fort Leavenworth, KS: US Army Command & General Staff College. Available at: www.terrorism.com/modules.php?op=modload&name=News&file=article&sid=5671 (accessed 29 Dec 2004). Reprinted in part in David J. Whittaker, ed., *The Terrorism Reader*. London: Routledge, 2001: 17–21.

US Census Bureau. 2001. *Statistical Abstract of the United States 2001*. Washington, DC: Government Printing Office. Available at: www.census.gov/prod/www/statistical-abstract-04.html (accessed 8 Feb 2005).

US Census Bureau. 2005. *Statistical Abstract of the United States 2004–2005*. Washington, DC: Government Printing Office. Available at: www.census.gov/prod/www/statistical-abstract-04.html (accessed 8 Feb 2005).

US CIA (Central Intelligence Agency). 2003. The War on Terrorism: terrorism FAQs. Available at: www.cia.gov/terrorism/faqs.html (accessed 12 Nov 2003).

US Congress. 2001. USA PATRIOT Act. Available at: thomas.loc.gov/cgi-bin/bdquery/z?d107:h.r.03162 (accessed 1 Oct 2005).

US Department of Homeland Security. 2005. Threats & protection advisory system: current threat level. Available at: www.dhs.gov/dhspublic/interapp/press_release/Copy_of_press_release_0046.xml (accessed 14 Feb 2005).

US Department of State. 1986. *Current Policy*, no. 820. Washington, DC: Department of State.

US Department of State, Office of the Coordinator for Counterterrorism. 2001. *Patterns of Global Terrorism – 2000*. Available at: www.state.gov/s/ct/rls/pgtrpt/2000/2419.htm (accessed 12 Nov 2003).

US Department of State, Office of the Coordinator for Counterterrorism. 2003. *Patterns of Global Terrorism – 2003*. Available at: www.state.gov/s/ct/rls/pgtrpt/2003 (accessed 24 Jan 2005).

US FBI (Federal Bureau of Investigation), US Department of Justice. 1998. *Terrorism in the United States 1998*. Available at: www.fbi.gov/publications/terror/terror98.pdf (accessed 13 Nov 2003).

US National Commission on Terrorism. 1999. *Countering the Changing Threat of International Terrorism*. Washington, DC: Government Printing Office. Available at: www.fas.org/irp/threat/commission.html (accessed 24 Jan 2005).

US 9/11 Commission. 2004. *The 9/11 Commission Report: Final Report of the National Commission on Terrorist Attacks upon the United States*. New York: Norton.

US OMB (Office of Management & Budget). 2005. FY06 budget priorities: Department of Homeland Security. Available at: www.whitehouse.gov/omb/budget/fy2006/dhs.html (accessed 23 June 2005).

US OTA (Office of Technology Assessment). 1993a. *Proliferation of Weapons of Mass Destruction: Assessing the Risks*. OTA-ISC 559. Washington, DC: Government Printing Office.

US OTA (Office of Technology Assessment). 1993b. *Technologies Underlying Weapons of Mass Destruction*. OTA-BP-ISC-115. Washington, DC: Government Printing Office. Available at: www.fas.org/ssp/starwars/ota/9344.html (accessed 16 Feb 2005).

von Neumann, John, and Oskar Morgenstern. 1944. *Theory of Games and Economic Behavior*. Princeton, NJ: Princeton University Press.

Waldron, Jeremy. 2003. Security & liberty: the image of balance. *Journal of Political Philosophy*, 11: 191–210.

Waldron, Jeremy. 2004. Terrorism & the use of terror. *Journal of Ethics*, 8: 5–35.

Walzer, Michael. 1977. *Just and Unjust Wars*. London: Allen Lane.

Walzer, Michael. 1988. Terrorism: a critique of excuses. In Steven Luper-Foy, ed., *Problems of International Justice: Philosophical Essays*. Boulder, CO: Westview Press: 237–47. Reprinted in *Arguing about War*. New Haven, CT: Yale University Press, 2004: 51–66.

Walzer, Michael. 2004. *Arguing about War*. New Haven, CT: Yale University Press.

Wardlaw, Grant. 1982. *Political Terrorism*. Cambridge: Cambridge University Press.

Weimann, Gabrielle, and Conrad Winn. 1994. *The Theatre of Terror: The Mass Media & International Terrorism*. New York: Longman/Addison-Wesley.

Weinberger, Jonathan. 2003. Defining terror. *Seton Hall Journal of Diplomacy and International Relations*, 4, Winter/Spring: 63–81.

Wellman, Carl. 1979. On terrorism itself. *Journal of Value Inquiry*, 13: 250–8.

Wellmer, Albrecht. 1984. Terrorism & the critique of society. In *Observations on 'The Spiritual Situation of the Age': Contemporary German Perspectives*, ed. Jürgen Habermas, trans. A. Buchwalter. Cambridge, MA: MIT Press: 283–307.

White House, Office of the Press Secretary. 2004. Fact sheet: three years of progress in the War on Terror (released 11 September). Available at: www.whitehouse.gov/news/releases/2004/09/20040911.html (accessed 15 Jan 2005).

Wilkinson, Paul. 1990. Some observations on the relationships between terrorism and freedom. In Martin Warner and Roger Crisp, eds, *Terrorism, Protest & Power*. Aldershot: Edward Elgar: 44–53.

Wittman, Donald. 1983. Candidate motivation: a synthesis of alternative theories. *American Political Science Review*, 77: 142–57.

Young, Robert. 2004. Political terrorism as a weapon of the politically powerless. In Igor Primoratz, ed., *Terrorism: The Philosophical Issues*. London: Palgrave: 55–64.

Zohar, Noam J. 2004. Innocence and complex threats: upholding the war ethic and the condemnation of terrorism. *Ethics*, 114: 734–51.

Index